# LIKE A COMPLETE UNKNOWN

JOHN HINCHEY

Stealing Home Press

Published in the United States of America by Stealing Home Press, Ann Arbor, Michigan.

Cover photo taken in 1966, © Lisa Law (flashingonthesixties.com)

Cover design by Mary Hunt



Library of Congress Cataloging-in-Publication data has been applied for.

ISBN 0-9723592-0-6

Stealing Home Press
802 Jones Drive
Ann Arbor, Michigan 48105

stealinghomepress.com

To the memory of John Bauldie

## CONTENTS

# *Introduction*

Bob Dylan is a poet and, as the world will gradually come to recognize, a great one. I realize that for many people–including many Dylan fans–a book about the poetry of Dylan's songs is a book about something that doesn't exist, or is of no real consequence. My aim is to show otherwise.

Even I recognize that Dylan is not merely a poet and that making poetry may not even be what he is best at. He's a recording artist, live performer, songwriter, and poet. But I do not believe, as almost everyone else who concedes this much seems to, that Dylan's art can be discussed only as all of these things at once. Dylan makes record albums and performs live concerts, both of which are sometimes works of art in themselves. These recordings and concerts are in turn made up of discrete performances of individual songs, usually his own compositions, and each of these performances is also a work of art, to be judged as good, bad, or indifferent, each on its own merit. The songs he performs are also works of art of varying quality, and they all contain lyrics that may–and in the case of Dylan's own songs, almost always do–engage our attention as poems. Like every other dimension of Dylan's polymorphous creativity, these poems may be sublime or awful, or any number of other things in between.

There is nothing unprecedented in this. William Blake's "The Tyger," one of the greatest lyric poems in English, also happens to be a song, as well as merely an element in one of those engravings combining text and image that Blake called "illuminated printing."

Shakespeare's "Full Fathom Five Thy Father Lies" is another great poem, also a song, that forms but a part of a larger work, in this case another poetic text, *The Tempest*, that is also a stage play, one that is regularly performed–splendidly, badly, decently, etc.–around the world. But when was the last time anyone seriously argued that "Full Fathom Five" is not a poem because its full meaning is inseparable from its rendition in a performance of *The Tempest*, or that "The Tyger" is not a poem because, well, unless you heard Blake sing it, especially that one summer morning when he suddenly broke into song while returning from London after the unfortunate incident with the vicar, you'll just never understand it?

Then there are the original troubadours. No one dismisses Arnaut Daniel–Dante's archetype of the vernacular poet–as "merely" a songwriter, though perhaps that is because his poems have survived only without their melodies; we have to read them, so no one can pretend they don't yield themselves to reading. Dylan is the archetype of the modern troubadour. More than anyone before or after him, he has doggedly tested and stretched the poetic limits of song.

Unlike the medieval troubadours, Dylan not only composes the poetry and the music of his songs but he also sings them; he is his own minstrel. And, yes, no one sings Dylan like Dylan; indeed, no one sings anything quite like Dylan. Taking hints mostly from earlier recordings of American vernacular music, he has absolutely redefined, for many of us, what it means to sing, so that it sometimes seems he has created an entirely new art form. But we shouldn't let the beguiling genius of his singing blind us to the strength that singing draws from the intrinsic poetry of what he is singing. (On the other hand, many of the people I know who regard Dylan as a superior poet also insist that he can't sing a lick. Go figure.) As a poet, at his best, he is arguably as good as Whitman and Dickinson, which, in the American tradition, is as good as it gets.

This is not a claim likely to meet with wide assent, perhaps even among likely readers of a book about Bob Dylan. This is one reason I have chosen to write about Dylan's poetry, which I view both as valuable in itself and as the matrix that energizes the musical compositions that, in turn, energize his powers as a singer. The poetry of his songs is the "substructure that holds it all together," as Dylan has called the lyrics of the songs on his 2001 CD "*Love and Theft*."* The poetry of Dylan's songs is a crucial, not just an incidental, element of their greatness.

## II

From the beginning, there has been widespread resistance, both from the academy and from the streets, to the notion of taking Dylan seriously as a poet. A lot of this resistance arises from extraordinarily constricted notions about what poetry is (and has been). This is true both of the guardians of culture who insist that it act and look like the (often narrow) range of existing poetry they happen to be familiar with, and of those Dylan fans who seem to have been taught, in college or maybe even high school, that poetry is just a diabolically encrypted mode of (often banal) philosophizing. The former consider Dylan unworthy of the name of poet, and the latter insist it is unworthy of him. I don't see any point in attacking these views head on. My own way of exploring Dylan's poetry either credibly establishes a way of looking at poetry to which Dylan's work answers, or it does not. But, to indicate at least where I am coming from, I will say that to my understanding poetry is an art that uses words not just to explore but to create our fullest awareness–emotional, perceptual, and intellectual–of what, without poetry, we merely and blankly "know." Poetry–all poetry worthy of the name–provides us with answers, of varying degrees of persuasiveness and indispensability, to the question at the center of Dylan's most crucial song: "How does it feel?"

Not all song lyrics, I know, are poetry. Often the words–as opposed to their mere meanings–are just along for the ride. They possess little or none of the imagistic vitality, rhythmic verve, auditory resonance, ver-

* "The music here is an electronic grid, the lyrics being the substructure that holds it all together," Dylan told *USA Today* music writer Edna Gunderson. "Dylan's Melodies Always Are A-Changin'," section C, p. 1.

bal wit, or other textural and structural features necessary to elevate mere verse into poetry, so they can't serve as the "substructure" for their music. In most songs, the words are merely fitted piecemeal to the musical structure. And there are also songs–like, for instance, those of Cole Porter or Lennon & McCartney–whose lyrics could justifiably be called poetic but rarely are because their poetry is so lightweight. These songs are fun to recite–one good test for poetry–but they don't really compel our attention unless they are sung. They are not bad poems, just weak ones. Dylan is not the only modern songwriter I would go to the bother of treating as a poet–the likes of Chuck Berry, Tom Waits, and Joni Mitchell leap immediately to mind, and there are certainly others–but even in this comparatively rarefied company, Dylan laps the field. The difference is that Dylan's best lyrics are not just fun but thrilling to recite; they don't just compel our attention, they enlarge it and set it free.

Let me put it this way. I have no musical talent. Though my wife says I have a nice voice, my singing keeps babies awake. So, as much as I love "Things We Said Today," I need to hear (or remember hearing) the Beatles perform it to get anything out of it. But I can delight myself by reciting "Buckets of Rain"–in a tuneless whisper, attending only to the sound and kinesthesia of my own voice. It works like a charm. (It is a charm!) That's my test for poetry worthy of the name, and Dylan's songs afford me this kind of pleasure regularly enough that I have to refer to them as poetry.

Dylan himself, when asked, has been notoriously self-contradictory on this issue, sometimes embracing and more frequently disavowing the title of poet. But his disavowals are always qualified in ways that muddy the issue. Sometimes he seems simply shy of seeming to put himself on a pedestal, or wary of being measured against "poetic" standards irrelevant to his work. Usually, there's a sense he'll give whatever answer that will enable him to defy his questioner's expectations and elude the grasp of any definition of what it is he does. The Muhammad Ali of interviewees–"float like a butterfly, sting like a bee"–he's mainly keen not to allow himself to be boxed in. To my mind, the most illuminating statement Dylan has ever made about the mode of his lyrics was made in late February or early March, 1966, during an interview with Martin Bronstein for CBC radio:

> I found myself writing this song, this story, this long piece of vomit about twenty pages long, and out of it I took "Like a Rolling Stone." . . . I'd never written anything like that before, and it suddenly came to me that that was what I do, y'know. I mean, nobody has ever done that before. . . . I think "Like a Rolling Stone" is definitely the thing which I do, man. That's write songs. . . . After writing that, I wasn't interested in writing a novel, or a play. . . . I wanted to write songs, y'know, because it was just a *whole new category*. I mean, nobody's really written songs before. Really, I mean, people have in older days, but those were sonnets and soft troubadour-type things." [emphasis added]*

What Dylan is insisting is that the songs he writes don't behave like what we are used to thinking of as songs. They do things that songs hadn't previously done, or as Dylan acknowledges, haven't done in a long time. What's new about his songs, I would say, is that they behave like poems–that's why his discovery of this new sort of song enabled him to cease dabbling in conventional literary forms. So, yes, we could say that Dylan writes songs, not poems, but only if we remember–which we won't–that we are using the word "song" to address that undefined new thing Dylan is struggling to put his finger on in his response to Bronstein. But, if you like, you can treat my insistence on talking about the poetry of Dylan's songs as merely an expedient to draw attention to the features of that "whole new category" Dylan was certain he had invented, or reinvented.

The other major obstacle to taking Dylan seriously as a poet is based on the apparent notion that poetry is a textual art, one that lives in print, on the page. In one sense, this is sheer silliness. Certain not very interesting experiments in concrete poetry aside, poetry does not live on the page; what you see on the page is to poetry as a printed score is to music. Poetry lives on the breath and tongue and in the ear. True, the oral and aural dimensions of most printed poetry have grown increas-

* John Bauldie, *The Ghost of Electricity*, p. 23.

ingly attenuated over the past two or three centuries, so that it now lives largely, as it were, on the mind's breath and in the mind's ear. But even Wallace Stevens, that great ghostly talking head of American poetry whom Dylan himself cited as the sort of "great poet [who] is not necessarily a great singer,"* writes a poetry that is, in Stevens's phrase, "blooded by thought." And there is no blood, not even of thought, on the page. In addition, one should keep in mind a counter-tradition, in American poetry, that runs from Whitman through Pound and Williams to Ginsberg and then to Dylan. It is a tradition that, in various ways and with varying degrees and kinds of success, has been trying to get poetry to lift itself more vigorously up off the page than now customary and to re-ally itself with music and even with dance.

But in another sense, this charge–"Dylan's songs don't stand up on the page"–points to a real problem. I agree that what one reads in the two printed collections of Dylan's words, *Writings & Drawings* (1973) and *Lyrics: 1962-1985* (1986)–or in their online version at bobdylan.com–is rarely poetry. But that is because these texts provide only the words and not (or not in any complete or reliable form) the "words and the spaces between the words," which William Carlos Williams identified as the constituent elements of poetry. Whoever assembled these two collections left out and/or obscured many of the "spaces" crucial to the poetic structures Dylan composed. The reason the poems you see in *Lyrics* do not stand up on the page is that their backbones have been shattered.

The problem with existing printed texts is that the only organizing principle they seem to acknowledge is line divisions cued by the rhyme scheme–and when the rhyme scheme is at all complex, or incorporates unrhymed lines, even this simple-minded procedure can collapse into desperate guesswork. The result is often doggerel:

*The sweet pretty things are in bed now of course*
*The city fathers they're trying to endorse*
*The reincarnation of Paul Revere's horse*

---

* Hubert Saal, "Dylan Is Back," in McGregor, *A Retrospective*, p. 245.

*But the town has no need to be nervous*

No one discovering "Tombstone Blues" from the above is likely to suspect that its author is a poet. But this is not what Dylan sings. What he sings is more fairly represented as this:

*The sweet pretty things are in*
*bed now of course*
*The city fathers they're*
*trying to endorse*
*The reincarnation of*
*Paul Revere's horse*
*But the town has no need to be*
*nervous*

"Tombstone Blues," like almost all of Dylan's songs, is comprised of poetry whose verses are best represented as a series (usually in quatrains) of metrically equivalent half-line pairs, or of couplets that function like half-line pairs. Representing them this way does fair justice to the internal shapes of the lines, their clusterings of syllables and their caesuras, their sculpted intensities, and exposes the genuine kinship between the music of the verse and the actual music we hear in the performed song.

Consequently, the text I rely on for the songs I discuss in this book is necessarily my own. Unless otherwise specified, I've taken the words from the recorded performances on their original release (silently correcting vocal flubs), and I haven't paid much attention to Dylan's revisions of the words, either in live performance or in the printed collections cited above. But I've had to determine how to represent the "spaces between the words" for myself. In transcribing Dylan's poetry to the page, I have generally stuck with the prosody, as I hear it, of the original recorded version.

The question of what constitutes the division of poetry into lines or half-lines is a nice point, to say the least. My own working definition is that verse is divided into lines by some principle of recurrence (e.g., alliterative or accentual-syllabic patterns) that establishes the metrical equivalence of one line with another, and that a line is subdivided into two (or more) parts by a break in (or breaking up of) the voice of a line for which the technical term is a caesura, which in Latin literally means a "cutting." Such a break is often but not always occasioned by the end of a sentence or another grammatical subdivision requiring punctuation.

The principle of recurrence that shapes Dylan's poetic line is a complex pattern comprising beats, accents, and rhyme–a cross pattern, as Dylan himself put it, of "rhyming and rhythm, what I call the mathematics of a song"* Look at almost any Dylan song, and you'll see that all the lines all contain the same number of beats and accents–or, if there is some variation from line to line, the same pattern of variation recurs from verse to verse. Occasionally, he'll even write a song in traditional English accentual-syllabic verse. But in most of his songs, the number of unstressed syllables and the placement of the accents change from line to line, yielding something that could easily be mistaken for free verse.

Dylan's use of the caesura is sometimes quite conventional, organized around major grammatical divisions, but like William Carlos Williams, he prefers to chase after the tonal surprises that can be released by severing a phrase from the syntactic train that hauled it into view. Thus:

*The sweet pretty things are in*
*bed now of course*

or this from "Visions of Johanna":

*Ain't it just like the night to play*
*tricks when you're trying to be so quiet*

or this from "Highlands":

*She got a pretty face and long*
*white shiny legs*

or this from "Sugar Baby":

* Bauldie, *The Ghost of Electricity*, p. 10.

*You went years without me, might as well*
*keep goin' now*

The caesura is properly part of the poetry of the lyric, while a mere holding (or rushing) of the breath is part of its performance. Thus, the opening couplet of the last verse of "All Along the Watchtower" normally goes like this:

*All along the watchtower*
*princes kept the view*
*All the women came and went*
*barefoot servants too*

Dylan might sing this evenly and straightforwardly, as if merely reciting, or he might stretch and squeeze the phrasing, with results like this:

*All along the . . . watchtower*
*princes kepttheview*
*All the women came and went*
*barefoot servants . . . too*

These changes don't affect or alter the poetry; they belong not to what Dylan sings but to the way he sings it. The way he sings his songs is a matter that I largely ignore in this book. This is not to deny that this performative resource–among many others–can greatly enhance (or degrade) the expressive power of what he is singing. Indeed, these sorts of changes, which arise from the way Dylan is living inside his song as he sings it, can even make a great lyric sound idiotic or a lousy one seem sublime.

But sometimes Dylan does more than play with the poetic phrasing; sometimes he revises it, so that we get–as we do in my favorite performances of "All Along the Watchtower"–a new prosody:

*All along*
*the watchtower*
*Princes*
*kept the view*
*All the women*

*came and went*
*Barefoot*
*servants too*

The result is a significantly revised poetic "substructure" for the song, something new–here a pervasive, unsettlingly dainty feline stealth–for his voice to play with from night to night. And because they belong to the poetic structure of the songs, these prosodic changes–when they work–are usually maintained for the length of an entire tour, or even longer, while the merely performative variations are, however similar to something done before, unique, fingerprints that enable a listener to identify a particular performance.

But what one notices, over time, is that whatever prosodic revisions Dylan makes, the pattern of alternating half-line persists. It is a pattern that is at once a dialectic, a dialogue, and even a dancing (left foot, right foot, left foot, right foot) or a shadow boxing (left hand, right hand, left hand, right hand.) When Dylan sings, in "Angelina," "My right hand drawing back while my left hand advances," he is describing, among other things of course, his prosodic signature.

In any case, I think that I have succeeded in fashioning a viable printed form of Dylan's poetry to this extent: readers of this book, when encountering quoted verses, will not be moved–as they would often likely be when reading *Lyrics*–to dismiss it as nonpoetry on the face of it. Its vitality as verse does not depend on its strictly musical setting, and–to make a related but considerably lesser point–that vitality can be indicated on the page.

And no, it does not bother me at all that Dylan himself apparently cares not a fig for all this. Why should he? He's the poet, I'm the pedant.

## III

Dylan's poetry is the aspect of his work I happen to be best equipped to write about, but it's also the aspect that has been least adequately appreciated, let alone studied, even among Dylan's admirers. Paul Williams, who is probably Dylan's most prominent critic, insists that Dylan can only be understood as a performing artist, and he strenuously resists the usefulness of thinking of Dylan as a poet–even on those occasions when Williams, usually with considerable insight, is himself discussing the poetry of Dylan's songs. Dylan's most prestigious critic, Greil Marcus, also considers Dylan's art only in its totality, as performances that Marcus regularly locates through their historical, cultural, or sociopolitical resonances. Marcus's writings about Dylan, as his writing about any number of things, rarely fails to fascinate and instruct, but he's never really addressed himself to basic questions about the elements of Dylan's art. And while there are a large number–a mountain, really–of short articles–most notably a handful of brief but incisive essays by the poetry scholar and critic Christopher Ricks–and even some books and monographs addressed to the poetry of particular songs or albums, or to a particular feature (usually thematic) element of Dylan's poetry, Michael Gray is the only critic who has preceded me addressing the question of what sort of poetry it is that Dylan writes.

Gray's *Song and Dance Man III: The Art of Bob Dylan* gives lively subordinate attention to Dylan's achievement as a vocalist, recording artist, and even public persona, but Gray focuses his attention primarily on Dylan's poetic art. Now in its third edition–the first appeared in 1971–Gray's ever expanding study is a wonderful and invaluable achievement. His tenacious research into the literary, scriptural, and folk traditions upon which Dylan draws are nothing short of staggering in its thoroughness and specificity. But what I like best about Gray's book is the severe intelligence with which he addresses and assesses the poetic texture, or personality, of Dylan's songs.

I don't agree with all of Gray's assessments of Dylan's work–the personality of any particular work of art inevitably appeals differently to different people–but the present study does not retrace the same ground, except incidentally. Nor do I suspect that Gray would agree with my confidence that the poetry of Dylan's art can be viewed and assessed separately from its other aspects, or that it would be useful to do so. Moreover, my approach to that poetry, unlike Gray's, is grounded in attention to its narrative and/or dramatic form, to the shape it takes–and the resources it employs–as it unfolds in time, as it discloses itself to listening. Finally, Gray's approach tends to emphasize the ways Dylan is like other great poets; my own emphasis is on the ways in which he is like no one but himself.

I would also emphasize that this book is but a preliminary study of its subject. Long as it is, this book–the first of three (or more) projected volumes–treats Dylan's work only through 1969, and it addresses only a fraction of what engages the attention of even my own necessarily limiting biases and interests. My aim in publishing this text is simply to arouse a wider interest in its subject, mainly by persuading my readers that thinking about Dylan's songs in terms of their poetry, and (to a lesser extent) along the lines I set forth, is a rewarding and even entertaining enterprise.

My aim in writing this book in the first place is even more modest: I was looking for a project that would provide me with a way of entertaining myself for the rest of my life. Since this volume, which covers nine years (1961-1969) of Dylan's career, took me six years (in my spare time, to be sure) to produce, I might even live long enough to catch up with him. Not likely, but something to shoot for.

Since this book was taken up in the spirit of self-entertainment (and self-education), the reader should take that as fair warning: I talk about what I want from whatever point of view seems right and for as long (or as briefly) as my interest sustains me. Moreover, I make no pretense that this study is in any way normative; indeed, I would be appalled were any reader to be moved, let alone feel pressured, to regard it that way. What I have to say about Dylan's poetry is simply a report on what it looks like, and feels like, from where I stand.

Indeed, I would go further than that. The form of criticism I practice is Emersonian, though I like to think of it as taking up the terms of Whitman's formulation of what I take to be the implicit contract any writer makes with his or her reader or listener: "What I assume, you shall assume." What Dylan assumes, I assume: I attempt to understand his songs by trying them on. Just as Dylan discovers what his songs mean (to him) by singing them, so I discover what they mean (to me) by singing them. The difference is that Dylan broadcasts his discoveries directly–and as he is making them–as public performances, while I chant and mumble to myself, usually under my breath, walking to and fro, and publish my discoveries through the medium of premeditated prose that hopefully is neither too long-winded nor too short-sighted. As a critic, I don't necessarily care why Dylan wanted to write his songs as he did; that information might come in handy, it might not. In the end, however, I care only to learn why I do (or don't) like them the way he wrote them, what it is about them that makes me want to listen to them and repeat them to myself, or discourages me from doing so.

This book then is really about the poetry of my songs–the songs written by Bob Dylan, that is, after I have taken them to heart and made them my own. And I, in turn, authorize my readers to take this book to heart in whatever fashion they must, including, if it suits them, as a textbook case in how to misread (or mishear) Bob Dylan's poetry.

## IV

I have said that, in the chapters that follow, I write about what I want to and from whatever point of view seems right. Well, that is not entirely true. There is something of a method underlying it all. This study explores the poetry of Dylan's songs from his first album, *Bob Dylan* (1962), through *Nashville Skyline* (1969). It covers all the officially released albums of new material from that period. I give some attention to almost every original song on those albums, and to some songs–singles, outtakes, demos, and other stray songs–not included on the albums. The only songs I systematically ignore are those from the 1967 Basement Tapes sessions, some of the best of which were released on the 1975 *Basement Tapes* LP but many of which remain even now available only on bootleg collections. These sessions, which include 27 copyrighted Dylan songs and another dozen incomplete Dylan originals, are simply too much for the present study to accommodate.

My first chapter treats only a single song, "Like a Rolling Stone," and the second covers Dylan's first two albums, both of which are miscellanies. After that, each chapter treats a single album (though the discussion of *Blonde on Blonde* takes up two chapters), and in these chapters, I give some attention both to the individual songs and to their place in the context of the album. My decisions about what to emphasize and what to gloss over are based partly on my judgments about the relative worth of each song or album and partly on my instinct for what is interesting or undiscovered about them.

And there is a theme, sort of. I was very conscious of not letting this study become in any way thesis-ridden, so sometimes my theme may seem to disappear for a stretch. It is allowed to do so when its pertinence is so peripheral or subtle that to insist upon it would be tediously pedantic, even to me. But even then, I suspect it only seems to disappear. My theme takes various guises, not all of which I bother to identify as such.

My theme is this: the most distinctive feature of Dylan's poetry is the way it is implicitly shaped by the changes (as Dylan imagines them) that are induced in his listener in response to the song as it unfolds. That is, when Dylan addresses "you" in his songs, he means it and acts like he means it. As the lyric unfolds, "you" are changed by what "you" hear, and anticipating these changes in the "you" he is addressing, Dylan's perception of and attitude toward "you" changes correspondingly. Moreover, these changes in his perception of "you" provoke in turn adjustments in his perception of and attitude toward himself. Dylan's characteristic song is a duet for solo voice.

Let me suggest a simple way to look at this difference, at least as it applies to Dylan's poetry. Ordinarily, when we listen to a song, we identify with the point of view of the singer or of the person or persons he is addressing. Or our identification might flip back and forth between these points of view, as if we were listening to a play. But Dylan's most characteristic songs require us to identify simultaneously both with the singer and with his implied listener; we experience ourselves as both "I" and "you." To what purpose he does this is a complex matter, but, at bottom, his way with words–as a poet and as a singer–is sustained by his deepest sense of his own psyche as a conversation, as the meeting (and mating) ground of an "I" and a "you" who are, audaciously enough, at once both objective (self and other) and subjective (spirit and soul).

This is the feature that lends his poetry a confidential intimacy, at once inviting and unsettling, that even Whitman does not achieve on such a minute and continuous scale. Dylan's songs kidnap our imaginations. This is why you can't listen to "Positively Fourth Street," for instance, without both enjoying its caustic temper and feeling somewhat scorched by it–no matter how much you may pretend not to. The listener's discomfort is a palpable presence in the singer's own words. This feature of his lyrics is also a major reason his evangelizing Christian songs caused such an unholy furor among the faithful. His fans were not just disappointed that their hero had done something they deemed embarrassingly stupid and couldn't imagine identifying with. No, what really inflamed them is that they couldn't believe that Dylan, of all people, would force them, who had been traumatized by their own experiences with Christendom, to hear themselves addressed in those terms all over again. And you can't listen to those songs–you just can't–without going through that particular gauntlet.

I have coined the term "lyrical dialogue" to describe those songs–of which "Like a Rolling Stone" is the first and most famous–in which this doubled "I"/"You" point of view plays itself out most directly. But the image of the poetic voice as itself a conversation takes various and unexpected forms in Dylan's poetry. Dylan playfully acknowledged this in a 1985 interview:

> Sometimes the "you" in my songs is me talking to me. Other times I can be talking to someone else. If I'm talking to me in a song, I'm not gonna drop everything and say, alright, now I'm talking to you. It's up to you to figure out who's who. A lot of times it's "you" talking to "you." The "I," like in "I and I," also changes. It could be I, or it could be the "I" who created me. And also, it could be another person who's saying "I." When I say "I" right now, I don't know who I'm talking about.*

* Scott Cohen, "Don't Ask Me Nothin' About Nothin' I Might Just Tell You the Truth: Bob Dylan Revisited." *Spin* (Dec. 1985), p. 39

Many of the forms this conversation takes do not engage the listener–that is, Dylan's actual audience–directly. Consider, for instance, the weirdly posthumous second-person ventriloquism of "The Ballad of Holes Brown" or the teasing use of "you," in "Subterranean Homesick Blues," to conduct what refuses finally, and with a provoking hipster disdain, to be anything more than an internal dialogue. Or one might consider how this line from "Highlands"–"I was talking to myself, in a monologue"–could occur *without any sense of redundancy* only in a Dylan song, where it names the most dreadful extremity of alienation.

Or consider "Mr. Tambourine Man," a song in which no listener is ever tempted to identify with the "you" addressed, who is a demigod. Indeed, given the exaltation of Dylan's quest, we may find it hard to identify fully even with this singer, except as a hero in the old-fashioned sense. "Mr. Tambourine Man" is an ode, one modeled, in obvious ways, on Keats's "Ode to a Nightingale," a poem that haunts many Dylan songs. But the poetry of "Mr. Tambourine Man" is not at all Keatsean; indeed, Dylan has little of Keats's genius (or appetite) for appropriating the taste and texture of the realities he addresses in his words. Nor does he achieve–or aspire to–anything of the sublime pathos of Keats's poem. Both Keats's nightingale and Dylan's Tambourine Man are tropes of each poet's own poetic voice, but the difference is that Dylan conceives of his voice as a man, with a (supernaturally wordless) human voice. This enables him to conceive a project for his song that Keats would likely have considered lunatic: he is going to sing just like that bird, or in his case, in the "jingle jangle" voice of the Tambourine Man. And somewhere in the dizzying figurative acrobatics of the song's third verse he does just that, by incorporating the tracings of the voice of the Tambourine Man as an element in the conversation that now, at last, constitutes his own renovated voice.

Yes, he actually does that, sort of, maybe. This points to another widely recognized aspect of the poetry of Dylan's songs that also derives from their conversational character: an indeterminacy of meaning that makes every interpretation a provisional and very personal completion of that meaning. Since we are listening to a conversation of two (or occasionally three) voices represented as a single voice, one of those voices we must imagine ourselves. Imagine "Boots of Spanish Leather," an old-fashioned ballad dialogue, without the verses spoken by the singer's departing lover. How would you then explain the course of the singer's thought from verse to verse? You'd have to imagine something like the three missing verses. But not only would you never–not in a thousand monkeys!–reproduce exactly the verses Dylan wrote, you would be free to start hearing a lot more than you now do, unexpected colors of feeling and awareness, in what the singer himself is saying. What you would hear would depend on who you are, the mood you're in, what you notice first in the song. Well, most Dylan songs–especially the best ones–are constructed in a way that requires a listener to flesh them out in precisely this way. Their distinctive ambiguities are not logical but emotional and, ultimately, vocal.

Not incidentally, songs constructed this way allow Dylan the singer to draw new wine from old bottles night after night from the stage–at least on those nights when he has the energy and heart for it. Dylan devised his poetic style in response to his need not just, as he put it, for "something to sing" but for something to sing that would challenge him to renew his voice on stages around the world, night after night, year after year. Dylan has devised a kind of song whose poetry is not fully created until he sings it, and the result, for us, is a kind of poem that is not fully created until we listen to it. As the English critic Frank Kermode observed, "[Dylan's] poems have to be open, empty, inviting collusion . . . a geometry of innocence which [his listener] can flesh out."*

Moreover, having so trained his vocal imagination, he is now able to draw new wine even from songs not so constructed. For every really good song, like every really good poem, is a conversation, if only with the poet or songwriter's unconscious, and that remains true even if this hidden conversation is papered over with one or another conventional logic. Dylan is often said to "deconstruct" songs in live performance,

* Frank Kermode, "Bob Dylan: The Light at the End of the Funnel," *Esquire*, p. 111.

and this is an apt characterization of what he often does with most of the pop songs and many of the folk songs in his repertoire. But it is deeply misleading about his usual way with his own songs and with those older songs, especially traditional ballads and blues, that unfold from verse to verse, or even occasionally from line to line, via jump cuts that throw the precise logic of these sequences up for grabs. These songs he does not deconstruct–they do that for themselves–but reconstructs.

## V

The jump cut, in various forms and under various names, has long been a staple resource of the American poetic tradition, from Whitman's catalogues to Emily Dickinson's fracturing dashes to Pound's juxtapositions to William Carlos Williams's dislocating metrics to Wallace Stevens's appositional meditations to the telegraphic syntax of Allen Ginsberg and other Beats. What distinguishes Dylan's "chains of flashing images," as he once called them, is that they are generated primarily as images not of mind but of voice.

Let me explain what I mean by returning to the comparison between "Ode to a Nightingale" and "Mr. Tambourine Man." This is how Keats opens his poem:

*My heart aches and a drowsy numbness pains*
*My sense, as though of hemlock I had drunk,*
*Or emptied some dull opiate to the drains*
*One minute past, and Lethe-wards had sunk:*

This is Dylan:

*My weariness amazes me*
*I'm branded on my feet*

Now, their lyrical panache notwithstanding, Dylan's lines, compared to Keats's, may seem hasty and superficial, a mere sketch of a state of consciousness he doesn't have the patience of mind to realize in its fullness. A lot of American poetry can seem this way, but the best of it finds compensation for what's lost in the nimble grace of its namings and in the mental flashes that occur when we shoot the gaps between the lines, or, as in the line from "Mr. Tambourine Man" cited above, across the caesura that divides a line in half. The movement of mind this line traces is especially startling, even for Dylan, but even here it is secondary to the brightness of the flash engendered by the movement of voice. Dylan "amazes" himself with what he hears himself saying, and the second-half of this line registers his amazement, even as it intensifies it. "Branded on my feet" means "my feet are on fire," an image that is Dylan's characteristic emblem of the prophetic voice. But we don't initially hear it that way because of the syntax, which emphasizes the passivity and involuntariness of his experience: it sounds like he is saying something like "my feet are manacled." He is possessed, and uneasily so.

But none of this is likely to register if we, as listeners, merely think about what he is saying; we must imagine him saying it or, better, imagine speaking it ourselves. It is not fair to say that we can satisfactorily read Keats or even the sublimely disembodied Wallace Stevens by merely thinking our way through their poems, but their poems won't stop us from doing that if we so choose. Dylan's poems will. To "read" Dylan properly we must take our eyes up from the page and let his phrases, each in its turn, pour from our tongue, left, right, left, right. Or as Dylan himself long ago told us, we must "know [his] song well before [we] start singing" so that we may "tell it and think it and sing it and breathe it."

So, yes, Dylan is not a poet of the page, but not because his poems cannot be represented on the page. They just won't lie still there. And no, I don't think Dylan will ever be (literally) read much, as a poet. Who needs to? We have it all on record, to listen to. Indeed, I rarely consulted even my own printed renditions of the poetry of his songs in writing this book; I never wrote more than a sentence or two about any song I did not know by heart. But I did learn a lot more from reciting these poems to myself than I did from listening to Dylan's recordings, or even from recalling his performances to my mind's ear. When they come out of my tuneless mouth, there is, helpfully, nothing left of Dylan's songs but their poetry. Dylan's performances contain so much more than mere poetry that I have a hard time wrapping my mind around them as performances, let alone as songs or the poems for which the songs find the music. In writing this book, Dylan's performances have served me mainly as a tuning fork–or lie detector–against which to test the persuasiveness of my readings of his poems. Otherwise, when listening to his recordings, I don't really think at all; I just let them take me wherever it is this time they are going to take me.

But, I can hear a voice or two object, why bother? We have, as you say, the records, and if you want to count the concert bootlegs, as we must, we even have multiple readings–for some songs well into the hundreds–for almost every notable song Dylan have ever written. What exactly are you trying to prove, Hinchey?

Good question. Why bother? A short answer is: because it's the truth. A less flippant short answer is that to look narrowly at the poetry of Dylan's songs, and to assess them as poetry, is to put yourself in a position to notice things you hadn't noticed before. One thing you notice is that the more vigorous the poetry out of which the song has been fashioned, the greater the potential of the song that can be fashioned from it, and of the potential of the performances that can be wrung from that song. I've heard performances of the early antiwar song "John Brown" that have almost taken my breath away. Almost. No matter how passionate and intelligent the attentiveness Dylan brings to its performance, he's still hindered by the fact that he's singing a so-so song erected upon a poem I could have written in high school. And believe me, that's weak.

And then there are the long answers, one version of which is this book. So read on.

# 1

# *Like a Rolling Stone*

## No More Mr. Nice Guy

"Like a Rolling Stone" re-ignited Bob Dylan's career. By his own account, he had been ready to quit. In May 1965, just turned 24, Dylan returned home from an apparently triumphant British tour in utter defeat. He was the champion of the folk world–indeed, he had made folk a champion in the pop world–but his crown weighed on him like a badge of imprisonment. He had won a world-wide audience, but his audience was strangling him with adulation. The "voice of his generation," he reflected his audience in the visionary mirror of his songs, and in the answering mirror of its enraptured idolatry, he saw himself debased with a certain alienating majesty. He hated them. And he hated himself for allowing himself to play along.

His hatred began pouring out on the plane ride home in page after page of "vomit" directed at his tormentors. Dylan had always been a good hater, but this was something else, a hatred so pure and so uncannily knowing it could make even "Masters of War" seem a mere fit of bad temper. Perhaps it was because the object of his venom had never before been so close, so inseparable from his most intimate sense of himself. Oddly, it wasn't the self-hatred in the mix that upped the ante.

(Retrospective self-hatred can even be a bracing comfort–witness "My Back Pages.") No, the element of self-hatred was important only because it closed the back door. There would be no escape.

The novelty of the situation was that for the first time, Dylan found himself hating what he also loved: the very idea of an audience. Like every performer, Dylan needs an audience, not just as a pretext for performing but as a tacit collaborator whose anticipatory openness serves as a kind of midwife to the performance. But by mid-1965, for various reasons, Dylan had lost confidence in his audience's good faith. This crisis was made even more acute, I suspect, because Dylan's rapidly developing creative instincts as a performer were outstripping his own courage to follow his muse. As Paul Williams has helped all of us understand, Dylan eventually developed an aesthetic of performance as an exploration of its own moment, which is always unknown, harboring surprise. But until the crisis his disastrous 1965 tour provoked, neither Dylan nor his audience–despite his pretensions otherwise–seem to have been prepared to abandon a notion of performance as a culturally conservative rite, a demonstration of the known.

Nevertheless, when he felt his audience was turning its back on his deeper instincts, Dylan thought of giving up performing in favor of the cloister of the written page, where the audience never intrudes. But it was already too late for that. His creative spirit had long since cast its lot with the performing muse. He couldn't just walk away from his audience: his hatred held him hostage.

So he poured out his hatred, somehow transmuting the vomited mess into a song that saved his career. After writing it, he abruptly abandoned his dalliance with conventional literary forms–written poetry, prose fiction, plays–re-committed himself to his performing muse, and never looked back.

## II

"Like a Rolling Stone" opens with a diabolically feline explosion of homicidal rage:

*Once upon a time*
*you dressed so fine*
*Threw the bums a dime*
*in your prime*
*didn't you?*
*People'd call*
*say beware doll*
*You're bound to fall*
*you thought they were all*
*kiddin' you!*
*You used to laugh about*
*everybody that was hanging out*
*Now you don't talk so loud*
*now you don't seem so proud*
*About having to be*
*scrounging*
*for your next meal*

The moral drama sketched here is familiar enough; indeed, it is the quintessential myth of the ethos we call the 60s. The contrast is between those who live vulnerably in the moment and those who rely on social status to insulate themselves from our common existential nakedness. It's easy to imagine how Dylan would have identified his audience with the phonies, but what made him think they had already gotten their comeuppance, that they had already been knocked off their high horse and knew it? The answer is, he didn't. But he meant to change that.

The song's opening scenario, that is, is pure wish-fulfillment, a sadistic fantasy tossed out as a prophetic gambit: the song it opens is the only scene of an imagined degradation his audience suffers the moment it submits to the song. "Once upon a time" is shattered only by the "now" of composition or performance, a "now" the audience corroborates by listening.

To lash back at his smugly admiring tormentors in this way must have felt awfully good, but in itself, revenge would not have been enough. It would have made a thrilling valedictory, perhaps, but there was no future in it. It changed nothing.

But something was changed. Dylan had stumbled onto a new kind of song, a new kind of poetry that liberated him from his audience's transfixing expectations. And he found it in words likely to make a conventional poet wince: "didn't you?" These words are not metrical filler, nor are they merely a set-up for their snarling rhyme. The question they ask is not–in the ordinary sense–merely rhetorical. Dylan means the question, though it's possible he didn't notice that himself, since so far as I know, no poet before him had ever so asked a question. Whatever he thought he was doing, Dylan had done something quite original, something that opened a whole world of possibilities for a poet who wrote songs to be performed before a live audience: he kidnapped his listeners from their seats and put them–as listeners–in his songs.

At the end of "Talkin' World War III Blues," Dylan had promised his audience that "I'll let you be in my dream, if I can be in yours." In "Like a Rolling Stone," he finds a form that finally fulfills that promise. But since his relationship with his audience has lost its innocence, it comes off not as a promise but as a threat: "If I have to be in your dream, then you're gonna be in mine."

"Didn't you?": the key to the whole song is that Dylan actually listens for an answer. The answer he hears, of course, is an imagined response, but it has a real effect. The answer Dylan imagines–to a serial questioning that culminates in the sadistic "How does it feel" chorus–changes his perception of "you," a change that in turn alters his own mood.

(I hereafter refer to "You" simply as you, without quotation marks. If that makes you, my reader, uncomfortable, well, that's what the song intends. I suppose I should apologize, however, for allowing myself to be forced into the role of the singer challenging you.)

In the second verse, Dylan's rage is suffused with a complicating compassion for your pain as "Miss Lonely," a compassion that blossoms into the mingled pity and terror with which he contemplates your incredulous encounter with "the vacuum," an unsheltering vacancy or emptiness at the heart of reality:

*You said you'd never compromise*
*with the mystery tramp but*
*now you realize*
*He's not selling any alibis*
*as you stare into the*
*vacuum of his eyes*
*And say,*
*"Do you wanna*
*make a deal?"*

The "mystery tramp" is in some sense Dylan himself, but the "mystery tramp" is not an alter ego, not even a visionary alter ego like the final verse's "Napoleon in rags." He is something finer–and spookier–than that. The "mystery tramp" is what Romantic mythologies call the "divine self," the figure Whitman called "the Real Me." It is the part of Dylan that is evoked by his art, a self into which Dylan the performer (if he is lucky) disappears. The song subjects the singer's ego to the same transforming ordeal to which it subjects you. Thus, to the extent that the "mystery tramp" is the agent of Dylan's revenge–or what starts out as revenge before turning into something more interesting–it is a revenge exacted upon himself as well. (That's one of the reasons the song's sadistic current is profoundly masochistic as well.)

And it is more than mere revenge. The second time around, the chorus has gone beyond sadism. The words haven't changed, but their meaning has–even on the page–because the context has changed. This is not as novel, or outrageous, a notion as it may first seem. Just as a word can change its meaning with a change in context, so can groups of words. That's the main reason, I think, that interpretation remains such an inextricably subjective enterprise: our sense of the right context is always chosen from a theoretically endless array of conceivable contexts.

When I first listened to "Like a Rolling Stone," blaring incessantly for months from the cafeteria jukebox in college, the beginning of the second chorus always seemed to be the place I stopped merely listening to the song and got excited by it. It's here that the song becomes something more than superb satire–like "Tombstone Blues"–and explodes into a realm beyond words, beyond music, beyond all sense, enveloping itself in the intoxicating accents of pure imagination.

The second time round the chorus inevitably strikes you as the voice of the "mystery tramp" himself, an invitation to enter a harrowing inner world uncompromised by the "alibis" of social and even psychological identity, to re-connect with the freedom of a "vacuum," or nothingness, deep within you and become a "complete unknown," even (or especially) to yourself.

The third verse represents another shift in Dylan's mood that once again coincides with a change in his sense of you. His response suggests you have accepted the chorus's offer too greedily, mistaking an escape from society's false identities for an escape from human relations and responsibilities. This verse suggests that the singer fears you may think you have been able to get away with making some kind of "deal" to keep your identity intact, after all.

But not only have you not escaped your human connections, suddenly your immediate relationship–with this interrogating voice– presses upon you with a discomfitingly knowing intimacy. For the first time your social identity is characterized as that of a patron of artists and entertainers, and your present crime as a betrayal of that relationship. This verse is animated by a sense that you owe an apology to all the "jugglers and clowns" (including the one singing this song). Indeed, you and the singer may owe each other an apology, for the double-edged opening couplet blends snarling indignation with self-implicating images of erotic degradation. "Did tricks for you" and "get your kicks for you" suggest a sado-masochistic circuit that links your voyeurism with his prostituting exhibitionism.

The image of Miss Lonely in her "chrome horse" with her "diplomat" and his "Siamese cat" has always struck me as a bit overcooked, but the diplomat himself is a wonderfully apt metaphor for the way the conventions of polite society (i.e., you buy the ticket, I put on the show) covertly function as antisocial mechanisms that enable us to hold each other at arm's length, as foreigners. But this diplomatic immunity is a soul-killing bargain, as Dylan points out. His tone here fuses disdainful cruelty with a compassionate generosity that implicitly offers recovery of a self beyond the reach of "everything he could steal." This time round the chorus carries the same meaning but the opposite feeling as the first time: to be a "rolling stone" is to reclaim a sense of shame–of the boundaries of your own being–as the mark of your common humanity.

The fourth verse opens with an assumption of an achieved complicity between Dylan and you. The "princess on the steeple" is an image of the "once upon a time" fairy-tale identity you were still clinging to when the song opened. You still have your "diamond ring," a symbol not so much of wealth as of sanctioned social identity, but Dylan now assumes you have so little attachment to it that you will readily "pawn" it. He also assumes that you are now challenged rather than "amused" by "Napoleon in rags": you are now prepared to recognize him as a fellow (and rival) emperor of "nothing." Dylan's "nothing" is an Emersonian poverty that is synonymous with spiritual wealth, the name for a freedom ("nothing to lose") that is decidedly not the mere "nothing *left* to lose" (emphasis added) of Kris Kristofferson's "Me and Bobby McGee." Dylan's freedom entails not a loss of identity but an immunity from his own identities: a capacity to own things without being owned by them that takes the form of a readiness to "pawn" anything and everything, to divest and re-invest an established identity at will.

I said that the fourth verse opens with an assumption of an achieved complicity between Dylan and you, but that is not quite accurate. Or its accuracy depends on what you mean by "Dylan." By this point, the singer–a fellow human just like you–has all but entirely disappeared, to reappear presently as "Napoleon in rags." The voice in the fourth verse belongs to the "mystery tramp," the song's presiding genius, who begins by offering some pointed advice and then re-introduces the imperious voice of the singer as a fellow character within your narrative. Finally, the mystery tramp's divine voice shifts to a tone of visionary exhortation:

*Go to him now he calls you, you can't refuse*
*when you ain't got nothing*
*you got nothing to lose*

*You're invisible now*
*you got no secrets*
*to conceal*

The song reaches its climax here, in the transcendental ecstasy of a visionary "now" that breaks the spell of the rage-filled "once upon a time" out of which the song arose. This "now" is identical to the emergence of your "invisible" self from the social covering that has made its nakedness a "secret." To be "invisible," in the sense intended here, is a radically dialectical notion, an appearance that is also a disappearance, and though it invites endless meditation, I'll just say that it seems to be Dylan's ultimate image for an authentic being-in-the-world. "You're invisible now," then, is a statement equivalent to "I see you," except it finesses the rude self-consciousness of such bad language.

This visionary "now" is thrown out as the consummation of an encounter between singer and listener–Dylan and you–on the common ground provided by the song. That is, "Go to him now, he calls you" is a fairly transparent trope whose literal meaning is "Come to me now, I call you." But Dylan doesn't say "I," not in this line, not anywhere in the song. He eschews the first-person pronoun throughout because this is your song, and you inevitably encounter him as "him," in the third person, or specifically (as it turns out) as "Napoleon in rags." Your sense of him as "I" is necessarily a leap of faith, an imagining grounded in your sense of yourself as "you." Similarly, his sense of you as "you" is grounded in his sense of himself as "I." In an important sense, then, Dylan has been saying "I" all along. Like any other maker of fictions, Dylan can address his fiction of "you" only because–and only insofar as–he can see you in himself. You are, first and foremost, an imagined "you," a fictional eye for Dylan's "I."

"You," in sum, are Dylan's most daring and transgressive trope for himself: he supplants his own audience by finding it within himself. Perhaps this is just a way of saying that, above and beyond the ecstatic release of his own truest voice in singing the song, Dylan enjoys your ecstasy at the climax of the song at least as much as you do. (Or I should say, as you might, if you have managed to keep pace throughout the song with his exacting imagination of you.) "You're invisible now" also announces an apotheosis of the singer's desire. The final chorus carries the same meaning it did after the second verse, but what once loomed as a forbidding ordeal is now joyously solicited–by the "mystery tramp" in both Dylan and you, both singer and listener–as a revelation of a naked self beyond identity, beyond personality, beyond its own creations.

As an image of self, the "rolling stone" transposes the self-cleansing nothingness of Emerson's "transparent eye-ball" from the realm of contemplation to the realm of social intercourse, while also imbuing the Emersonian divine self with an unmistakably Dylanesque negative theology. This is Emerson in his *Nature*: "I become a transparent eye-ball. I am nothing. I see all. The currents of the Universal Being circulate through me; I am part or particle of God." This (in essence) is the Dylan who first discloses himself in "Like a Rolling Stone": "I become a rolling stone. I have nothing. Home is wherever I go. I travel the streets everywhere, inscrutable and self-sufficient."

## III

"Like a Rolling Stone" is a song about freedom, but then, in one way or another, so is every song Dylan would write until the 70s, when marriage usurped its place as his central imaginative obsession. But "Like a Rolling Stone" dramatically expanded the scope of his freedom as a performing artist because it showed him a way to retrieve his freedom from his audience without simply abandoning that audience.

Dylan retrieves his freedom, as I have argued, by putting his audience into his song. What this means pragmatically is that he must find a voice for that audience within himself. "Like a Rolling Stone" thus emerges from Dylan's dialogue with himself, a dialogue in which "you" figure as an evil twin he cannot expel but must forever confront.

But this "you" also still carries the sense of other people, of external listeners, real or imagined. Otherwise, it wouldn't have resolved Dylan's impasse with his audience, and you would not feel (as we all do) invited into the song. Moreover, without the driving force of his passion–his hatred–for his audience, I doubt that Dylan would have found the courage to ferret out his inner demons. I suspect, in fact, that Dylan had been projecting onto his audience–not that they didn't offer an easy target–his own failures of nerve. (After all, during that 1965 British tour, even after he had released a whole album side of rock-'n'roll, he was still playing artistically and commercially safe acoustic shows to adoring audiences.)* But when he hauled his audience into the court of his imagination, he found their crimes–surprise!-in his own divided imagination.

This psychologizing, I concede, is rank speculation, and I certainly don't claim either that Dylan understood his breakthrough in these terms, or that we need these terms to understand this song. But I do believe you'll find that this point of view will come in handy when you try to talk about "Like a Rolling Stone," and I do know that what he had done in creating "Like a Rolling Stone" opened his art to a whole other level. In the short run, it exploded into a year of performances that we might retrospectively dub the Mystery Tramp Tour, a series of concerts (culminating in the legendary 1966 tour of the British Isles) built around several other new songs that also interrogated "you" with a shamanistic wit at once lethal and frightfully tender.

Dylan's Mystery Tramp persona burned out rather quickly. But the artistic discoveries that fueled its peculiar confrontational intensities have had a lasting impact on Dylan's career. For one thing, whenever Dylan has faced–or wanted to provoke–controversy with his audience, he has come up with a new batch of material dominated by you-baiting second-person songs. He returned to this form–with a vengeance–in the late 70s, at the beginning of his "born-again" phase: on *Slow Train Coming* the mystery tramp is Jesus, and you are usually non-believers–within and without. In many of these songs, however, the I-you

* Carolyn Sumner's "The Ballad of Dylan and Bob" (*The Telegraph* 14, pp. 38-52) is a superb discussion of the strain of self-interrogation in the relationship between the fictive "I" and "you" in Dylan's songs. The pseudonymous Hugh Dunnett's "Weary Hugh Tonight" (*The Telegraph* 23, pp. 92-97) explores the same theme in "Like a Rolling Stone."

rhetoric is turned upside down, in a way that reflects Dylan's religious experience of grace as an intervening "you," so that you are often either the Divine Self Himself or one of his angels. Dylan returned to this song form again in the late 80s–in the early years of a so-called Never-Ending Tour, when he might perhaps have begun to wonder whether anything more than habit kept him or his audience listening. For instance, the *Oh Mercy* song "What Was It You Wanted?" is a baffled elegy–both for love and for the ties that bind performer and audience–that fuses Dylan's old confrontational ferocity with a sublimely weathered mournfulness.

What Dylan discovered in writing "Like a Rolling Stone" was what might be called the essential dialogic nature of his own creative identity. Interestingly, he seems not to have realized what he discovered until a couple of years later. As he told his first biographer, Anthony Scaduto, it was only in writing the songs for *John Wesley Harding* that he "discovered that when I used words like 'he' and 'it' and 'they' and talking about other people, I was really talking about nobody but me. . . You see I hadn't really known before that I was writing about myself in all those songs."*

The force of this insight informs even songs that don't rely on projected second-person points of view. Consider, for instance, another *Oh Mercy* song, "What Good Am I?" I would submit that the fundamental meaning of this song would be the same had he written it as "What Good Are You?" Indeed, had he written it that way, he would have made explicit an I-you dialogue that is central to what he did write: a self-that-questions addressing a self-that-is-questioned, who plays dumb. A song that asked "What Good Are You?" would lack the overt rhetoric of self-questioning–a rhetoric that is crucial to its tone of moral bafflement–but the reality of self-questioning–the reality of the humbled spiritual yearning the song expresses–arises from something deeper than its superficial rhetoric. There are lots of bad songs pretending to express moral humility–Dylan's own "My Back Pages" springs to mind–and

* Anthony Scaduto, *Bob Dylan*, p. 286

they are bad because they are hypocritical in the literal sense of the word: the morally superior questioning "I" overwhelms the cross-examined "me," who is little more than a straw man for the questioner's implicit assertion of redemption. "What Good Am I?" persuades because it does not cast out the questioned "I" but affirms it as an inevictable part of the questioner's identity.

In Dylan's most characteristic songs you can almost always substitute "I" for "you" or "you" for "I" without changing their essential meaning. Sometimes, performing this exercise helps to break the spell of narrowly (and misleadingly) literal interpretations. Imagine, for instance, that Dylan had written "Is My Love in Vain?" or "You Want Me" or "You Don't Believe Me (She Acts Like We Already Have Met)." Changing the pronouns changes the point of view, but after "Like a Rolling Stone," point of view in Dylan's songs is almost always comparatively superficial, because he is always, as he says in "Where Are You Tonight?," "fighting with [his] twin, that enemy within."

Before "Like a Rolling Stone" Dylan is less consistent. "My Back Pages," for instance, is a song that seems to announce a new maturity beyond the crudities of "good" and "bad." But the problem with this manifesto is that it tries to disown Dylan's moralizing impulses rather than to transform them. For instance, "Masters of War," one of his greatest "finger-pointing" songs, defines "good" and "bad" with a prophetic authority undiminished by the recantations of "My Back Pages." But "Masters of War" also tells us more than "My Back Pages" does about the nature of the self-righteousness Dylan needed to outgrow: his lurid eagerness to see the war profiteers dead and buried is an anxious defense against recognizing anything of himself in an adversary whom his imagination, knowing better, nonetheless addresses as "you." Ironically, less than a year after writing "Masters of War," Dylan got himself into a heap of trouble when he accepted an award for his civil rights work by telling his audience that he saw something of himself in Lee Harvey Oswald.

The lessons of "Like a Rolling Stone" also profoundly affected Dylan's approach to performance. His deliverance from the tyranny of his audience also had a liberating effect on his relationship to the songs he sings. It's a cliché among Dylan fans that he never sings a song the same way twice, but that has not always been the case. Early in his career, Dylan's singing was conventional in one important way: you always felt he was concerned mainly to do right by the song. His sense of what is "right" was highly idiosyncratic, but his performance always seemed to be at the service of some demand the song made upon his imagination. And composed songs–even (or maybe especially) one's own–are full of demands that impose all sorts of constraints upon the creative freedom of performance.

They impose constraints upon performance to the extent that the performer regards them as establishing standards of expression he must meet, as something he must live up to. And in retrospect, Dylan's early performances do sound like the training exercises of a young genius expanding his powers by absorbing the models against which he measured them. Indeed, his powers blossomed so rapidly that he quickly outgrew the exercise equipment he inherited and began inventing his own, but he still approached the performance of his own songs the same way he had approached traditional material–as models of an excellence to which he was still only aspiring. Thus, the original *Bringing It All Back Home* recording of "It's Alright Ma"–the song in which he announced he has "nothing, Ma, to live up to"–gains a certain piquancy from the way his text-bound singing, almost reverentially literary, belies the text's irresistibly persuasive assertion of independence.

After "Like a Rolling Stone" and the subsequent 1965-1966 tour, Dylan rarely sounds like he's seeking an imaginable perfection; in fact, the better he knows a song, the more he sings it as if he's sounding the unknown–even though the lyrics and the basic musical structures he performs remain composed, not improvised. The difference between the original recording of "It's Alright Ma" and any number of the live versions of the song I've heard in the past two decades is the difference between a precocious youth who knows more than he can yet do and a mature artist delighting in the confidence that even he doesn't know what he's going to do until he does it. He knows what he's going to say, but he doesn't yet know how it's going to feel when he says it.

Dylan is able to sing with this kind of freedom, I would suggest, because in writing "Like a Rolling Stone," he had learned to find whomever he is singing to or for or about within himself. He had learned that his relationship to whatever song he is singing could be realized as a version of his dialogue with himself. And any tension in this relationship–as in his relationship with his audience–would be transformed from an obstacle to performance into one of its prime resources.

Dylan is an artist who is energized by conflict–with his audience, with his material, with himself. But he is even more fundamentally energized by something beyond distinctions between conflict and cooperation, if not beyond good and evil. Let's call it engagement, and the engagement that energizes Dylan is engagement with what he has to be able to call "you"–something or someone, that is, that answers him and that he can answer back. His initial success brought him an audience that answered him with an enthusiasm that must have exceeded even his wildest dreams. But it responded in a way that inevitably seemed to exclude him from the conversation. Applause turned him into an icon and turned the stage into a museum. The air up there was getting musty enough to make a feller sneeze.

"Like A Rolling Stone" is the sneeze heard 'round the world. In writing it Dylan stumbled onto a formula that opened "the language that he used" to his deepest intuitions about himself and his relationships with his audience and his art. He discovered that he could address you by talking to himself, and vice versa. He discovered, in short, a way to get himself and his audience under each other's skin. "Are you hard on them because you want to torment them, or because you want to change their lives and make them know themselves?" Dylan was asked during the legendary San Francisco press conference in December, 1965. "I want to needle them," came the impish reply.*

* "Bob Dylan '65: Meeting the Press," transcribed in *Rolling Stone Rock 'n' Roll Reader,* p. 216.

# 2

## *Ain't Too Big to Tell*

### Dylan's Early Songs

Bob Dylan began writing songs when he was still a child, but "Song to Woody" is really his first song. The earliest of the two original songs on his eponymous first LP, it was the first song he kept and, as Dylan told a radio interviewer in 1984, "the first song I ever wrote that I performed in public."* In many ways, it is also his most directly autobiographical song, since it is a song about writing one's first real song. Not surprisingly, it also turns out to be a final homage to the folk tradition that nourished him, and a dramatization of the process by which, in making that tradition his own, Dylan both carries it forward in himself and leaves it behind.

"Song to Woody" opens with a definition of the psychological site of its own origin. "Out here a thousand miles from my home/Walkin' a road other men have gone down," Dylan imagines himself a displaced person, a follower in other men's footsteps. But this mood–at once reverential and incipiently anxious–doesn't last for long. He covers his confusion so quickly we barely have a chance to hear it in his voice, and he covers it with an unconscious sleight-of-mind that seems to me to reveal one of the fundamental imaginative needs that defines him as artist:

* Bernard Kleinman, "Dylan on Dylan," in Benson, *The Bob Dylan Companion*, p. 33.

*I'm seein' your world*
*of people and things*
*Your paupers and peasants and*
*princes and kings*

Who is this “you” Dylan abruptly invokes? Woody Guthrie? Well, yes, of course–but not so fast. Woody Guthrie doesn't turn up until the next verse, where Dylan must still get his attention (“Hey hey”) and introduce himself by presenting the credentials, as it were, of his own Guthriesque vision of a “funny ol' world.” It is only in the third verse that Dylan resumes the familiarity of address he employed at the outset.

So who is he talking to? He's talking to “you,” the primordial “you whoever you are” implicit as a silent correspondent whenever we talk to ourselves. This “you” is invoked in what sounds like a revelatory slip-of-the-tongue. It's as if Dylan had started out to write a song for (and in the manner of) Woody, but the pressure of an unconscious need to talk to someone–or more precisely, to talk back to someone–broke through and pushed the song he was writing to another level.

Dylan himself, at the beginning of the second verse, certainly sounds surprised to discover he's written a song to Woody, to find himself talking to him, and not just about him. There is more to his delight than satisfied hero worship; this is the song in which Dylan outgrows his need for a hero, his dependence on the “other men” who pioneered the road he travels. He does it quite gently, smashing the idol while leaving the man intact. And he does it by addressing his hero as an aspect of what I've called the primordial “you,” as an aspect of his own soul. You could say that “Song to Woody” announces the separation of Woody Guthrie into two distinct beings, one the actual man and one now an interlocutor within Dylan's psyche.

The actual Woody is now a part of Dylan's past: Dylan sings “I wrote you a song,” even though that line was written as part of the song that was still largely unfinished. For Dylan, the actual Woody, like the rest of the “good people” saluted in the fourth verse, is already “gone with the wind;” the Woody he speaks to as he writes the song is a freshly discovered internalized presence. That's why Dylan is not at all anxious about acknowledging that Woody "knows all the things that I'm a-saying and a-many times more." It's as if Woody's knowledge is now an interior treasure, Dylan's to explore in the leisure of his own creative life.

Dylan's creative life is still mostly a matter of the future, a promise of "tomorrow." It could begin today, he tells us, but today he is taking one last backward glance. This is humility, but also simple honesty. The ethos of this song–its peremptory intimacy of address aside–belongs to Woody as much as, perhaps more than, to Dylan. The son moves vividly out from the father's shadow in only one of the song's images–the distinctly Dylanesque vision of a world whose death throes and birth pangs are indistinguishable–and in a pervasive fastidious elegance in the song's verbal music. The most characteristic touch is only half realized: "Somewhere down the road someday" is an awkward first instance of Dylan's characteristic use of "some" (among other modes of vagueness) as a kind of visionary prolepsis; that is, an anticipation of an imagined future as if it were a present reality.

What he foresees for that visionary "someday" is in many ways the best thing in the song:

*The very last thing*
*that I'd want to do*
*Is to say that I've been hittin'*
*some hard travelin' too*

To say "I've been hittin' some hard travelin' too" is to be able to say to Woody that "I know what you know." That will be the last thing he will say because the "someday" he has in mind will arrive only when–at "last"–he has mastered Woody's legacy. But even then, to say this would be (in the ordinary sense of the idiom) the last thing he would want to do–because when he is finally in a position to make such a statement, he will say it in way that sounds like Dylan and not (like these lines) an echo of Woody Guthrie.

## II

"Song to Woody" presents a revealing portrait of the early Dylan, a period of creative innocence that leaves its mark on most of the songs on his second album, *Freewheelin'*. Written sometime in January or February 1961, when Dylan was not quite 20 years old, "Woody" is most recognizably Dylanesque in its carefree blend of a generosity of spirit with a lethally ambitious self-confidence. "Song to Woody" praises and buries its subject with equal energy and conviction.

The combination of sweetness and aggression is an abiding feature of Dylan's temperament, but here it also reflects a striking innocence in his early sense of his audience. The world he writes about is almost always an inhospitable one, but he instinctively writes as if the "you whoever you are" he sings to is an equal who understands and accepts him. There is a seductive conspiratorial air about Dylan's songs of this period that lets us know that he's singing among friends. It's a quality that had a lot to do with Dylan's early popularity: At once brash and unassuming, he treated himself as one of us, and even better, he treated what was most free in our spirit as if it were what made us normal, our truest (and only) common denominator.

Dylan's implicit confidence in the intelligence and good faith of his audience may have charmed us, but it also worked wonders for him. Dylan identified you, his listener, as a part of himself, as a manifestation of his own friendliness. This identification was uncomplicated, intuitive, innocent; the dialogue with himself in Dylan's early songs is unconscious. Its pragmatic consequence is that even though almost all the songs of this period (including many of those on personal subjects) take the form of topical explorations of the "people and things" of his "funny ol' world," from the start Dylan's songs possess the vital intimacy and openness of a man talking to himself.

Or maybe I should say a precocious boy talking to himself. On his first album, Dylan sounded like an earnest, reverential, but supremely self-confident apprentice; on *Freewheelin'*, he sounds at once older and younger: older in that he sounds (and audibly revels in sounding) like no one but himself, and younger because–no longer feeling the need to ape his mentors to fit in–he sounds his age. In fact, he acts and sounds like a close kin to the innocent adolescent whose passing he laments in the album's only song addressed to himself alone, "Bob Dylan's Dream":

*By the old wooden stove*
*where our hats was hung*
*Our words were told*
*our songs were sung*
*Where we longed for nothin' and were*
*quite satisfied*
*Talkin' and a-jokin'*
*about the world outside*

The biggest difference is that in the other songs on *Freewheelin',* Dylan is "talkin' and a-jokin' about the world outside" from within its midst, and not from within the cozy cocoon of adolescence.

Sometimes, the change in venue doesn't make much difference. The best example of this is the song that made him famous, "Blowin' in the Wind." It sounds like the very sort of song a teenage boy (granted, a very talented teenage boy) might have sung to his friends, as they sat together and talked, wondering and worrying about the "world outside." "Blowin' in the Wind" is a political anthem, but Dylan sings it to "my friend" (not even "my friends," as I heard it sung at political rallies in the 60s). This private address seems to open the lyric to intense spiritual yearnings that override any imaginable political objectives and even confound the very idea of political progress. The images of the white dove sleeping in the sand, the mountains washed into the sea, or even the man looking blankly at the sky evoke apocalyptic desires for deliverance from mortality, not political yearnings for release from social oppression. These political and spiritual dimensions coexist in a partly coincident and partly contradictory tension–a provoking duplicity that has everything to do, I feel, with the song's resilient appeal.

"Masters of War" probably would have ended up sounding a similar note had Dylan opened the song by singing, "Those masters of war, my friend, they lie and deceive..." He's still the same callow youth, and he still is only half-aware of what he's railing against, or why. In the *Freewheelin'* liner notes, Dylan says he was simply "striking out against" injustice, but as an analysis of the causes of war, the song is both off-center and overblown.* Had he merely done what he intended, the song would be forgotten, like even the smartly written *Freewheelin'* outtake "Let Me Die in My Footsteps."

His decision to confront his nemesis, however, transports him to the "world outside," and that changes everything. The song transcends its fallacies, because in addressing these cynically manipulative arms merchants directly, as "you," Dylan allows them to get under his skin. Feeling infected by them ("you put a gun in my hand"), he casts his song in the form of an exorcism, deploying his penetrating knowledge of his enemy (he can "see through" their "masks," "eyes," and "brain") as a kind of protective charm.

And where does this knowledge come from? Not from experience (Dylan concedes he's "young" and "unlearned"), but from within, from a young man's intuitive knowledge of the exploitative psychology of the anxiety-ridden adult ego. In "Masters of War," for the first time Dylan finds a name for and vividly identifies Satan, the genius of division and strife who, under various names (including, ironically, "Man of Peace"), will bedevil his imagination throughout his career. Though conceived as a song of social protest, "Masters of War" is one of Dylan's most Blakean songs, a visionary confrontation between Innocence and Experience.

It's a confrontation that Experience wins because the self-knowledge that enables Dylan to "see through" his nemesis remains unconscious. The song ends in a visionary stalemate, with Dylan awaiting the time when "I'm sure that you're dead." It's a time that will never come,

---

* Dylan may or may not concede that as an analysis of the causes of war, his song is off base, but it appears, from his statements in a 1980 interview, that he would defend it as a revelation of the essence of most wars: "My thing was to pull the mask off whatever was going on. It's like war. . . . war--unless people need another people's land--is a business. If you look at it that way, you can come to terms with it. There are certain people who make a lot of money off of war the same way people make money off blue jeans. To say it was something else always irritated me." Robert Hilburn, "I Learned That Jesus Is Real and I Wanted That," in Benson, *The Bob Dylan Companion*, p. 165.

for the figure Dylan has conjured is not a mortal individual but (in Blake's terms) a permanent state of each human soul, including his own. Indeed, it is only from this Blakean perspective that the notion that "even Jesus will never forgive what you do" makes sense. In Blake's mythology, Jesus forgives individuals, not the states they pass through. This line troubled even Dylan, and indeed it makes no sense in the narrowly socio-political context in which he consciously conceived his adversary.

I don't want to give the impression that I feel that the adolescent psychology of this or other early songs in itself necessarily diminishes their aesthetic value. The fact that thirty years later, Dylan is still singing "Masters of War," often with passionate conviction, might suggest that the truths of adolescence it articulates never entirely lose their force; indeed, the song's projected sense of an innocent soul engulfed in a alien world reflects an abiding Gnostic element in Dylan's temperament that reasserts itself off and on throughout his career.

Tellingly, however, in the fall of 2001, Dylan made a small but crucial adjustment in the lyric to accommodate a radical change in his approach to performing it. For the first time the tone of Dylan's voice–cutting yet intimately confidential–suggested he was really talking to this demon, and not just through him. In performances of the song during the 90s, the line "I'll stand over your grave until I'm sure that you're dead" had often inspired a bloodthirsty roar from Dylan's live audiences. But not this time. Dylan's delivery had–apparently deliberately–drained the thrill from the line.

Dylan then ended the song by repeating the first verse. Ah-ha! So the vampire is still alive, still wearing the mask of decency we can now all see through, as he always will be. Suddenly the original concluding verse, now displaced, was no longer a fantasy of some final once-and-for-all triumphant riddance of evil. It was, more modestly, just Dylan's way of letting the devil know that "I'm never going to let you out of my sight or take my eyes off you." Suddenly that fantasy of disappearance into the grave sounded like the devil's own desperate fantasy of escape.

The adolescent temper of "Masters of War," even in its ascendancy, was only one element in a famously mercurial temperament. *Freewheelin'* also includes "Talking World War III Blues," a delicious comedy that features Dylan as a latter-day Ishmael with a wryly engaging awareness of his ambivalent superiority to and complicity with the anxious isolato* psychology that spawns hatred and war. "Talking World War III" may be the lesser song of the two–it's somehow easier to take for granted than its dark Ahabic twin–but I grow less sure of that judgment every time I listen to *Freewheelin'*.**

"Talking World War III" is one of several early songs where Dylan projects himself into a picaresque persona to express a more complex sense of himself than he was yet able to get into his lyrical songs. It is the only one of these songs, though, that really pushes past amiable farce to consolidate this consciousness in a fully articulated self-awareness. I'm referring, of course, to the song's concluding two-part moral.

*Half the people can be part right all of the time*
*Some of the people can be all right part of the time*
*But all the people can't be all right all of the time*
*(I think Abraham Lincoln said that)*
*"I'll let you be in my dream if I can be in yours"*
*(I said that)*

The first part is the sanest summation of the moral comedy of our unreliable common nature Dylan (or anyone else, for that matter) has ever come up with–not to mention a pointed rebuke to the apocalypse-mongering paranoia out of which the song arose–and the second part a barbed revision of the Golden Rule it would take Dylan years to absorb fully into his songwriting and performance.

---

* Melville coined his irreplaceable word, which a Google search reveals to have some currency in American literature studies, in Chapter 27 of *Moby-Dick:* "They were nearly all Islanders in the Pequod, Isolatoes too, I call such, not acknowledging the common continent of men, but each Isolato living on a separate continent of his own."

** See John Bauldie's "Stranded" in *The Telegraph* 15, pp. 31-38, for a engaging & persuasive account of the song's deeper resonances, which Bauldie locates in the spiritual trauma of birth into this world.

This ending comes as a surprise–wisdom and imagination always do–but it is not simply tacked on. Unlike Dylan's other talking blues or the allied *Freewheelin'* song "Honey, Just Allow Me One More Chance," this song's narrative has all along been making a bid for self-understanding–and not just self-justification. The role of refusing consciousness has been foisted, ironically, onto the hapless psychiatrist. Moreover, Dylan's nuclear dream is largely shaped by a theme of willfully thwarted communication that (by way of the mythical "Rock-A-Day Johnny") also implicates his own artistic credibility. The song's conclusion comes as a brilliant stroke that unties its Gordian knot of paranoid isolation by finding "somebody to talk to" in the audience that (up to now) it was being sung at.

"A Hard Rain's A-Gonna Fall" is addressed to the early Dylan's most accommodating audience, and the result is closer to "Masters of War" than to "Talking World War III": a luminously intense but severely circumscribed self-awareness. "Hard Rain" is the first in a series of progressively demoralized apocalyptic prophecies Dylan would address to a mother figure who always seems to induce in Dylan a self-revelatory expansiveness verging on logorrhea. Whatever Dylan's actual relationship to his mother (it seems to have been unusually positive), "mama" is Dylan's poetic name for a muse that never tires of hearing him talk. The early songs addressed to this mother-muse are among Dylan's longest: "A Hard Rain's A-Gonna Fall," "It's Alright, Ma" and "Stuck Inside of Mobile." This tradition seems to culminate in "Visions of Johanna," the 1966 song Dylan introduced, at a concert in Melbourne, Australia, on April 19, 1966, as "Mother Revisited." After that, the mother-muse is replaced by a lover-muse (or wife-muse), and "mama" (with the single exception of "Knockin' on Heaven's Door") appears only as an aspect of his lover-wife or (in malign form) as an inhibiting mother-in-law figure.

"Hard Rain" is also Dylan's first visionary song, his first song in which the "funny ol' world" is wholly metamorphosed into images of his feelings about it. In their range and sequence, the song's catalogue of images has an improvisatory feel to them, but despite the conclusions of most commentators, it possesses a definite logic, a logic shaped (as one might expect in a song provoked by a mother's questioning) by Dylan's hopes and anxieties. And despite Dylan's claim that the song is a response to anxieties provoked by the Cuban missile crisis, the anxieties that shape it are fundamentally psychological.

Overtly, the song is a visionary apocalypse of a human world gone horribly wrong, a world the singer foresees–with an anxious relish–will soon disappear in a cleansing "hard rain." This much is true. But I've always felt–long before I stopped to think about it–that this social and moral prophecy gets caught up in and nearly swept away by a rather more deeply unsettling cosmic apocalypse. In its own visionary terms, "Hard Rain," in a nutshell, is about Dylan's fears that his life is a highway that leads down a mountain into a dark forest that exits only into the depths of the ocean; or in simpler terms, it is about his fears that he is a mountain sinking inexorably into the ocean of death. That is, it addresses Dylan's fears about the futility of his own creativity in the face of the universality of death, a world of death in which the human political and cultural institutions he encounters on his journey seem to be collaborating.

The sense of this futility–of creativity wasted and unrealized–is powerfully conveyed by the very structure of the song, a series of five successively longer catalogues of beckoning images–Dylan once described them as the first lines of songs he feared he might never have the chance to write–that, one by one, are sucked back into the whirlpool of fate as quickly as they are thrown up by it. Although all these images–with a single exception–are of wounded lives (or of the wounding forces themselves), the accumulating pathos of the world the singer sees is matched, if not surpassed, by a corresponding pathos of his seeing, inasmuch as his visions, rushed along by the structure of his song, remain only partially realized. The largest sense conveyed by this exercise of his visionary power, that is, is of chances missed, of realities unfathomed, of insights lost to the rising tide in which his whole world is rapidly being submerged.

Everything, that is, except his visionary power itself. Perhaps this is the significance of the one exception to the bleakness of the song's imagery: "I met a young girl and she gave me a rainbow." Unlike the rainbow in the sky, this one is no emblem of divine protection against an apocalyptic flood–the "hard rain," the chorus insists, is "a-gonna fall"–but it does resonate enigmatically with the immunity of the singer's visionary imagination to the corruption it beholds.

Nonetheless, that immunity is but the flip-side of its futility–innocence is always both unharmed and helpless–and it won't last forever anyway. The singer's concluding determination–to sing until he sinks–simultaneously defies and surrenders to his anxieties without resolving them. It's hard not to conclude that the inundating ocean in "Hard Rain" is the dark side of the mother-muse to whom the song is addressed. If one had to reduce the song's emotional core to a single slogan, it would be "Thank you, Great Mother, for poisoning me with life." The song's most striking imaginative quality is its innocence, the absence of any developed sense of irony: the gratitude and the resentment simply co-exist in equal proportions.

The innocence of this relationship is more troubling–because more unstable–than the innocence of Dylan's relationships to the friends and other strangers his early songs are usually addressed to. Indeed, at this stage Dylan seems to have found it difficult to impossible to say no to any woman: that's why his "no's" are often violent and vicious. A good deal of the drama of his early love songs arises from his efforts to find satisfying ways to put a limit to women's claims on his soul.

## III

*Freewheelin'* contains three songs that fall into this category. The earliest is "Down the Highway," a superb traditional blues that chooses, with fierce reluctance, a life on the gamblers' highway over life (or death?) in the "middle of the ocean" that "took my baby." Except for the desperate plea to his absent lover that erupts at the end of the fourth verse, the song is addressed to a shadowy "Lord" of the highway who fifteen years later (in a similar context) will reappear as "Senor." Here he is little more than an unconscious invocation of an embryonic sense of self. Something similar is going on in "Girl of the North Country," a lovely idealization of lost love that is mediated through a presumptively male "you" who is barely (if at all) distinguishable from Dylan himself and whose fellow sympathy for the pangs of unrequited love is the song's true emotional center.

The third *Freewheelin'* love song, "Don't Think Twice, It's Alright," is one of Dylan's most sublime creations. It takes the form of a farewell to an ex-lover, but since this farewell is sung after he has already left, it is really a farewell to that part of himself that can't stop wanting a woman whom he "once loved" and who wants him but (apparently) never really loved him. There is no good reason for her not to have loved him, but then there is no good reason for Dylan to give up on her just now. And that's his problem, the motive for his song: to reconcile himself with what he's done by finding something within himself more precious than this woman.

He hasn't found it when he starts his song. He seems to have left in a pique, but his recrimination ("you're the reason") rings hollow, and by the second verse he acknowledges, reluctantly, that he is beyond her reach. His claim that "it doesn't matter anyhow" seems aimed at comforting her, and in any case it is certainly premature in regard to his own feelings. This is one instance, however, where saying begins to make it so. That is, what do ring true are his insistently repeated negatives, his insistence upon the finality of his disappointments, an insistence upon saying "no" born of an emergent sense of the urgencies of his own life.

This urgency of self finds its voice in the concluding charge that "you just kinda wasted my precious time." This line sounds like a throwaway, a final shrug of the shoulders, but it reverberates as a triumphant final surprise. This sense of triumph has nothing to do with revenge and even little to do, at this point, with the woman he's left behind. It has everything to do with Dylan's still somewhat toddling discovery that the "long lonesome road" is his home. He is, for the first time, his own rooster crowing.

There are two other related songs I would like to discuss in this context, "Tomorrow Is a Long Time" and "Mama, You Been on My Mind." This first of these, apparently composed a couple months earlier that "Don't Think Twice," is a *Freewheelin'* outtake, a live version of which was released in 1971 on *Greatest Hits, Vol. 2*. The lyric is rather slight–the middle verse is the only one whose language registers with memorable force–yet it is also a wonderfully acute evocation of the disorienting identity loss that accompanies first love. What's interesting about it is the way the singer's recovery of his sense of self arrives, as in "Don't Think Twice," as a surprise so quiet we probably don't even notice it:

*There's beauty in that silver*
*singin' river,*
*There's beauty in that*
*sunrise in the sky,*
*But none of these and nothing else can*
*touch the beauty*
*That I remember in*
*my true love's eyes.**

The decisive touch here is the interpolation of "that I remember," a touch that retrieves the center of his identity from his "true love's eyes" and restores it to his own mind.

The same theme returns in "Mama, You Been on My Mind," a 1964 outtake from *Another Side* released in 1991 on *The Bootleg Series*. This song is something of a companion to "Don't Think Twice," both musically–it's easy to mistake opening chords of the one for the other in live

---

* Dylan sings "rainbow in the sky" in the live version, from April 12, 1963, of this song that was released on *Greatest Hits, Vol. 2*, but the original lyric–which can be heard on an unreleased publisher's demo made in December, 1962–has "sunrise in the sky," which is also the published text and the one he continues to sing. "Rainbow in the sky" strikes me as a sentimental banality, while "sunrise in the sky"–mainly because of the alliteration of "sunrise" with "silver singin'" in the previous line, and the way the phrase is palpably shadowed by the sense of the "sun risin' in the sky"–possesses a real kinetic force, and genuine sense of awe.

performance–and thematically. The singer is now well along on that "lonesome road," utterly free now of any lingering bitterness toward or desire for the woman he left behind. Indeed, it takes the middle three of the song's five verses for him to satisfy himself that–even though she is merely an imagined listener–that his old love will credit the new-found disinterest with which he salutes her memory. (In concert, happily, Dylan usually ditches two of these verses.) The core of the song, however, is its first and last verses. The opening verse is a dead-on evocation, shivering in its delicacy of perception, of just how lonesome the lonesome road can get–it sounds like a more refined version of similar moments in Huckleberry Finn. Shaken by the onset of loneliness, the singer resurrects her memory to keep him company, and he sounds as surprised as he expects she would be to discover what pleasant company that memory provides. His surprise turns, in the final verse, into a kind of visionary giddiness:

*When you wake up in the mornin', baby,*
*look inside your mirror.*
*You know I won't be next to you,*
*you know I won't be near.*
*I'd just be curious to know if you can*
*see yourself as clear*
*As someone who has*
*had you on his mind.*

This quatrain is suffused with the rampant playfulness characteristic of *Another Side*–the second line translates roughly as "look, Ma, no hands"–but what's new here is that in this song there is no doubt that the singer notices–and consciously relishes–the revisionary powers of his imagination. Underneath that tender solicitude he shows for a memory he clearly treasures, you can almost hear him giggling.

## IV

"Long Time Gone" is a brilliantly revisionary adaptation of the traditional "Maggie Walker's Blues" that is still available only on bootlegs.

(The lyrics are included in *Lyrics.)* I wish it had somehow made it onto Dylan's first LP. It doesn't appear to have been written yet when *Bob Dylan* was recorded in November 1961, and the date of the initial reported appearance of the song–in a performance at the Minneapolis home of Dave Whitaker on August 11, 1962–suggests it might have been composed with material that found its way onto Dylan's second LP. But its emotional flavor–a stark, weirdly weathered innocence–fits better with the mood of Bob Dylan, and if I'm going to re-imagine history, I might as well have it my way.

And since it's my fantasy, I'd also edit it. For starters, I'd get rid of the 2nd, 6th, and 7th of the song's eight verses. The 2nd and (especially) 6th verses are childish excesses that just slow the whole song down to a peevish, pouty slog. The 7th verse is a tediously obvious artistic manifesto, although I do hate to lose the delightfully sly hot-dogging of "But I know I ain't no prophet/An' I ain't no prophet's son."* I'd also move the wonderful 4th verse ("I once loved a fair young maid/And I ain't too big to tell") after the 5th verse, so it would be the next-to-last of the remaining five verses. Finally, if I could get Dylan to collaborate with my fantasy, I'd have him re-set this verse's music as a bridge passage.

What's left is a Portrait of the Artist as a Demon Child, a rather more centrally Dylanesque flip-side to the Portrait of the Artist as Huck Sawyer, or Tom Finn, we get from "Song to Woody." It's the nutshell story of a beloved only child propelled, as if by the very tenderness of his parents' love, out of his home and onto a long road where nothing is stable yet nothing changes either, a road where only the faces that belong to children (like his own) seem really real. Children's faces and the "empty air" of his own incessant thinking.

There was also a girl, a girl who gave him the broken heart that started him talking to himself and so started him walking. The link between talking to himself and walking–as between thinking and doing–runs

* Stephen Scobie's "No Prophet's Son," in *The Bridge* 2, pp. 7-20, offers an illuminating discussion of the Bible-and-blues-derived ambivalences of this couplet that also fully squares with my own sense of the vaulting imaginative reach of the entire song.

deep in Dylan. As he puts it in the early song "Walking Down the Line," "My feet'll be a-flying/To tell about my troubled mind." One thinks also of "You're Gonna Make Me Lonesome When You Go," the *Blood on the Tracks* song in which the girl's departure makes Dylan "give myself a good talking to" that takes him all the way from "Honolulu" to "Ashtabula."

In any case, it's the girl who got his "mind mixed with rambling," which means the girl has an effect on him a lot like Mom's. Certainly the "single time" or "ten or twelve" times she broke his heart is an awful lot like the "twelve and one" years he spent not running away from home and ma–and not just "ma" either but (according to the text in *Lyrics)* "Maw." Yipes!

So maybe there wasn't even a girl, exactly, and maybe it was a good thing he got away before that tender love turned voracious. But anyway, here he is, "a long time coming" and soon to be "a long time gone." The song's refrain deepens the aura of divinity, Whitmanesque if not Biblical, surrounding this demon child, but it also defines his presence as a provoking negativity, an explosion that happens when the long foreground that nurtured him collides with his endlessly reverberant future. Never to be captured in the actual flesh (let alone flag an actual ride!), he emerges finally–"before your eyes"–from the ashes of an apocalyptic demolition of "youth" and "beauty," wielding his own "gravestone" as the herald of his imminent arrival.

This is the song I remember hearing for the first time over thirty years ago, as I listened to a scratchy, borrowed bootleg recording of a voice that sounded not like an old man but an old woman, and not even that so much as the elfin ghost of an old woman haunting the wind. I've never heard anything more preposterous before or since. Utterly unforgettable.

# 3

# *The Times They Are A-Changin'*

## Sinking Suns

I've never been very enthusiastic about Dylan's third album. I first took to Dylan because I was excited by the lively intelligence of his lyrics and his voice. *The Times They Are A-Changin'* is not exciting; it's grim, all but barren in its feeling, and more than a little depressing. It's Dylan's only album where he doesn't appear to be having any kind of fun.

To a large extent, of course, that was the point. *The Times They Are A-Changin'* was designed to showcase Dylan's ascendancy as the "the voice of his generation," as the nation's presumptive social and political conscience. It was a grim task–just look at the face on the album cover–and the resulting album is suitably grim in mood, tone, and manner.

The best songs on the album, however, do achieve a grim beauty and even sublimity unique among Dylan albums. Along with "Percy's Song," a contemporaneous composition that remained officially unreleased until its appearance on *Biograph* in 1985, these songs–"With God on Our Side," "The Ballad of Hollis Brown," "The Lonesome Death of Hattie Carroll," "Only a Pawn in Their Game," and "North Country Blues"–are by far the best of the "finger-pointing" protest songs Dylan was churning out from late 1962 through early 1964. But they do so only by transcending their genre, and in a way that implicitly betrays Dylan's temperamental unfitness for the role of protest singer, at least as most of his early fans and champions understood it. Those who heard him as the voice of their generation believed–or wanted to believe–that his songs could change history. But Dylan, like Joyce's Stephen Daedalus, instinctively saw history as irremediable, as the nightmare from which his songs, if they were good enough, would help him awaken.

This is certainly the thrust of "Percy's Song." Its story–a good friend gets life in prison for an accidental homicide–is too anomalous to comprise a representative anecdote about the injustice of the "system," but it makes all-too-perfect sense as a Kafkaesque vision of cosmic injustice:

*Too late, too late,*
*for his case it is sealed,*
*Turn, turn,*
*turn again.*
*His sentence is passed*
*And it cannot be repealed,*
*Turn, turn to the rain*
*And the wind.*

Dylan's deepest intuition about human history is that its "case is sealed," beyond appeal. He may from time to time rebel against his own imagination– *Times* includes two such insurrections–but he never really overturns it.

The album's two revolutionary anthems–"The Times They Are A-Changin'" and "When the Ship Comes In"–are both superbly realized, but listened to outside the context of a political rally, they both sound facile, mere wishful thinkings. And yet their imaginative reach, which is genuinely apocalyptic, exceeds that of any political effort to effect social change. "The Times They Are A-Changin'" is cast as public prophecy, but it is most persuasive, I find, when viewed as a repressed communal prayer–a prayer for change and, secretly, a prayer that one's own spirit be a part of whatever change may come. And the triumphalism of "When the Ship Comes In" rings truest, I feel, when we hear it as a repressed vision of spiritual renovation, so that the "foes" to be overcome are recognized as inner fears that "keep the ship confused," psychic specters each shipmate is sloughing off, to be "drownded in the tide" that is carrying them home to daybreak. I know I'm on shaky ground to present these two songs as evasions of their own imaginative impulses, but that is how I hear them.*

At his best, in any case, Dylan has always sought not to change history but to escape it. This album's five core songs are bound together by a common concern with how it is that people get trapped in history, and how they may rise above it. Their grimness is a matter of the scarcity and tenuousness of such images of transcendence as emerge from the

* On the other hand, apparently I'm not alone on this shaky ground. Listening to (or watching) Dylan's performance of "The Times They Are A-Changin'" during his 1993 appearance on MTV's *Unplugged,* Greil Marcus hears the voice of a "detective, investigating his own songs," and what that detective unearths, as Marcus hears it, is this: "Emphasis was the motor of the performance, with quietly stinging guitar notes highlighting especially 'If your time to you is worth saving,' a phrase that in 1964 felt certain and today can feel desperate and bereft--a deeper challenge. Or perhaps those words, sung and played as they were, were now a challenge for the first time. The song took on a new face . . ." ("Bob Dylan After the 1994 Congressional Elections," *Double Trouble*, p. 106). This "new face" of doubt and anxiety is, I suggest, the face obscured by the repression of that prayer I hear haunting the lyric.

Finally, to make my point perfectly clear, this is a nonpoet's version--mine--of the repressed communal prayer I hear whenever I hear Dylan sing this song:

*Come gather round people*
*wherever you roam*
*And admit that the waters*
*around us have grown*
*We must accept that soon we'll be*
*drenched to the bone*
*If our time to us*
*is worth saving*
*Let us start swimming*
*or we'll sink like a stone*
*If the times*
*they are to be a-changing*

darkness that enshrouds the lives that people these songs. Listening to them, I have the sense that Dylan is exploring–at arm's length–how to escape the feelings that fueled the fury of "Masters of War": confused feelings of guilt and betrayal, of some obscure, almost Faulknerian sense of inherited dispossession and defeat, a feeling of personality buried in the debris of fate.

## II

Before turning to a discussion the album's five central songs, I want to discuss three songs whose connection to this album's theme is rather oblique: "Boots of Spanish Leather," "One Too Many Mornings," and "Restless Farewell."

"Boots of Spanish Leather" is an immaculately executed ballad, in traditional style, that chronicles, in the form of an epistolary exchange, the breakup of a love affair. The narrator's girl, who has just sailed for Europe, writes him four times, offering each time to send him a gift, and he responds each time insisting the only gift he wants is her return. It gradually becomes clear–for her as well as him–that she won't be coming back to him. After her fourth letter, which announces "I don't know when I'll be coming back again/It depends on how I'm feeling," the singer sees his fate and writes back to accept it.

Yes, his fate. The singer's fate–the loss of a "true love"–is a trivial burden compared to those of Hattie Carroll, Hollis Brown, and the other ill-fated protagonists of the album's protest songs, but it poses the same kind of problem that fate always poses for the individual spirit. The heart of the song's affecting loveliness is the gallant delicacy with which the two soon-to-be ex-lovers continue to address each other all the way through to the end. They are unable to resist the fatality that separates them–a fatality we identify, I think, with both her wayward heart and his possessiveness–but they do master it to the extent that they do not allow it to disfigure their humanity. The narrator almost loses it in his third letter–"How can how can you ask me again"–but he recovers enough to transmute recrimination into a reaffirmation of his fidelity.

He also almost loses it in his fourth and final letter, although he manages exquisitely to conceal all traces of his inner turmoil:

*So take heed take heed*
*of the western wind*
*Take heed of the*
*stormy weather*
*And yes there's something*
*you can send back to me*
*Spanish boots of*
*Spanish leather*

The "western wind" and "stormy weather" are both the literal dangers she faces on her journey and, well concealed in that literal sense, tropes for the foul weather of his own mood. His final concession–the specification of the gift she been urging on him all along–is meant to quiet his mood by reducing her memory to–or externalizing it as–a souvenir.

Though it treats similar themes, "One Too Many Mornings" is an entirely different kind of song, one that resonates with the rest of the album only on its evocation, in its marvelous opening lines, of a consciousness embattled by an enveloping cosmic fate:

*Down the street the dogs are barkin'*
*And the day is getting dark*
*When the night comes in a-fallin'*
*The dogs'll lose their bark*
*An' the silent night will shatter*
*From the sounds inside my mind*

Beyond this, the remainder of the song–which is pretty good but frankly doesn't live up to the promise of its opening lines–takes a tack that, while suitably grim-voiced, has more in common with the songs on *Another Side* than with those on *Times*. It is a telescoped drama of moral-self discovery in a dying relationship neither the singer nor his love have been able to bring themselves to shake. All that still binds the two lovers is a spiritual timidity–evoked with a wholly apt creepiness in the middle verse–that has left both of them "one too many mornings and a thousand miles behind" their own lives.

Until the final verse, where he is finally able to release himself and his "love" from their joint bondage, the singer has–as he surely knows–more in common with the dogs cowering before nightfall than with the night-shattering powers of his own mind. He is able to break the spell that holds both of them, and thereby restore both to the righteous freedom of their separate selves, only by coming clean about his motives:

*It's a restless hungry feeling*
*That don't mean no one no good*
*When everything I'm a-sayin'*
*You can say it just as good*
*You are right from your side*
*And I am right from mine*
*We're both just one too many mornings*
*And a thousand miles behind.*

He had been held "behind," it seems, by some sort or false and self-flattering idealism, unable to make a move that did not cast him as some sort of moral hero. Ironically, it is only after confessing his selfishness that he has (what sounds like) his first mutually regarding conversation with his love in "one too many mornings."

"Restless Farewell" was written–in response to a *Newsweek* expose of Dylan's background–and recorded after the rest of *Times* had been completed. The final verse–with its defiant confidence that his art can "pierce through" the "dust" of any fate that awaits him–makes it a fitting finale for *Times,* but with its youthful brio and studied eloquence, it's completely unlike anything else on the record. Its genre is provokingly mixed: part tavern song (it's an adaptation of the traditional Irish song, "The Parting Glass"), part final testament, and part manifesto. Indeed, its status as a manifesto emerges as the song proceeds, so that our initial impression that the singer, with a gallant blend of pride and humility, is taking his leave yields gradually to the suspicion that he might just be leaving us in his dust, as he turns to "meet the dawn."

Despite the undeniably disarming nobility of its sturdy, sometimes penetrating (and occasionally impenetrable) truth-telling, the song's greatest interest, I think, is as a manifesto. The final verse has always gotten the most comment, but for me the most centrally revealing lines occur in the preceding verse:

*But it's not to stand naked under*
*unknowin' eyes*
*It's for myself and my friends*
*my stories are sung*

What this means, I would suggest, is not that Dylan sings only for his (existing) friends but that his songs exist only to solicit an audience that will listen to him as friends. This tells us a lot, I think, about Dylan's psychic investment in his art and what that art requires to keep it honest.

## III

"My name it is nothing." In opening "With God on Our Side" with these words, Dylan is not identifying himself with the anonymity of the masses or any folk community. He is doing just the opposite, taking refuge (not for the first or last time) in an alias to elude conscription in the patriot game that grinds its soldiers into fodder. Despite this defiant opening gesture, however, in this song Dylan fails–courageously–to slough off entirely the inward grip of a spiritual inheritance that deifies history. The song's shockingly abrupt climactic question–Did Judas Iscariot have God on his side?–arises from a gnawing fear that he's been "brought up" right, that "God" is merely Manifest Destiny, the triumph of history over charismatic personalities like Jesus Christ–or Bob Dylan. Dylan believes in the individual, but just as his words "fall to the floor," his faith falls flat in the face of his implicit certainty that God won't "stop the next war," because God has forsaken us, as he forsook Christ, to Judas and to history.

Dylan's faith in the individual is more than a political or even cultural matter; indeed, for Dylan, politics and culture, as ordinarily understood, are shadow states that usurp the reality of individual lives. Tradition is our living relationship with ancestral individuals, not with their institutionalization in culture: Woody Guthrie and Leadbelly are real, not folk music; the Founding Fathers are real, not the United States of America; Jesus Christ is real, not his betrayal by history we call Christianity.

This is the faith that succumbs to confusion in "With God on Our Side." Or seems to. The verse that confesses Dylan's intellectual confusion (the one about Judas) is also the verse that re-asserts, poetically, the primacy of the individual conscience by resort to Dylan's signature voice of direct address to "you." This gesture turns the song into a kind of incipient conspiracy against its own overt resignation to fate.

Dylan's antinomian faith survives its confrontations with history on *The Times They Are A-Changin'*, but it survives only by taking a hermetic turn: real history turns out always to be some sort of secret history. This seems to me to be the thrust of the album's other four protest songs. The story of a man undone by poverty, "The Ballad of Hollis Brown" casts its grim narrative largely in terms of a revisionary second-person–and insistently present tense–witness to the tortured inwardness of a man who kills his family and himself because his spirit has lost all connection to life, even his own. Yet Dylan's mode of address implies a mutual connection, even an intimacy, between them. The narrator, preposterously, is the "friend" that Hollis Brown "ain't got," and he's talking to a man who, even before he kills himself, has, in a fundamental sense, already ceased to exist. The song's terrible poignancy turns on our recognition that "Hollis Brown he lived" and "you prayed to the Lord above" refer to two different (and now incommensurable) entities, one a creature of history and the other a spirit entombed in that creature.

"Only a Pawn in Their Game," a song about individuals who have unwittingly traded their souls for their own paltry history, pointedly withholds any such gesture of friendship. This song is, in spirit, nearly a mirror image of "Masters of War": Dylan's polemical interest in those who put guns in killers' hands (here the "South politician") yields to an appalled–and appalling–sympathy with the plight of his "pawn" (here the poor whites who killed civil rights leader Medgar Evers). Dylan's stark narrative reverses the initial relation between victim and killer: Evers is "lowered . . . down as a king," while his assassins have become their own epitaph.

To achieve this reversal Dylan relies primarily on a blend of daringly dislocating metonymies that reduce the poor whites to the white skin on their backs with a merciless rhyming that enfolds them in its immobilizing glare. The rampant rhyming has been focused on the "pawn" with some deliberation. The first line (and only the first line) of each verse is unrhymed. The sole exceptions are the fourth verse–which is also the only verse whose first line focuses attention on the "pawn"–and the fifth verse, which affords the account of Medgar Evers burial not one but two unrhymed lines.

"Only a Pawn in Their Game" is one of Dylan's truly great songs, and what puts it over the top–for me anyway–is its unmatched tone. Its anatomy of the poor white possesses a fiercely unwavering balance of condemnation and pity, but it possesses something else, too, a mute sublimity, a reserve of silence emanating from Dylan's knowledge there is nothing he can to say to his subject. Dylan is speaking to himself, and to us, but not to Medgar Evers's killers. This epitaph to the living is as uncanny as the conversation with the dead in "Hollis Brown."

"The Lonesome Death of Hattie Carroll" is a variant on the themes of "Pawn": its racist killer, William Zanzinger, is damned by a similar reduction to his (much greater) social power, but he's accorded none of the sympathy that informs Dylan's portrait of the poor white. Instead, he functions largely as a foil to his victim, Hattie Carroll, who is as much a prisoner of her social condition as is her killer, except–and it changes everything–she "empt[ies] the ashtrays on a whole other level."

This outrageous pun, which lays claim to a secret truth that resumes its secrecy in the lyric as abruptly as it had flashed forth from it, has always struck me as the most Dylanesque moment on the entire album. "Whole other level" refers both to a mundane kitchen (or maybe basement) on another floor of the hotel and an inner reserve, a secret spiritual plane that transcends social identity altogether. We believe this claim for her because from the start Dylan's representational language accords her a special status.* Unlike William Zanzinger, unlike the poor whites in "Pawn," and unlike poor Hollis Brown, Hattie Carroll is rendered not through her social or bodily circumstance but through actions taken and privations endured. She is not defined in terms of her fate; her fate is re-defined in terms of the way she handles it. She alone outsizes her fate, a phenomenon wonderfully suggested by the way the triple rhyme on "table" (in a song unusually spare of rhyme) mimes both the reiterative tediousness of her life and her irreducible singularity:

*Who carried the dishes*
*and took out the garbage*
*And never sat once*
*at the head of the table*
*And didn't even talk to the*
*people at the table*
*Who just cleaned up all the*
*food from the table*
*And emptied the ashtrays*
*on a whole other level*

The song doesn't end with its poignant canonization of Hattie Carroll, however: Dylan wants justice. I don't think Dylan cares much what happens to William Zanzinger–he's beneath even revenge–but he wants Hattie's loss publicly acknowledged. This element in the song–which is carried by its refrain–has always bothered me. The impulse behind it needs no defense, and certainly the measly six-month sentence handed out does add insult to injury. My problem, I guess, is that Dylan puts too much weight on this issue. The song is addressed, after all, to "those who philosophize disgrace and criticize all fears"–the

---

* For an examination of other ways in which the song's verbal texture establishes our sense of Hattie Carroll and the world she endures, see Christopher Ricks's "The Lonesome Death of Hattie Carroll," *The Telegraph* 42, pp. 77-82.

intellectual quislings who collaborate with the judge's indifference to Hattie Carroll as surely as the judge collaborates with Zanginger's. Dylan's narrator knows that he is all alone in his possession of a truth about Hattie that, no matter how many listeners he might come to share it with, would remain a secret–a truth that anybody can but not everybody will recognize. Despite its underlying realism, "Hattie Carroll" is deeply infected, in its refrain, with the wishful thought that when the truth is revealed, as Dylan fantasizes in "When the Ship Comes In," "the whole wide world [will be] "watchin'." One has to wonder if the tears the narrator finally solicits are for his own disillusionment.

## IV

No one is watching, or listening, to the woman who sings "North Country Blues." It begins, like "The Times They Are A-Changin'," with an invitation to "come gather 'round," but in this case this initiating social gesture is wistful, ironic, and incalculably sad. Hers is one of those cruel songs that "make the hour twice as long," an inconsolable admission of defeat and uncompensated loss. It is just about the bleakest song I've ever heard.

It's also my favorite song on this album, an odd preference, I suppose, considering it's one of the few *Times* songs Dylan never performs. (As far as I can tell, he has sung it only once, at a 1974 benefit concert for Chilean refugees and political prisoners.) It's also virtually unique among Dylan's songs in its effort to render–without any detectable ironic distancing–the inner experience of another person, not to mention the only Dylan song to give itself over to the voice of a woman. What makes this distinction especially intriguing is that "North Country Blues" is one of the finest early examples of Dylan's mature poetic voice.

By poetic voice I refer simply to a signature sound we hear in the words, an imaginative shape in the music of the words themselves. This is Dylan talking:

*Come gather 'round friends*
*and I'll tell you a tale*
*Of when the red iron*
***pits ran plenty***
*But the cardboard-filled windows*
*and old men on the benches*
*tell you now that the*
***whole town is empty***

The crux of this sound lies in the structure of the second half-lines (in boldface) of the second and fourth lines in each of the song's ten verses. These half-lines kick in with a syncopated bite that quickens the verse with new energies, a resource Dylan uses (in this song and many, many others) to unsettle, complicate, or even overturn its established emotional cadences.

In most lines, what happens is that a single syllable is shifted from its expected place at the end of the first half-line to the beginning of the second. Thus, the completion of the first cadence is delayed, but when it comes it arrives with a rush, on the crest of the second cadence it initiates. Sometimes the effects of this shift are relatively easy to isolate and identify. For instance, the final half-line of the fifth verse ("shift with no reason") reverberates like an explosion through the whole song, illuminating its underlying theme of arbitrary dislocations, of displacements that transform time from a biological blessing ("filled every season") into a social and psychological curse ("the hour twice as long").

The larger effect, however, has to do with the way this altered cadence–at once slightly retarded and slightly rushed–bears pervasive witness to a resistant force of personality not present in the mere sense of the narrator's words. What we hear in this voice is not sadness and defeat but an elemental resilience, an unvanquished contrariness, an unspoken insistence on the psychological primacy of her own experience powerfully at odds with the steadily accumulating measure of her losses. This quality of voice comes across, for me, most forcefully in two places: at the end of the song, where "here now to hold them" quietly enforces a claim for the narrator's enduring affection that belies her overt acknowledgment that (for her children) there is "nothing here now," and at the end of the eighth verse:

*As I waited for the*
*sun to go sinking*

Part of the effect here is that the metrical phrasing audibly resists the possibility of "As I waited for the sun–to go sinking," a deflating cadence that would have played into the overall theme of expectations dashed.

Instead, the line insists that it was the sinking sun she waited for. The image of the sinking sun is both a symbol of her life's sad story and the actual sinking sun, an instance of the beauteous natural rhythms of life whose violation is the source of that sadness. The narrator's delight in her experience of natural beauty does not cancel her sadness, nor is it mere consolation; rather, her anticipation of the sinking sun enfolds her losses in a sublimely inviolable self-possession that finally outlasts her defeats.

## V

Who is this woman? We don't know. Unlike the people in the album's other protest songs, she's anonymous and (probably) fictitious. I'd suggest, though, that there's more of Bob Dylan in her than in any other character on this album–including the speaker in "One Too Many Mornings," whom she most resembles. Her son perhaps.

I'll give you something else to chew on. She's Bob's mother. No, not Beattie Zimmerman. This is poetry, remember? You know, nonsense in rhyme. She's Emily Dickinson–Emily Dickinson in Hibbing. America's original Girl of the North Country, Emily was the first to note that "certain slant of light/winter afternoons"–when the sun goes sinking.

God is a woman. Bob Dylan said that. Emily Dickinson is Bob Dylan's mother. I said that.

# 4

## *Another Side of Bob Dylan*

### Coming to his senses

"I can't understand." That's the opening line of "I Don't Believe You," one of the best songs on Dylan's fourth album, *Another Side of Bob Dylan*. But it could stand as a motto for this entire album. Something happened to Dylan–something internal, measured by no track of hours–in the process of completing his previous album. Something let go. The insecurities that energized (and partly plagued) his work up until this time simply disappeared–poof! It was if he had suddenly realized he no longer had to fight for his own life. He had somehow won.

*Another Side* is animated by an unusually anxiety-free self-confidence that isn't just a by-product of the famously large quantities of wine Dylan consumed during the recording session. He's so at ease with himself in these songs that he's almost delighted with his ignorance. Any number of his best earlier songs–from "Masters of War" to "Hard Rain" to "Don't Think Twice"–could be said to arise from the pain of what "I don't understand." But on this album, what he doesn't understand is greeted as "mystery" and "myth," and his own failure to understand is exploited as a comic resource, a license to explore.

The only two songs on the album to fall flat–and they fall as flat as any songs Dylan has ever put his heart into–are "Ballad in Plain D" and "My Back Pages," the latter a song for which Dylan and most of his fans retain an unfortunate fondness. In these two songs, exposition of what he knows overwhelms all exploratory impulses–not to mention any trace of humor. The problem with them is not self-consciousness, immaturity, self-absorption, or any of the other essentially moral objections usually raised against them. Actually, they strike me as morally and psychologically insightful, even precocious. But while they might be cognitive triumphs, they are also aesthetic failures because Dylan sounds too glib about the lessons of these experiences to invest them with any freshness of feeling or perception. "Ballad in Plain D" has, to my ears, only one good line–"beneath a bare light bulb the plaster did pound"–and "My Back Pages," apart from its admittedly fine refrain, is composed in the archly dense, hyper-allegorical lingo not of a poet but of a poeticizing bore.

These two failures are also exercises in self-criticism, and their profound humorlessness suggests, perhaps, that Dylan at this stage lost the ability to write directly about himself. In a sense, his newly achieved self-confidence had drained the imaginative urgency of his struggles with his identity. That's why, I suppose, in songs like "My Back Pages" and "Ballad in Plain D" he sounds like he's beating a dead horse, and that's why the humor of "I Shall Be Free #10," the album's other exercise in self-definition, lacks the edginess that makes its *Freewheelin'* predecessor, "I Shall Be Free," a memorable minor song. The humor of the earlier song has real bite, because its singer is still more than a little uncertain that he is free, or can be, or deserves to be. "I Shall Be Free #10," a song untroubled by such complicating anxieties, never amounts to more than facile stand-up comedy–except in the anomalous verse about "my monkey," a gnomic allegory about the status of blacks in America worthy of Richard Pryor.

There is a good deal of lively, absorbing introspection on *Another*

*Side,* but it is all indirect, a by-product of his explorations of the "mystery" outside himself. The album's one successful self-exploration is "Chimes of Freedom," but this extraordinary song draws its imaginative energy from an augmenting sense of self disclosed (implicitly) in the singer's discovery of his connections with others–with the "strung out ones and worse" he sings for, with his fellow storm-watchers, and most of all, with a god-like spirit in the storm itself that feels indistinguishable from the imaginative energy with which Dylan salutes it.

Indeed, in this song, the imagination rushes daringly ahead of the perceptions that fuel it. It does this first in Dylan's images of the storm (e.g., "the sky cracked its poems in naked wonder"), a series of precipitous visions that remind me of Hart Crane, except Hart Crane never succeeded so well in persuading us to hear his visions as plain talk. Then, in the song's benedictory quasi-refrains, the singer's enchanted mind flashes forth in litanies that range from visionary catalogues, a la "Hard Rain," to hyperbolic abstractions held together as images only by a miraculously infallible sense of rhythm, cadence, and the musicality of words:

*Tolling for the aching ones*
*whose wounds cannot be nursed*
*For the countless confused accused misused*
*strung-out ones and worse*
*An' for every hung-up person*
*in the whole wide universe*

Like much of the writing on *Another Side*, this should be awful. Instead, it is magnificent, because–well, who knows? Let's say it's because Dylan has a gift, a gift provisioned by the "majestic bells of bolts" that strike "shadows" in his "sounds."

To be sure, this heart-on-sleeve rhetoric is something of a dead end, a one-shot wonder. As poetry and as prophecy, it is perhaps the most extravagantly self-indulgent song Dylan has ever gotten away with. But he does get away with it here–because he sounds like the rejuvenated poet "My Back Pages" merely chatters about. Superficially similar rhetoric in "My Back Pages" ("Crimson flames," "confusion boats," etc.) rarely amounts to anything more than fancifully baroque allegorizations of what Dylan understands perfectly well. "Chimes of Freedom," on the other hand, sounds like the inspired utterance of someone who has no idea what he wants to say–until he says it.

## II

"Chimes of Freedom" is an anomaly on *Another Side*, where the "mystery" that arouses Dylan's imagination is mainly the mystery of women. In Dylan's songs, the mystery of woman is ultimately absorbed in the larger mystery of "you," a poetic trump card that may be Dylan's single greatest invention. This particular poetic logic, central to his art, informs several songs on *Another Side*, but its presence is usually subliminal, suggesting that at this stage in the development of his poetic art Dylan was still feeling his way toward it.

For instance, "Spanish Harlem Incident," with its striking observation that this anonymous "gypsy gal" has got her admirer to "wondering all about me," seems merely to stumble onto insights about the mysterious kinship of intimacy and solitude, insights that receive a fully realized expression only in "You're Gonna Make Me Lonesome When You Go," the much later *Blood on the Tracks* song. "Spanish Harlem Incident," like other songs on this album, is largely absorbed by the mystery of sex, while the later Dylan sees other mysteries through it.

"All I Really Want to Do," with its insistence that Dylan just wants to be "friends" with his "baby," readily lends itself to such transcendental interpretations, but this song is mainly concerned to announce a turning away from the rational mind that is central to this album's distinctive aesthetic. In this song, Dylan assures his would-be "friend" that their relationship will be liberated from the prejudicial definitions of the analytic mind. Instead, as we learn from "Spanish Harlem Incident" and other songs, their relationship will be based on exploratory energies released by their aroused senses. Of course, Dylan doesn't actually abandon the mind, but on this album's best and most characteristic songs, the rational mind either trails breathlessly behind a rising tide of excited sensual discovery, or it is momentarily assimilated into sensation, where it re-emerges as a flashing perceptual wit. Both these conditions of mind are exemplified in the spectacular concluding verse of "Spanish Harlem Incident":

*I been wondering*
*all about me*
*Ever since I*
*seen you there*
*On the cliffs of your wildcat*
*charms I'm riding*
*I know I'm round you but I*
*don't know where*
*You have slayed me*
*you have made me*
*I got to laugh halfways*
*off my heels*
*I got to know babe*
*will you surround me?*
*So I can know if I am*
*really real*

"To Ramona" relies on this sort of language to engender passionate conceits like "the strength of your skin" and blithe paradoxes like the proposal that Ramona should shut her eyes so that her "senses will rise." This song's emotional tenor is also grounded in Dylan's handling of its distinctive meter, an eleven syllable line comprised of three amphibrachs and an iamb: *daDAda daDAda daDAda daDA*. The base rhythm is a kind of lullaby–tender, solicitous, cuddling–an effect enhanced by the fact that it consists almost entirely of rhythmic repetitions of Ramona's name. The missing final unstressed syllable at the end of each line has the effect of a swallowed sob that implicitly supports the lyric's exhortation to stanch "the pangs of your sadness." (The lyric also employs a rare–for Dylan–tripartite line to counteract the tendency of the base meter to devolve into sing-song.)

"To Ramona" also manages to smuggle in–with remarkable credibility–the language of moral definition that Dylan abjures in "All I Really Want to Do" and that sinks "My Back Pages" and "Ballad in Plain D." Perhaps because Dylan uses this language here as if to inoculate Ramona against those who would "hype and type" her, he is able to come up with abstractions as suggestive as "finishing end" or finely tuned as "fixtures and forces and friends." Another reason the analytic language in this song comes across with the persuasive intensity of direct perception is that it is borne along on the current of an erotically charged rhythm. To paraphrase Whitman, it's only the lull we hear, the hum of his valved voice.

But unlike music, talking, however finely tuned, eventually wears itself out and "turns into a meaningless ring." Dylan awakens to this truth just in time, for during the course of the song's middle verses, the incurable prosiness of mere talk has been steadily proliferating extra syllables that have made it harder and harder for him to hang on to the "Ramona" rhythm. And so, as if having noticed what was happening, he concludes his song by returning to pure lullaby, expressed through a couplet that relinquishes his song to his faith in Ramona's inner strength:

*Everything passes everything changes*
*just do what you*
*think you must do*
*And someday maybe*
*who knows baby*
*I'll come and be cryin' to you*

"It Ain't Me Babe," the final song on *Another Side*, is one of Dylan's most popular songs, and deservedly so. Sometimes dismissed as a pale remake of "Don't Think Twice," it is in fact a mirror image: the song the woman in that earlier song might have sung to Dylan to help set him on his "long lonesome road" and get him thinking about just how much he was worth to himself. It's a very different kind of anti-love song than

"Don't Think Twice." "It Ain't Me Babe" is a song of resistance to the seductions of sex, a resistance that makes it something of a palinode to the mood of the entire album.

"It Ain't Me Babe" turns the album's sensuousness against itself. Each of the song's three 12-line stanzas opens with a quatrain commanding a former lover to depart. The language of these openers possesses a pungently sleek eroticism that progresses, as in a series of cinematic jump cuts, from a self-delighting renunciation ("go away from my window") to a shared delight in her escape ("go lightly on the ledge . . . I'll only let you down") to a self-abnegating delight in her recovery of a freedom that she experiences as her own disappearance:

*Go melt back into the*
*night babe*
*Everything inside is*
*made of stone*
*There's nothing*
*in here moving*
*And anyway I'm*
*not alone*

As she melts, he hardens into an effigy– before re-emerging as one who is "not alone."

To be perfectly honest, I don't know exactly what to make of this last image. I don't think it means simply that he already has another woman with him; that's never felt right to me, although when I first heard the song, I couldn't imagine what else it might mean. My sense now–influenced, to be sure, by Dylan's use of the word "alone" in subsequent songs–is that it means something pretty close to "I'm not lonely": not open and vulnerable, not receptive. Dylan commonly uses the word "alone"–as in "To Be Alone with You" or "'twas then she felt alone" ("Simple Twist of Fate")–to designate a specific inward state. He might also mean that he's not alone because, spiritually and imaginatively, she is still with him–as literally (since he's singing to her) she still is. This final paradoxical extension seems like a stretch even to me (who will believe anything), but I find that now that it has occurred to me, I can't get rid of it.

The middle quatrain in each stanza forms a different sequence of images, one that moves in an opposite direction: the corrupt excesses of the woman's erotic will yields to her abusive suppression of the singer's senses, which yields, in turn, to his enslavement on this proto-Maggie's love-farm, an image whose bitter tone turns on a sly pornographic pun on "come."

These two narrative sequences intertwine to create a resonant emotional fabric that I won't attempt to trace in detail. It is worth noting, however, that Dylan uses the refrain-like final quatrains in a way that anticipates the choruses of "Like A Rolling Stone." The reiterated refrain consolidates and measures the song's evolving emotional fabric, so that, for instance, the tone of "no no no" shifts from defiance to a kind of ecstasy, and "it ain't me" takes on an increasingly visionary flavor. This effect is further complicated by the fact that the refrain is confined to the last three lines of the final quatrain of each stanza. The first line of each final quatrain summarizes the preceding middle quatrain, and they do so in a way that introduces yet another image pattern, one that connects erotic excess with an attempted evasion of death: "open each and every door," "die for you and more," "life and nothing more."

My reading of "It Ain't Me Babe" may seem excessively fine, but I think that's a measure of its special greatness: it's an emotionally complex lyric that does not advertise its complexity. It goes down like candy. For this reason, I suspect it will prove the most durable song on *Another Side*, the one most likely to have a wide audience in a century or so. But it's not the richest song on the album–for one thing, its humor is too restrained–and it's not my favorite.

## III

"I Don't Believe You (She Acts Like We Never Have Met)" has been one of my favorite Dylan songs from the time I first discovered it and recognized it, in tone and attitude, as Dylan's first real rock 'n' roll song, a more genuine rock 'n' roll song than anything (except maybe "Maggie's Farm") on *Bringing It All Back Home*.

This claim is probably impossible to defend–what exactly is that hydra-headed beast we call rock 'n' roll?–but I can at least explain it. Rock 'n' roll, to me, is, among other things, a form of exhibitionism whose range encompasses shamanism at one extreme and pornography at the other. It almost inevitably takes the form of amplified music with electric instruments because its exhibitionist aesthetic invites a BIG NOISE, a noise that engulfs its audience: you don't listen to rock 'n' roll music; you swim (or drown) in it. A little more than a year after recording *Another Side*, Dylan would begin to make a bigger noise–literally and figuratively–with his songs (including "I Don't Believe You") than anyone had yet imagined possible. But rock 'n' roll is not its instruments; it's an attitude and a stance, a noise you make with your mouth that commands the electricity to support it.

So when I call "I Don't Believe You" Dylan's first rock 'n' roll song, I mean that it is his first song that feels like it was written for a rock 'n' roll singer to perform. Part of this is the way it violates poetic conventions governing the relation between audience and speaker. In a conventional lyric–like "To Ramona"–we are to imagine that we overhear the speaker pouring out his emotion. In "I Don't Believe You," Dylan discloses directly to his audience private feelings that are none of its business: he is talking to himself and (indirectly at first, directly at the end) to the woman who has upset him. Nor can you say he is merely talking aloud to himself, as if to an audience: the lyric is shaped at every point by a concern to convey the spectacle, alternately maddening and amusing, of his experience. He is using his experience to put on a show. That's rock 'n' roll.

As a final comment, I'd suggest that this song's only real rival for nomination as Dylan's first rock 'n' roll song is "One Too Many Mornings," a song with a very similar theme and structure. But "One Too Many Mornings" loses its nerve in a middle verse that retreats into a pretense of private musing belied by its extreme self-consciousness. Along with "I Don't Believe You" (and a greatly re-written version of

"Baby Let Me Follow You Down," his adaptation of a Reverend Gary Davis song that appeared in Dylan's first album), "One Too Many Mornings" was one of the few songs from his acoustic repertoire to receive an electric treatment during Dylan's first rock 'n' roll tour in 1965-1966. But where "I Don't Believe You" readily yielded to the transformation, "One Too Many Mornings," proved a bit recalcitrant: Dylan has to bull his way through the middle verse, and his shouted rendition of a line like "where my love and I have LAAAAIID" comes across as unwittingly hilarious, an unintended foretaste, as it were, of the wittily alienated erotics of the Talking Heads.

The lyric of "I Don't Believe You" is also, to my mind, a more adventurous, inventive, and realized performance than any earlier Dylan song. To say this is not the same as saying it is his first rock 'n' roll song, but given Dylan's rock 'n' roll soul, it is no mere coincidence, either.

"I Don't Believe You" is a mock protest song: it is a protest against its own discovery of the limits of Eros. The song is about Dylan's (comically baffled) discovery that erotic intimacy–no matter how real or fulfilling–leaves us still strangers, still apart, because we are still separate individuals:

*I can't understand*
*she let go of my hand*
*And left me here*
*facing the wall*
*I'd sure like to know*
*why she did go*
*But I can't get*
*close to her at all*

The underlying emotional structure of this song is an alternating rhythm between clenched petulance and bewildered vulnerability, between an insistence upon control and an openness to surprise. This emotional rhythm is grounded in a prosody that alternates between rhymed pairs of half-lines in strict iambic/anapestic (rising) meter and unrhymed half-line pairs that pivot on a substituted trochaic/dactylic (falling) foot. The metrical substitutions–which Dylan italicizes in performance–focus the emotional changes that ripple through the song like an electric current. At the beginning of the first verse (quoted above), "facing" and "close" underscore the singer's sense of betrayal by a world of appearances that has suddenly turned opaque, a realization that itself hits him in the face. "Close to" has a wonderful felicity here: the singer wants to be connected with a woman he finds himself merely next to, and he expresses that feeling (as we commonly do) by using a phrase that literally means "next to" to try to say "connected with." An old trope that we now wield as a trusty cliché has reasserted its literal meaning with a vengeance.

I could complicate things by suggesting that in acting "like we never have met," the singer's paramour has initiated a crisis of faith in his identity as a poet. But I won't. We'll just say she's left him feeling rather futile as a lover. That's our story, and we're sticking to it.

In the next verse, though, we find our frustrated lover in remarkably good humor:

*It's all new to me*
*like some mystery*
*It could even*
*be like a myth*
*But it's hard to think on*
*that she's the same one*
*That last*
*night I was with*

The key to this verse–and to the ingenuity of the baffled lover's response–is the antecedent to the pronoun "it." "It" is the situation he to which he has awoken, but evidently, from what follows, "it" is not the fact that he is lying next to a stranger. The truth, as (apparently) he has had the wit to take it, is that he is lying next to a lover who acts like a stranger. His response, that is, is to attempt to embrace the contradiction between what he sees and what he believes.

This response re-opens the situation to thought, to "mystery" and "myth," but thus also to forms of thought upon which thinking itself founders. His sense of what's real seems like a vanished dream, yet he wonders, provokingly, if he is still dreaming, as if his confusion were but a further phase of a dream from which he hasn't yet fully awakened. He wants her to talk–to reassure him that he is real, that she is real, that they are real–but her voice is locked, as if under some enchantment.

It is beginning to sound like a myth, isn't it? Our hero flails about in slapstick confusion for another two verses (is she sick? did I do something wrong?) before finally and abruptly coming to his senses. He let's go of her ("I'll be on my way"), reasserts his own counterbalancing privacy ("Of this I can't say very much"), and breaks her spell by addressing her directly, as "you," as someone he must somehow talk to in order really to touch:

*But if you want me to*
*I can be just like you*
*And pretend that we*
*never have touched*
*And if any*
*body asks me*
*Is it*
*easy to forget?*
*I'll say it's easily done*
*you just pick anyone*
*And pretend that you*
*never have met*

To address a body as "you" is an act of faith that remains forever at risk, even (or especially) after we "have touched." To "forget" here means to disregard (as in "forget it!"), a deliberate pretense which acknowledges that we are not one but two. "To forget," it turns out, is as easy as using the impersonal "anyone" when thinking about and talking to someone you know. "Anyone," that is, is the singer's witty trope for the woman he has been addressing as "you." His trope is an act of creative will, his way of pretending not to know her in acknowledgment that he cannot really, fully know her. To forget, in short, is as easy and as necessary as saying "hello" all over again.

Or as easy–and as difficult–as saying no. *Another Side*, in the final analysis, is a collection of songs not about the poetics of Eros but about the erotics of negation. The pleasures of the senses, Dylan here discovers, open him to the desire for an intimacy whose attainment requires a final refusal of mere erotic pleasure. Dylan's "no, no, no" possesses a dialectical ambivalence that makes its effect surprisingly akin to the Beatles' "yeah, yeah, yeah." Ramona closes her eyes not to stop her pain but to possess it in her heart, so that when she re-opens them she can look on a world unblighted by her loss. Similarly, Dylan-as-sex-addict must learn to forget so that he can recognize what he has to remember, and "Babe" must go away if she is ever to find someone "inside" the man she is "looking for." *Another Side* is a crucial album because it is here that Dylan discovers the resources of "no," a "no" that is not simple denial but an interposition of the spirit–for release, for respite, and for renewal.

# 5

## *Bringing It All Back Home*

### The snotty and the sublime

When I listened to *Bringing It All Back Home* for the first time, soon after my college roommate introduced me to Dylan, I was stunned. I was already an immense fan, but I wasn't prepared for a collection of songs that would make his earlier work seem, by comparison, almost dull. I've had a similar experience listening to new Dylan records several times since, but never as intensely–although *Slow Train Coming* came close. *Bringing It All Back Home* was the first and last Dylan LP to give me vertigo.

No doubt, the singularity of its effect on me had mostly to do with my own innocence: the psychology of the first kiss. I mention it here because listening to this record again, I have the feeling that the intensity of my relationship to this record somehow blinded me. For all my delight in the aesthetic qualities of these songs–their poetry, their wild humor, their musical inventiveness–I somehow never managed to listen to this record. I've never noticed until now what this record is all about, how its songs fit together, their particular personality. I'm not saying I had a mistaken, or inadequate, sense of this record; I'm saying that I apparently didn't have any sense of it at all.

And what a surprisingly odd record it turns out to be. For one thing, it's virtually two different records, so different is side one from side two: side one is extremely funny, side two has a Sunday solemnity; side one is mostly social satire, side two strains toward a visionary apocalypse; side one is mutant rock 'n' roll, side two is a mutant poetry reading.

Let's start with side one. One of the pleasures of revisiting Dylan's old records (and some not-so-old ones) is the opportunity it affords to marvel at his profligate invention. Dylan's catalogue is littered with pathbreaking gestures never followed up. Of all Dylan's one-shot wonders, however, "Subterranean Homesick Blues" is the most remarkable.

This song is a miracle of what Dylan would dub "tonal breath control," of rhythms fashioned with such immediacy from the bounce and spin of words that the sense of the words become indistinguishable from voice. To a degree equaled by few other poems I know, there is something indescribably exhilarating about the way the kinesthesia of this lyric renders its precise meanings not irrelevant but redundant, like subtitles in a movie whose original language we already understand.

The exhilaration this song provides depends equally, though, on the fact that the sense of the lyric does command our full attention. A seriocomic bohemian's survival guide, "Subterranean Homesick Blues" is an exploding digest of alternately gnomic and plain-spoken tips on eluding the traps society sets for our freedom. As such, it is a fitting introduction to a set of songs that portray society as the enemy of the artist. What I have been surprised to discover, however, is that compared to "Subterranean Homesick Blues," the rest of the songs on side one imagine society's hostility to the artist in terms that are drastically simplified. The sense of menace and hidden malice that pervades "Subterranean Homesick Blues" is reduced to meanness and mediocrity of spirit, and these other songs excise entirely the discomforting sense that social oppression is allied with biological nature: "the girl by the whirlpool" (or is it "Whirlpool?"), after all, leads directly to the nightmarishly mechanistic archetypal biography ("get born keep warm/short pants romance") that opens the final verse of "Subterranean."

The transition from "Subterranean Homesick Blues" to "Maggie's

Farm" is like going to sleep in a Dostoyevskyan underground and waking up in *Huckleberry Finn* on Aunt Sally's farm. The issue is still freedom, but its antagonists have shrunk from demons to fools. The song offers wonderfully on-target satire of the pettiness of normal social life, but the pettiness of normal social life is not a plausible threat to–or provocation for–the "head full of ideas" exploding from Dylan's brain.

There is, I would suggest, an oddly sophomoric hysteria just beneath the surface of these songs that you won't find anywhere else in Dylan's work. They sound like they were written by a man who's just discovered he almost took the road traveled by the gray-flanneled dwarf in "Gates of Eden," a road that would have taken him to Maggie's farm in suburbia and a commuter job in Tin Pan Alley. Or maybe they are songs written by a man compelled to tell himself some such story–as a stratagem for stopping his ears to the siren song of that girl by the whirlpool. "Bob Dylan's 115th Dream" is an interesting case in point. It's something of a throwback for Dylan: like the *Another Side* song "Motorpsycho Nightmare" (which would be more at home on the first side of this album), it is a late evolution of his talking blues. It's also the only song on this LP in which the singer functions as a source as well as an observer of the humor. Inserting himself as a picaresque hero makes his critique feel more generous, less privileged. Also, its social critique is from a much more free-floating (to put it mildly) perspective. This song is inspired stream-of-consciousness farce, a true dream: phobias come flying from all directions, like the boiling fat in the exploded kitchen. But I guess I have to notice how many of those phobias–as in "Motorpsycho Nightmare"–circle around issues of domesticity. And after all, taken seriously (which is all but impossible to do: good dream work there, Bob) this is a song that concludes with the image of a great quester unmanned by a terrestrial fat girl.

Whatever its underlying psychology, this oversimplified myth (sensitive artist vs. venal society) sometimes backfires on Dylan. "On the Road Again" still seems as funny as when I first heard it, but now I also hear in its lurid images of home life a somewhat pathological fear of domesticity. "Outlaw Blues" wastes a superbly menacing surliness of tone and one great couplet ("don't ask me nothin' about nothin'/I just might tell you the truth"), because in this song Dylan reduces his rebel stance to antic capering. It's delightful, but it's a delightful trifle.

And it's a shame that "Maggie's Farm" should find Dylan complaining about having to scrub the floor. Does he expect the servants to do the cleaning? Sure, I know what he's really protesting–the "sing while you slave" ethic–but his words miss the mark. His words misfire because he's shooting at shadows: the song's protagonist is besieged by cardboard caricatures. Dylan's comic reductions of the bourgeois mean-spiritedness of Maggie and her family are both deliciously witty and plainly hilarious, but these are not people who in any way really get under his skin. "I just get bored," he finally admits, and it shows. The song never delivers on the promise of its superb opening couplet:

*Well I wake up in the morning*
*fold my hands and pray for rain*
*I got a head full of ideas*
*that are driving me insane*

The prayer for rain is prompted by his need for something to water and cool off the fevered soil of his mind. But remembering Maggie and her scrub brush, we might start to wonder if he's really just praying for his workday to be washed out.

All of which is perhaps to say that *Bringing It All Back Home* is not *Highway 61 Revisited*: Dylan does not yet deign to converse with his real enemies. The songs on side one feel like they have been unconsciously circumscribed to allow Dylan to focus on a single issue: his assertion of artistic freedom from "them," of his right to the riches of the imagination. "Subterranean Homesick Blues" escapes these limitations because in this song Dylan actually addresses himself to someone not beneath talking to, the anonymous "kid" who is tantalizingly not his audience–i.e., you and me–but his own best image of himself. His song is a talking to himself to keep up his courage as he stands on the corner, chewing gum, and trying his best to remain invisible. In this song, instead of hearing about the "head full of ideas/that are driving me insane," we hear those ideas broadcast live and taste the incipient insanity.

"She Belongs to Me" and "Love Minus Zero/No Limit" are the other two songs that manage magnificently to escape the limitations of the simplistic myth that informs side one. In both songs Dylan invokes his muse–perhaps for no better reason than to flaunt her before the bourgeoisie–but having invoked her, he finds himself in the presence of someone beyond his reach. Her very inaccessibility seems to activate Dylan's deepest artistic impulses, forcing him to acknowledge–and provoking him to attempt to overleap–the limits of his imagination.

"She Belongs to Me" demolishes bohemian sentimentalities from the inside, with a surprising portrait of the muse as an unapproachable yet imperious dominatrix. Rejecting domesticity for art, it appears, is to go out of the frying pan and into the fire, to be saved from becoming the "new fool" of the "girl by the whirlpool" only to become the mesmerizing muse's "walking antique." (Indeed, on the studio recording sheet this song is identified by the title "Worse Than Money!")* This song is a straight 12-bar blues, and Dylan would later sing it that way on the *Renaldo and Clara* soundtrack. But here he sings it with a rapt affect that turns it–disconcertingly–into a devotional hymn. The title, of course, is wholly ironic: he belongs to her, but she belongs to no one. Indeed, he cannot even address her directly. Personal pronouns are often readily interchangeable in Dylan's songs, but you can't change "she" to "you" in this song without destroying it utterly. She is someone whom he still lacks the wit, or the nerve, or the grace, to talk to directly.

Or maybe she is someone you don't have to talk to. This imaginative leap implicitly underlies "Love Minus Zero," the very best thing on side one. By all accounts Dylan was a somewhat snotty, callow youth when he wrote the songs on this LP, and in places it shows. Indeed, "Love Minus Zero" sounds like a song that might initially have arisen out of a mood of smug self-satisfaction: "My love, she speaks like

---

* Michael Krogsgaard, "Bob Dylan: The Recording Sessions (Part 1)," *The Telegraph* 52, 107.

silence"–while yours blabbers artless inanities. But it doesn't retain this tone long enough so as you would even really notice it. "My love, she speaks like silence": this is a lie, and Dylan knows it is a lie, the kind of exploratory lie poets tell, and this self-knowledge changes his tone.

We first hear that altered tone in the reverential delicacy that permeates his images of "my love" and belies his cocky air. And we hear it in the quiet pathos that informs his representations of conventional society's hapless flower-bearing lovers. This quality grows even more overt in the second verse, where the dullards of convention are represented as dime-store and bus-station rappers, images that suggest not the bourgeoisie but the bohemian world Dylan elsewhere embraces as his own. It is as if in recognizing the lie in his claim of easy intimacy with his muse, Dylan is forced to recognize–implicitly, emotionally, if not consciously–his kinship with those who are not her acolytes. Implicit is the recognition that he is closer to them than he is to her.

All this lends to "Love Minus Zero" a humane sweetness largely absent from the rest of side one, but I think the song's real power derives almost entirely from its extraordinary final verse:

*The bridge at midnight trembles*
*the country doctor rambles*
*Bankers' nieces seek perfection*
*expecting all the gifts that wise men bring*
*The wind howls like a hammer*
*the night blows rainy*
*My love she's like some raven*
*at my window with a broken wing*

This verse emerges from the song that engenders it like a butterfly from its cocoon, utterly transforming what has preceded it. Here Dylan finds the wit–and the humility–to draw on images of conventional society for images of a chastened sense of self, transforming pity into a sobering self-recognition. The "perfection" which, by virtue of his coziness with "my love," he had imagined for himself is conceded to be the pipe dream of pining bankers' nieces. The howling wind blows away any residual sense he may have that mere individual sensitivity governs access to an elemental wisdom, or, as Dylan delightfully puts it, "all the gifts that wise men bring." Dylan sees himself in that rambling country doctor, and the trembling midnight bridge is his tentative, tenuous, suddenly quite unstable access to his "love." For this sublime lady, whom he has encouraged us to imagine as if sitting next to him, is now revealed to be at once less accessible and more invisibly inward than that. She has metamorphosed into a raven whose presence, a temporary and arbitrary gift of the indifferent storm, is but an imagined thing, and not just an imagined thing ("like a raven") but an imagined imagined thing ("like some raven"). This little word, "some," an untranslatable idiomatic shrug of the mind, is a characteristically Dylanesque evasion, but here it is deployed against himself, to acknowledge that his deepest intuitions of truth and beauty all but evade his ministering mind.

All this seems to me an accurate account of the cognitive processes that inform this final verse and that sustain what you could call its moral authority. But all this humility and compassion is in fact but a minor element of its overall effect; indeed, a minor element that is the mirror image of its deepest effect. By yielding to the truth–or seeming to–Dylan has reclaimed and vindicated his lie. By acknowledging his kinship with rambling doctors and overreaching bankers' nieces, he has in fact appropriated them as images of himself. He has put the denizens of Maggie's farm, as it were, to work for his own imagination.

And though he has been forced to allow his muse her inscrutable distance, he has indeed persuaded her to speak to him–"with silence"–in the image of the raven she offers him. The raven is an emblem of her inaccessibility, her indomitable silence, yet as a poetic emblem, it speaks–as surely as Poe's raven speaks. Indeed, it delivers in silence the same message as Poe's talking bird: "nevermore." For in representing the muse as a bird, this emblem bespeaks her human silence, her refusal to enter through the window at which she appears.

## II

"A poem is a naked person," Dylan tells us in the liner notes he wrote for *Bringing It All Back Home*. By that severe definition, "Love Minus Zero" becomes a poem only in its final line, a line that turns the final verse into an incandescence that consumes the song that engendered it. I have tried to trace the path that leads up to this climactic flash, but what's important is not what it is "about." The image of "some raven" is not really "about" anything, not even, as is sometimes said of such images, about itself. It is an image, at once perfectly translucent and perfectly opaque, that manages to get to a place where it does not have to be "about" anything. It offers itself rather for what, literally, it is: a trope, a turning of a mind that finds and loses itself only in its own perpetual turning.

I don't intend to get sidetracked here in the sinkhole of literary theory, but I think it is important to draw attention to the flavor of this sort of image because, somewhere about the time he wrote "Love Minus Zero," Dylan had gotten addicted to the taste of it. It gave him a thrill–and not just any old thrill but the very thrill whose allure had first drawn him onto the stage. Dylan may, as he claims, have become a poet quite incidentally, as a by-product of his songwriting–itself an activity he claims to have taken up only because he neede something suitable to sing. (And if the truth be told, he probably became a singer only because no other singer knew how to create a suitable context for his harmonica solos.) But it seems pretty clear to me that in 1965 Dylan-the-poet was light years ahead of Dylan-the-performer. He was beginning to thrill himself with his poetry in ways he still could only dream of doing as a singer or musician.

The thrill in question is the illusion of presence, of seeming to be here now. This is the conquest of time that Dylan would later define as the "heroic" task of all art. Meaningfulness is a function of our existence in time, a measure of connections between then and now, or between now and again, or between here and there. Dylan's raven trope is like the mythical snake's head that swallows its own tail, a turning of the mind on its own thought that momentarily dissolves thinking in an incandescence that, technically speaking, is meaningless. Meaning eventually returns, to be sure, but only in retrospect, from the vantage point of a succeeding incandescence. Thus in the great triple shock of images that concludes "Love Minus Zero," the uncanniness of the raven is domesticated somewhat by that of the window, the uncanniness of which is displaced in turn by that of the broken wing, which, since it comes last, remains (ironically) untamed. The broken wing is the final form of the muse's temporary availability to Dylan's poetic ministration, but it is also an emblem of the irreducibly enigmatic character of her availability. The muse insists upon her unaccountability.

What I am talking about, I guess, is the triumph of liveliness–of life–over mere meaning. At the most mundane level, the purpose of all tropes, of all figures of speech, is to make our language vivid–which means to vivify it, to make it life-like, and in that sense, to make it seem real. By 1965 Dylan had reached the point where he was able–as only the best poets can–to subordinate the life-likeness of his tropes to the immediate liveliness of his troping. "Some raven"–like few images before it in Dylan's songs–matters less as an image than as an act, less for its meaning than for its power, a power that arises from the way we recognize it as an act of a restless mind, wrestling with its world. The larger verisimilitude of such an art comes to rest on our recognition that the poet's activity is representatively human–that, insofar as life is the difficult art of seeming to be here now, living itself is a kind of troping, a kind of figuring. A poet (and such a performer as Dylan would soon become) is just doing what we're all trying to do, except that as an artist, he is doing it in a way that clarifies and celebrates just what it is that we are trying to do: to hold our ground, here and now.

## III

Whether or not my own account of the nature of Dylan's poetic advance is judged to be adequate–or even on-target–I don't see how anyone can listen to side two of *Bringing It All Back Home* without noticing that somehow, somewhere, Dylan the poet has turned things up a notch. Indeed, this extraordinary quartet of songs sounds very much like Dylan's self-conscious celebration of his discovery of a new power. These four songs have little in common–in theme or method–except their poetic muscle-flexing.

The poetic exuberance of these songs remains astonishing. To stick with Dylan's conceit, the modulations of imagery in "Love Minus Zero" are like a series of costume changes that hint at but never directly reveal the "naked person" underneath–at least not until the climactic raven image. But the songs on side two are almost entirely comprised of the equivalent of raven images. Each of these songs unfolds as a series of uncoverings, of dis-coveries, of their own imagery, so that we are offered successive naked truths that are continually unmasked as the faces of still lower layers. Each of these songs finds its final end in what will become Dylan's signature gesture: a self-disclosure that takes the form of a disappearing act.

More or less. Dylan's creative energy sometimes flags, falters, and flails about. "It's All Over Now, Baby Blue" doesn't always stay on the right side of the thin line it treads between the irresistible emotional momentum of variably suggestive imagery and the numbing effect of endless reiteration, and even "Mr. Tambourine Man" is not perfect: its third verse ("Though you might hear laughing spinning . . .") is one of Dylan's most powerful and brilliant pieces of visionary writing, but like the third verse in "Love Minus Zero," it is a sidelight to the main lyric that is presented as if it were just another verse. Not much of a flaw, perhaps, but think about it this way: had Dylan been able to incorporate this visionary swerve as a structural element in his song–say, like the stanza-length bridges in the 1989 *Oh Mercy* song "What Was It You Wanted?"–maybe he would not have chosen to skip this verse in nearly every live performance of "Mr. Tambourine Man" (until the mid 90s, when he began skipping the second verse instead!). Finally, like most of Dylan's long-winded prophecies of this period, the other two songs on side one could use some editing. Most obviously, the splenetic fourth section of "It's Alright Ma" (the one about the "ratrace choir" and "society's pliers") is a turgid, melodramatic dud, fueled not by the imagination but by self-righteous rage. (Dylan seems to agree with this assessment: he has long since dropped this section from his live performances of the song.) And the "motorcycle black madonna" verse in "Gates of Eden," splendid as it is, disrupts the momentum of a song in which it probably doesn't belong in the first place: it sounds like the beginnings of the lyrical idea that eventually found form as "Ballad of a Thin Man."

This said, these songs are largely driven forward by a poetic exuberance that expresses itself as Dylan's impatience with the terms of his own imagination. In "Gates of Eden" Dylan's appetite for self-surprising turns takes on a desperate, even mournful cast. This song enacts a struggle to escape its own nightmare vision. Its opening stanzas are the very definition of the portentous. They are full of significances that, when deciphered, turn out to be quite banal. On the other hand, that seems to be the point. These opening stanzas deliver their poetic truth viscerally, in a feeling they convey about a too-humanized cosmos, as oppressive as it is impressive, that delivers truths that forever fail to satisfy our hunger for the truth. There is something clotted and constricting in the enfolded imagery, corkscrew syntax, and short-winded rhythms of these opening stanzas that evokes a world in which matter suppresses spirit and in which force substitutes for authority. Their banality is the banality of evil, the hollowness of truths whose light–like the waxy glow of the cowboy angel's candle or the lamppost-cop safeguarding hungry babies' right to wail–serves only to render the darkness visible.

The rest of the song is a progressive series of attempts to dissolve this pasteboard-mask world that bars the singer from Eden. First come two stanzas in which Dylan holds the world at arm's length by twisting his nightmare into a more overtly sardonic, even comic allegorizing mode. In the fifth stanza, Dylan finds the withering visionary tone that will see him through the song, a tone that allows him for the first time to assert his own presence in this song. But in identifying his voice with that of the "lonesome sparrow," he both gets ahead of himself (that particular tone doesn't enter the song until his lover comes to him at the end of the song) and underestimates his power here. In these middle stanzas, Dylan's voice allies itself rather with the "precious winds" that blow away the "kingdoms of experience."

And it is as the voice of the wind that Dylan blows away even the "foreign sun" in stanza eight. This stanza is one of my sacred texts: it blew right through me when I first heard it, long before I could even pretend to understand what it might mean. Yes, the sun "squints" in vain to find me, because whoever is to be found lying in my bed, it isn't really me; and yes, "friends and other strangers" scurry about at sun-up to get on with the imperatives of life (and life only); and yes, the only real freedom we have in this world is the freedom to die. And yes, everything matters, because nothing does. This is Dylan at his most primal, an apocalyptic spirituality that beggars all religion, that thrills and frightens me in equal measure.

What it earns Dylan's song is a moment of splendor in Eden, a "dawn" presided over not by the sun but by his own imagination, with a "lover" who, like the "hugging and loving Bed-fellow" who, under similar circumstances, visits Whitman in section 6 of "Song of Myself," is neither friend nor stranger, let alone a mere actual lady. But she brings him a gift of her dreams that neither of them violate–as I no doubt have violated Dylan's vision–by talking about. And finally, it has earned him a truthfulness for the words in which he tells us all this, a truthfulness we had better catch as it comes, for it won't last any longer than it takes for them to reach our ears, outside the Gates of Eden.

"It's Alright Ma (I'm Only Bleeding)" covers similar thematic ground but is otherwise as different from "Gates of Eden" as night and day. For one thing, it is a much better song, in part because it *is* a song–a virtuoso piece for what you might call boy oracle–while "Gates of Eden" (which Dylan rarely performs) is neither very musical nor easily adaptable to different interpretive moods. It is also, if not a better poem, then certainly a more remarkable and daring poetic invention. "Gates of Eden," wonderful as it is, is a rather conventional Romantic poem–a blend of Blake and Shelley by way of Eliot. "It's Alright Ma" is something completely different, a prophetic comedy whose idiom is a post-Beat adaptation of the headlong vernacular of Woody Guthrie's talking blues but whose tone blends the peremptory, harassing severity of the Old Testament prophets with the charismatic aphoristic wit of the Gospel voice of Jesus.

This last assertion may seem a stretch, but I find it inescapable. The voice we hear in "It's Alright Ma" is fashioned to a crucial degree out of Dylan's self-aggrandizing identification–as a poet–with the voice of Jesus, much in the same way that his earliest performances were prompted by an equally self-aggrandizing identification with the voices of Hank Williams, Robert Johnson, Woody Guthrie, and others. I would suggest that "It's Alright Ma" is best approached as the sort of song with which we might imagine Jesus to have regaled *his* mother during what John Prine calls "The Missing Years." This is pretty much unprecedented, at least in my experience. Lots of poets and fiction writers have done what Prine does in his song–appropriate the story of Jesus for their own ends–but who has ever tried to sound like Jesus? And not just sound like him, but do so in a way that uses Jesus's voice to midwife their own?

I call this song a prophetic comedy to draw attention to the behavior of its voice, which I hear as a thoroughly comic protagonist, a sort of picaresque seer. The first of the song's five three-verse sections is composed in an oblique allegorical mode similar to that with which "Gates of Eden" begins, but already there is a crucial difference. Dylan projects himself into his visionary Vanity Fair, and he puts himself there as part of the problem.

The "you" addressed here is clearly Dylan himself, but Dylan before (or just as) he first saw what he now sees, just as his free spirit is about to dissociate itself from his earth-bound ego. Thus the tone of lines like "you know too soon/there is no sense in trying" comes across in a delicious double-take: an initial depressed disillusionment gives way immediately to a sense of liberation from oppressive illusions. This movement is recapitulated in the refrain, when, stepping forth in his own voice to assure "Ma" that the "foreign sound" she hears really is him, Dylan dismisses the world of death as a mere exhalation–"just sighing"–of his invisible spirit.

The remaining four sections, by this measure, are the sound of Dylan just breathing to himself, a sound that we *see* as it blows through the song's apocalyptic images of the world we think we live in. Dylan represents the spirit's mastery of the ego by threading the lyric with a largely hidden opposition in which sound, or voice, is privileged over sight, or image. This privileging of voice over image comes through most forcefully in a way that is so obvious we don't even notice it. I'm referring to the speed and apparent freedom with which Dylan's voice moves through the elaborately overdetermined, almost absurdly over-rhymed verse structure he fashioned for this song. This is partly a function of a super-charged aphoristic wit with which line after line erupts from and dissolves its context while still advancing it. It is also partly a result of a elliptical syntax that Dylan nowhere else employs and that here allows him to leap-frog more ground than he should be able to. Listening to this song is like watching a man continually pour a gallon of whiskey from a pint jar. The eventual effect is to undermine our confidence that the material limits of pint jars count for much.

By the end of the song, even these syntactic liberties are barely adequate to keep pace with the astonishing cognitive leaps with which this whirlwind lays bare the hollowness of the respectable world:

*Old lady judges watch people in pairs*
*Limited in sex they dare*
*To push fake morals insult and stare*
*While money doesn't talk it swears*
*Obscenity who really cares*
*Propaganda all is phony*

The crux of this passage is the transition that links conventional sexual mores and money as varieties of materialism, and does so in terms that link an obsession with keeping up appearances with a desecration of "talk." This association allows Dylan to define both as forms of "obscenity," because both attempt to entrap the spirit in material form where it can be watched and measured. (The imagery and logic of this verse strikingly resembles a passage from Allen Ginsberg's "Howl" that identifies one of the "three old shrews of fate" as the "the one-eyed shrew of the heterosexual dollar.")

This opposition between voice and image is also worked into the lyric's narrative plot. Dylan's alter-ego "you" returns in the song's third section as his spirit's anxiety-ridden Blakean spectre, an incorrigibly gullible psychic side-kick forever seduced by the "advertising signs" that commonly pass for the real world. The lyric's pivotal moment occurs in the second verse of this section–the song's exact mid-point–when this spectre, forced to confront "life outside," encounters a fellow spirit in its primary form as a living voice:

*You lose yourself you reappear*
*You suddenly find you got nothing to fear*
*Alone you stand with nobody near*
*When a trembling distant voice unclear*
*Startles your sleeping ears to hear*
*That somebody thinks they really found you*

I have never been able to listen to this verse without feeling instinctively that this "you" is more than a little frightened to discover you have "nothing to fear." "To stand alone" feels like it's too much for "you," so that it's no surprise when "you" make the usual materialist mistake and mishear that "trembling distant voice unclear" as just another advertising sign, "somebody [that] thinks they really found you."

I've always been delighted by the miraculous vernacular pungency of this denouement. To say that a voice finds us would be to say that it captures our attention, and to say it "really" finds us would be to say that it finds the attention of what is the deepest and truest in us. But Dylan's phrase focuses ominously on what–as "you" hear it–the "somebody" behind that voice "thinks" they found out about you in capturing your attention. This is the voice not of a solitary human spirit seeking the company of another but of an advertiser trawling a target market.

"You" are compelled to hear another voice this way because to hear it as it is–"trembling," "distant," and "unclear"–would require you to embrace your own solitude. But as Dylan rebukes his backsliding ego in the next verse, "there is no answer" and the self "belongs to" no one: we have nothing to fear precisely because we cannot be found out, by ourselves let alone by each other. We can only talk back and forth across the abyss that secures the unfathomable solitude out of which we talk and sing.

The abyss itself is secured by death. This song that began by invoking (or seeming to invoke) "being born" and "dying" as touchstones of good and evil, respectively, concludes by invoking "death's honesty" as our universal calling card. Having concluded his argument, for the finale Dylan enters his prophecy in his prophetic persona for the first time, and he does so to offer a paradoxical image of a voice that eludes the snares of all images, the ruthlessly iconoclastic voice that throughout the song has been illuminating the "darkness at the break of noon" by shattering everything we see:

*My eyes collide head-on with stuffed graveyards false gods I scuff*
*At pettiness that plays so rough*
*Walk upside down inside handcuffs*
*Kick my legs to crash it off*
*Say okay I've had enough*
*What else can you show me?*

The imaginative force of the entire song is encapsulated in the final line quoted here, in the way that what Dylan has to "say" swallows and nullifies anything the world has to "show" him.

This sublime clowning opens the song's final refrain to a prophetic exultation that is positively Biblical in its severity. This refrain begins with an almost contemptuously ironic image of the prophet's martyrdom, a martyrdom that will never happen because the prophet's "thought-dreams" can not "be seen" but must be *heard,* and the materialists who might martyr him are precisely those who do not know how to listen for a spirit that must be heard to be apprehended. And even if they could hear his "thought-dreams," his voice–the unborn voice of the universal spirit of prophecy–cannot be killed because it does not merely live. This voice, as Dylan said of traditional music, "is too unreal to die."*

Dylan concludes by staking out the highest ground imaginable from which to reassure "Ma" of his safety, a better place disclosed negatively, in the immensely reverberant implications of his final word:

*But it's alright Ma*
*It's life and life only*

Dylan stakes out his high ground by replacing the polarity between "living" and "dying" with which the song opened with an implicit opposition between the natural world of life-and-death and an unnamed realm from which Dylan's spirit will shrug off its merely natural fate as "life only."

"It's Alright Ma" is the first song in which we hear the unmistakably prophetic accent that has since become a recurrent central element of what we all recognize as Dylan's voice. Crucially, this prophetic voice first arises as a kind of interior doppelgaenger, a previously hidden "foreign sound" that emerges like a phoenix from the ashes of an ego under the stress of a humiliating powerlessness: "To understand you know too soon there is no sense in trying." Who said that? Whoever it is, he wasn't around when Dylan wrote "My Back Pages," a song that treats a similar–if not an identical–psycho-spiritual crisis. "My Back Pages" is a protest song; the voice we hear in it is a retrospectively self-critical ego. "It's Alright Ma" is prophecy; the divine voice we here in it pounces upon the poor ego in the very instant of its greatest vulnerability and confusion.

This prophetic spirit is manifested as an inner voice that displaces the ego, the "I," into a "you." Sometimes, as in "It's Alright Ma," the prophetic voice appears as a new, transcendental "I," but technically, this voice is no "I" at all. Indeed, its "foreign sound" tends to undermine

* Nat Hentoff, "The Playboy Interview: Bob Dylan," in *McGregor, A Retrospective*, p. 130.

our belief in the reality of any "I" or "you," except for the instrumentality each of us possesses as the current sender or receiver, respectively, of an essentially anonymous transmission of voice. Or, as Dylan himself puts it in the liner notes to *Highway 61 Revisited* (and with a crucial pun that links this issue to the opposition between the visible world and the voice), "I cannot say the word eye anymore" because "there is no eye–there is only a series of mouths."

"A series of mouths"–as if ear and mouth were but the flip sides of the same organ, or as if the voice were transmitted in a kiss. This is a fantastical vision, a transcendental intuition rather than an actual experience. The voice in Dylan's songs is always beset by some form of displacement between "I" and "you," between mouth and ear, and this existential rift is also usually compounded by a deep resistance by "you" to the transcendental terms of address. Whether he is courting himself or another, Dylan almost always finds himself addressing a recalcitrant listener.

## IV

"Mr. Tambourine Man" is an exception to this rule, and I think that helps explain what makes this song, perhaps Dylan's best, so special. "Mr. Tambourine Man" is a prayer, a prayer in which the ordinary ego, hungering for a freer, stronger consciousness, addresses the transcendent power that gives it life. But it is a remarkably (for Dylan) innocent prayer, utterly exempt from the self-doubt and even self-hatred that both plague and enrich later prayer-songs like "What Can I Do for You?" or "Every Grain of Sand." "Mr. Tambourine Man" is one of Dylan's few songs in which he is not at all struggling against himself, and it is the only such song to which he brings all his powers and ambition.

Dylan's prayer is addressed to an element of his own spirit; specifically, to the power through whose grace he makes his music. Mr. Tambourine Man is invoked as the genius of song, as the liberated and liberating presence the singer feels within himself as he writes his poems, as he sings his songs–as he gets naked. The greatness of this song arises in part from the singer's richly ambivalent relationship to this transcendent power within himself. The tone he takes in addressing his genius is at once commanding and imploring: his prayer is both a celebration of and a plea for a nakedness he does and does not possess. It is both a neo-Whitmanesque rhapsody about a secret self and a neo-Keatsian ode addressed to a power beyond his reach. The song itself is the "trip" it seeks but, paradoxically, still fails to apprehend, except as a memory or an expectancy, an echo caught in the "vague traces" of its "skipping reels of rhyme." The entire song is possessed of this double consciousness that Dylan describes with such delightful good humor in the third verse. This is the double consciousness of a creative will beside itself with joy, an ego that is at once nothing in itself and the maddeningly inextinguishable medium through which its genius discloses its presence.

And yet. To say this much does not go far enough. "Mr. Tambourine Man" is a rare song, a rare poem. It does, and it doesn't, true. But it does, and it doesn't, and it does. The double consciousness I speak of is finally a red herring. The astonishing thing about this song is the way its unsleeping ego is reduced to a piquant shiver in the greater voice that swallows it. The voice we hear at last is neither Whitmanesque nor Keatsian but Emersonian, the mercury voice of pure spirit, heartless and unaccountable as the turning wind:

*Though I know that evening's empire*
*has re-turned into sand*
*Vanished from my hand*
*Left me blindly here to stand*
*but still not sleeping*

The sense of this passage, and the emotions attached to that sense, are both blown away by its poetry. Dylan always sings "re-turned," not "returned," a small change that makes a big difference: It turns a mournful, melancholy recognition of loss into an wholly aestheticized appreciation of change, of the spirit's incessant metamorphoses. This shift in perspective, and its accompanying liberation, is precisely what the singer is requesting when, at the end of the last verse, he asks, "Let me forget about today until tomorrow."

Dylan's pun on "returned" is one of only two instances where the sense of the lyric itself insists on a level of awareness and feeling that we otherwise glean exclusively from a disparity between the lyric's literal sense and the sound of its voice. Though "Mr. Tambourine Man" is not a "drug song," it is truly psychedelic. But its power lies in the way its psychedelia co-exists with the sober plain sense of a man still seeking to make a connection. Listen again to the opening verse:

*I know that evening's empire*
*has re-turned into sand*
*Vanished from my hand*
*Left me blindly here to stand*
*but still not sleeping*
*My weariness amazes me*
*I'm branded on my feet*
*I have no one to meet*
*And the ancient empty street's*
*too dead for dreaming*

The sense of this is plain enough: after a sleepless night spent in visionary yammering, probably with friends, the singer emerges into the morning sun, probably from a bar or coffeehouse (OK, there are drugs involved–but they are wearing off), where he finds himself suddenly bereft, an inflamed spirit in a diminished body stranded in the labyrinth of an alien world. "Branded on my feet" is an especially crucial image for Dylan, one which recurs as the title of the *Basement Tapes* song "This Wheel's on Fire" and in the announcement, by the enigmatic title character of the *John Wesley Harding* song "The Wicked Messenger," that the "soles of his feet" are "burning." In the light of the intimate linkage of walking and talking in Dylan's poetry, I'd suggest that "I'm branded on my feet" is the equivalent of "My tongue is on fire." Thus,

"I have no one to meet" means "I have no one to talk to, or to sing to."

But who's kidding who, here? These lines may say something like this, but their quotidian sense is only a vestigial element of the feeling they convey, which is a feeling of imaginative power and freedom. Of course, he may not have anyone to talk to, but he has found one, or invented one: Mr. Tambourine Man. This opening verse is itself the very sound of the Tambourine Man's "jingle-jangle morning," a tripping kaleidoscope of "sand" and "hand" and "stand," indifferent to the logic (and the psychology) that connects them. In this song, reason is just a pretext for rhyme.

A similar relationship between sound and sense obtains in the second and fourth verses, where the singer's yearning for transport and for deliverance from the womb of time, respectively, are realized poetically in the "jingle jangle" of his words. For the most part, the lyric's double consciousness–of yearning ego and celebratory spirit–are, like matter and anti-matter, sealed off from each other. The largest exception to this is the remarkable third verse, where this issue is addressed directly, and with a blend of cognitive sophistication and nonchalant charm that would make even the most erudite deconstructionist weep with envy. I've read a fair amount of erudite literary criticism myself, but I've never read anything that fully acknowledges, let alone so persuasively addresses, the way our language-bound consciousness both does and does not suffice the claims the spirit makes upon it.

This verse functions as a gloss on the rest of the song, but that is only part of the story. It also turns the song's point of view on its head. It's as if, overhearing the sound of his own sound, the singer recognizes himself as the Tambourine Man's voice. But since he is still addressing the Tambourine Man, he must be addressing something deeper or finer or purer in the Tambourine Man than his audible music, an unheard music that the song itself, "your tambourine in time," merely traces and shadows:

*And if you hear vague traces*
*of skipping reels of rhyme*

*to your tambourine in time*
*I wouldn't pay it any mind*
*it's just a ragged clown behind*
*it's just a shadow you're seeing*
*that he's chasing*

The "shadow" the Tambourine Man sees is this song, a song whose music "he," the singer, is pursuing. But the voice of this line, its implicit "I," is thereby distinguished from the "I" (now "he") who sings the rest of the song. For this one giddy moment–just about the time it takes for us to get our heads spun around by the syntax of this line–the singer addresses the Tambourine Man as an equal, face to face, or addresses himself in the voice of the Tambourine Man.

The final verse represents a falling off from this sublime perch. It resumes a more recognizably human perspective, but with a difference. The relationship between its dual elements–sound and sense, rhyme and reason, spirit and self, imagination and will, call them what you will–has changed. The ironies that have shadowed the lyric until now yield to an uncanny harmony, a kind of duet in which the singer seems to outrace the "reels of rhyme" he leaves in his wake, a "parade" from which he has always just disappeared. Listening to this final verse, it's hard to be sure which is the singer and which the song, or (to borrow a Yeatsian figure that's wholly appropriate here) which the dancer and which the dance. It's as if, the "jingle jangle morning" in which he follows his genius were, at last, nothing other than his own brightening:

*Take me disappearing through the smoke rings of my mind*
*down the foggy ruins of time*
*Far past the frozen leaves*
*the haunted frightened trees*
*out to the windy beach*
*far from the twisted reach*
*of crazy sorrow*
*Yes to dance beneath the diamond sky*
*with one hand waving free*

*silhouetted by the sea*
*circled by the circus sands*
*With all memory and fate*
*driven deep beneath the waves*
*let me forget about today*
*until tomorrow*

This I am not moved to call neo-anybody. This is just plain new. This is Dylan: the voice of a self-possessed yearning that both provides its own answer yet remains full of an unquenched expectancy.

## V

"Mr. Tambourine Man" presents Dylan at his most naked: It is a poet's poem, a singer's song. But he has never since written a song like this; he has never since sought a similar incandescence of voice. What he did instead was to write "It's All Over Now, Baby Blue." "Mr. Tambourine Man," which dates from early 1964, was probably composed before any of the other songs on *Bringing It All Back Home*, but "Baby Blue" is the only song here that sounds like it was composed in its aftermath. And unlike its progenitor, "Baby Blue" is a prototype for hundreds of songs to come.

At one level, "Baby Blue" is a simple song, obvious in attitude and unequivocal in tone. It takes the "chain of flashing images" aesthetic of "Mr. Tambourine Man" and turns it into an ethic: the self is an incessant turning in the wind and the rain in which nothing survives change except that which suffers change–the wind and the rain, the spirit and the soul, I and you. "I" know this, and "you" better learn it fast. Period. End of song.

But this is to rob the song of its essential drama, which arises from Dylan's highly inventive handling of the relationship between the singer and Baby Blue, or, more specifically, between the song's (unstated) "I" and its "you." Beginning with this very song, this "pronominal romance"–to borrow a term Leslie Fielder coined to describe the courtship dance of "I" with "you" that animates Whitman's "Song of Myself"*–moves to the center of Dylan's poetry, where it becomes an extremely volatile and ambiguous affair of sometimes dizzying complexity. "Baby Blue" *is* a simple song, but even here the psychology of this relationship between the speaker and his imagined listener is slippery enough to imbue the song with a layered richness of tone and implication utterly beyond anything Dylan had previously written.

For starters, the singer is a double agent. For the most part, he speaks as an impersonal spirit, a kind of guardian angel, kindred to Mr. Tambourine Man. However, the magnificent blast with which the song opens (truly one of Dylan's greatest single lines) sounds at first very much like the enraged shout of a man with a very personal stake in these goings-on. He's throwing her out; what is over is a love affair, hers and his. "You must leave now" is not far from "Go away from my window." But this is the only time we are permitted to hear this tone; indeed, it disappears so rapidly that we might even wonder whether it was ever present: maybe "you must leave" means "there is a necessity that you go" and not "I order you to go."

Well, who knows. The human voice is such a mercurial thing, as Dylan himself, as much as anyone, has helped us realize. But I do hear in this opening shout the accents of a fiercely personal exigency, one whose almost palpable repression, throughout the remainder of the song, is a major source of its power. For instance, in the second line, when the singer tells Baby Blue "whatever you wish to keep you better grab it fast," he is not threatening to throw her belongings in the dumpster if she doesn't clear them out immediately. But the violence of that thought does shadow this line's overt meaning–Baby Blue's need to accommodate herself to the radical discontinuities in human identity to which this rupture has exposed her–and it inflects the pathos of the succeeding image of "your orphan with his gun, crying like a fire in the sun." This uncanny figure seems, in part, to represent the singer's mere-

* Leslie Fiedler, "Walt Whitman: Portrait of the Artist as a Middle-Aged Hero," p. 70.

ly personal identity: wielding a gun, he is all menace and malice. But it is a child's harmless toy gun, and his primal "cry" is swallowed up in and nullified by the life-source that engenders it. His former identity is the orphan of a spirit that has abandoned it.

Baby Blue is in the same boat, and in pointing himself out to her, the singer is implicitly asking her to recognize her own orphaned self. But while the singer is reconciled to this change (and thus is able to sing this song), his ex-lover is being taken by cruel surprise. But the singer's cruelty is now secondary, a by-product of other motives. What may have begun as a kiss-off song has turned into a transcendental come-on, an invitation to accept a self Baby Blue does not yet recognize or desire to acknowledge.

The cruelty of Baby Blue's surprise is intended, that is, as a liberating violence, and the wonder of this song is that is pulls this off. In fact, I doubt that most listeners hear even a hint of nastiness or meanness in the song. This is largely the result, I think, of the fact that the singer never says "I." The lyric's "I" is wholly implicit (as a necessary speaker), in the same way that, in a soliloquy, a "you" is always implicit (as a necessary listener). In fact, this song is a second-person soliloquy. Just substitute "I" for "you" in the lyric, and this aspect of the song's rhetoric becomes obvious. Perhaps the singer addresses her in the voice of a guardian angel because that's who he is, an inner voice harassing her toward the embrace of a sublime spiritual nakedness. This is how I usually hear the song, probably because Dylan often sings it with an enraptured joyousness that nearly dissolves awareness of anything beyond his own augmenting ecstasy of anticipation. The singer is Baby Blue's spirit, giving *herself* a good hard talking to, or, if you will, Baby Blue is just the singer's name for his own wounded heart, which he is trying to retrieve.

Boy-girl song, a girl's soliloquy, a boy's soliloquy–pick whatever scenario you want, it hardly matters. Dylan's songs are famously open-ended and ambiguous, but this is where it begins. "Baby Blue" is his first song that is simultaneously a continuous fiction–a story–and a discontinuous series of figurations; and it is his first song that is simultaneously a self-exploration and an interrogation of another. And these and other firsts flow directly from the fact that is it also his first song that is a truly open-ended address to a "you" who is not a pronoun but, as it were, a pre-noun: not "you" as in some particular ex-girlfriend or even some particular composite of ex-girlfriends or whatever, but "you" as in whoever you are or might ever be who's listening to me. Baby Blue may have begun as a composite of all the women (or even all the men, women, and children) Dylan ever left behind, or even as a composite of all his own experiences of having been abandoned. But unlike the female figures in "Don't Think Twice," "It Ain't Me Babe," or "I Don't Believe You," Baby Blue does not remain a figure from the past; she becomes a figure out of the future, an image of emotions as yet unknown and unfelt. What we encounter here for the first time in Dylan's work is the second-person equivalent of the "egotistical sublime," Keats's term for the mind's confrontation, in Wordsworth's poetry, with its own illimitable greatness. "Baby Blue" is "you" as an ever earlier morning sky, an infant listener whose response, evermore-about-to-be, realizes the song's naked truths.

I suppose this must sound a bit like gibberish, and I must admit I am having a difficult time here finding adequate words to reconcile what I think I understand with what I know I hear. So let's cut to the chase. Dylan often sounds like not only is he making up what he sings as he sings it but also like he is singing it specifically and personally to me. This is an illusion–an illusion resulting from the fact that his songs are often structured in a way that requires me (or you) to complete them. They are structured, that is, in a way that asks "how do you feel" about this. We always have some answer; our answer is never exactly the same. Dylan never sings a song the same way twice; but more importantly, we never listen to it the same way twice. And beginning with "Baby Blue," Dylan's songs–most of them, anyway–begin to take this into account. Dylan changes during the course of "I Don't Believe You," but I (and you) must change during the course of "Baby Blue." The lyric requires our answer, an answer the singer never hears.

I said earlier that "Baby Blue" is a simple song, and it is. Dylan's lyrics begin to get increasingly complex with his very next song, "Like a Rolling Stone," in which he discovers that although he can never hear your answer, he can imagine it and respond to what he imagines. Beginning with "Like a Rolling Stone," Dylan ropes his listener into shadow dialogues he conducts with himself. Listening to these songs is like listening to one end of telephone conversations or (in the case of songs like "Visions of Johanna" or "She's Your Lover Now" to one end of conference calls.)

By this measure, the four verses of "Baby Blue" boil down to "Hello? Hello? Hello? Good-bye!" The key verse is the third, another of the album's disguised bridges:

*All your seasick sailors*
*they're all rowing home*
*All your reindeer army*
*they're all going home*
*The lover who just walked out the door*
*has taken all his blankets from the floor*
*The carpet too is moving under you*
*and it's all over now baby blue*

Baby Blue's retreating sailors and soldiers are a fairly transparent image of the futility of her ego defenses, and their nausea reflects the radical unmooring of her reality. But this verse is itself seasick with repetition, not only in the reflexive rhyme on "home" but also in the redundancy with which the moving carpet echoes the folding sky in the previous verse. Baby Blue's world may be going to pieces, but the singer's words here are full of an unpleasant sense of re-treading the same ground, of running in place. (Indeed, Dylan, perhaps becoming disoriented, actually sings "empty-handed army" on the album cut, a lyrical flub that imports "empty-handed" from the "empty-handed painter" in the previous verse.) By the end of this verse, the refrain "it's all over now" begins to sound a bit desperate, like wishful thinking.

He resolves this growing impasse by shifting his rhetoric, in the last verse, from declaration to exhortation, thereby bequeathing the lyric's realization to Baby Blue, who is hypostatized as "you" in a second reflexive rhyme. The final time round, the refrain refers less to Baby Blue's former world than to the song, which at last relinquishes itself to her listening. But Dylan also somehow manages to make this final verse seem to be something very much like the sound of her listening. There is a uncanny sense that Baby Blue has suddenly stepped forth from the shadows, even though the singer (whoever or whatever he is) is of course still talking. Part of this, I guess, has to do with the way the lyric embeds within itself images of the song ("something that calls for you") and the singer, with whom I identify the "vagabond who's rapping at your door." Insofar as the singer might also be her ex-lover, he is also present here as the most recent of the "dead you've left." But notice it is "the dead you've left," not "the dead you leave." Baby Blue has stepped forward, her naked listening confronting and containing within its attention the voice that is "standing in the clothes you once wore." There is a sense that the acts of speaking and listening, the polarities of "I" and "you," have somehow been folded into a single hushed moment. When it comes round the final time, the refrain embraces more than the end of something; Baby Blue is "all over now" the way a dawn suddenly floods the morning. No "fire in the sun," she's "another match."

## VI

"Another match" is also another mate. "It's All Over Now, Baby Blue" is a love song. Although it has taken me a long time to see it that way, I've always heard it as a love song. It sounds like a love song–not just the song, the music, but the lyric, too. The words sound like a greeting. "Baby Blue" is an anti-love song that turns into a friendship song that turns into a love song. It is, to be sure, an extraordinarily antithetical love song, attaining to a virtually disembodied eroticism that is, depending on your point of view, either a sublime paradox or impossible nonsense. I've put my money on the former, but not without hedging my bet: I have referred to Baby Blue as a kind of morning sky in part because it fits Dylan's imagery but mostly because I find it impossible to think of her as another person, male or female. She is too rarefied, too internalized. She is a mood, an inner weather; she is Dylan's rosy-fingered dawn, an Americanized Aurora.

She also enables Dylan, it seems to me, to recover by song's end an innocence that began to disappear from his songs in "Girl of the North Country," a song about the uneasily shared affection two boys feel for the same girl. This innocence appears without irony only in the song that (ironically) announces its disappearance from the singer's life: "Bob Dylan's Dream" is a song about a companionability so innocent Dylan doesn't even mention–or maybe even have to remember–whether these "first few friends" include any girls. The issue, of course, is not girls, or even sex particularly. The issue is adulthood, which Dylan experiences–always–as an adulteration, as a loss of an unselfconscious togetherness indistinguishable from solitude. In adulthood, one becomes two, and the many replace the few.

"It's All Over Now, Baby Blue" retrieves this lost innocence, emotionally and imaginatively, in the completeness with which the singer identifies with Baby Blue's second-person sublime. What I am struck by is how great a distance Dylan traveled–in less than two years! I am also struck by the even greater psychological distance that separates "It's All Over Now, Baby Blue" from his next major song, composed less than six months later. "Like a Rolling Stone" opens the very Pandora's box that "Baby Blue" so blithely finesses. Suddenly, we are two again, and soon we will be very many indeed, with a vengeance.

In composing "Baby Blue" Dylan had attained a maturity and completeness of vision that short-circuited the travails of adulthood, but that, for that very reason, could not be sustained. Indeed, "Farewell Angelina," a *Bringing It All Back Home* outtake not officially released until the *Bootleg Series* (1991), is something of a halfway house between the innocent intimacy of "Baby Blue" and the duplicities of "Rolling Stone." (It actually feels like an early version of the lyrical impulse that found its resolution in another *Highway 61 Revisited* song "Queen Jane Approximately.") Strikingly similar to "Baby Blue" thematically–its images of the shifting grounds of social and psychological identity are even more hauntingly pentrating–"Farewell Angelina" tells a very different story. The singer has little or no faith that Angelina can ever usher in her own new dawn, and with a oddly gallant mournfulness, he simply abandons her, "a table standing empty by the edge of the sea," to a deterioration her pride seems to invite.

Dylan has (as yet) never written anything as luminously transcendental, as angelic, as "It's All Over Now, Baby Blue," let alone "Mr. Tambourine Man." Measured by the aesthetic that informs these songs, even the best of Dylan's subsequent work is noisy, muddied by all sorts of psycho-sexual duplicities. At times still an angel, perhaps, but with a certain inevictable darkness in his eyes. I don't think the artist who made *Bringing It All Back Home* was ready for this–perhaps that is what is behind the mournfulness of the prescient "Farewell Angelina." Though Dylan says (in the album's liner notes), "I have given up at trying for perfection," he hasn't, or hadn't when he wrote and recorded these songs. And though he says "I accept chaos," he hadn't. This LP is a grand refusal of chaos, and in its best moments, a sublime triumph over it. After all, isn't that what it means to bring it all–ALL!–back home?

# 6

## *Highway 61 Revisited*

### Let's rock!

Bob Dylan is a

1) folk singer
2) rock 'n' roll singer
3) blues singer
4) pop singer
5) gospel singer
6) country singer
7) all of the above

A good desert-island topic, don't you think? Since 1997, I've been marveling at the way Dylan has been turning himself into some sort of country singer, but for a very long time, I've thought of Dylan as, first and foremost, a blues singer. It's his most congenial mask: aggressive, suspicious, devious, wildly shy, disarmingly humorous, incorrigibly mean, slyly charming, insolent, upset and upsetting in every way.

The blues is the first (and only?) individualist's folk music–a concept that would be an oxymoron anywhere but America. The blues is the voice of Whitman's "simple, separate person" chafing under some form of social or existential bondage and struggling to free his spirit from its grip. At its simplest, the blues–when sung by a male–is the voice of a man trying to exorcise the memory of a woman or repossess it as desire. At its most complex, it is–well, it's the voice of Bob Dylan on *Highway 61 Revisited*.

*Highway 61 Revisited* is, in an important sense, Dylan's first LP as himself. It's the first Dylan record on which he isn't groping to discover who he might become. At last, Dylan–poet, musician, performer–is just doing what he does. The songs on *Highway 61* possess the same poetic intensity as those on the second side of *Bringing It All Back Home*, but they wear their poetry lightly. For the first time, Dylan's writing makes no concessions to the claims of high art. Instead, he entrusts his powers to the pungency and verve of the way he talks. His voice finally sounds completely at home with itself.

And home base is the blues:

*The sweet pretty things are in*
*bed now of course*
*The city fathers they're*
*trying to endorse*
*The reincarnation of*
*Paul Revere's horse*
*But the town has no need to be*
*nervous*

This is very funny, much like Huck Finn's droll observations of similar insanities. Like Huck, Dylan refuses to be surprised, let alone outraged, by an outrageous world. He shrugs it off with an insouciance that out-Hucks Huck.

The brash, gleefully mocking humor of "Tombstone Blues" connects it with the so-called talking blues, a form that Dylan used in several earlier songs. Talking blues are almost always songs of alienation; every line functions as a kind of cathartic variant on the question "*Who ARE these people?*"–or, as the album's liner notes reduce it, "*WHAAT?*"

They always seem to be sung by a vagrant persona too young, or too lazy, or maybe just too bemused to have gotten around to moving on to the territory ahead where, presumably, folks don't act so crazy, or (better) there aren't enough folks to matter. They've always struck me as a poor white variant on authentic blues–which may be why they always remind me of Mark Twain, and why in his early days Dylan was often compared to Huck Finn.

The backbone of *Highway 61 Revisited* is comprised of three mutant talking blues–"Tombstone Blues," "Highway 61 Revisited," and "Desolation Row." "Highway 61 Revisited" is the only one that stays wholly within the talking blues ethos. It revises the form in a way that brings its imaginative and emotional core–*"I have nothing to do with any of these people"*–to its logical conclusion. It does this by eliminating the first-person narrator and presenting the action as a succession of discrete dramatic episodes. The result is an updated version of the King and the Duke sections of *Huckleberry Finn*, with the Mississippi River replaced by the highway that runs its length as an image of despoiled freedom.

In Dylan's vision, like Twain's, America is a place where everyone sacrifices their own lives and their loved one's lives to a fear of God that is really a worship of the devil, a denial of death and the terrible nakedness of their own lives.* Though Dylan's song begins with a parodic allusion to Abraham's sacrifice of Isaac, the killings that get done here are mostly the self-defined glory of our culture: the financial killings of a society whose prosperity is founded on its ability to buy and sell (and re-sell) everything and everyone. Dylan's song ends with the prospect that this society will finally cashier itself in an nuclear holocaust in which, sitting in the promoter's makeshift "bleachers in the sun," we will pay to see ourselves reduced to bleached bones.

"Highway 61 Revisited" is a diabolically funny song. The puritani-

* For a survey of the various guises the figure of the devil takes in Dylan's poetry, see Bert Cartwright, "Talkin' Devil with Bob Dylan." *The Telegraph* 49, p. 76-99.

cal self-hatred of its protagonists is perfectly matched by the song's narrative tone. The prospect of this crazy world self-immolating in a nuclear holocaust is an occasion not for horror, as in "Hard Rain," but for a vicious glee. "Tombstone Blues" possesses a good deal of this kind of humor, and it also does so in ways that link homicide and war to the civilities of capitalism. These images range from the sublime (Jack the Ripper at the head of the Chamber of Commerce) to the ridiculous (Gypsy Davy's "fantastic collection of stamps"). Stamp collecting, when I was a kid, was the perfect medium for boys' fantasies of conquering the world *and* making a killing in the market. Here, it represents the spoils of war gathered by Gypsy Davy, the marauding hero of the song's middle section in which an imperialist war–implicitly, the Vietnam War–is presented as a puerile adventure, as an apocalypse of boys who never grew up. Dylan's "commander-in-chief," to my ears, is just Tom Sawyer grown old.

But "Tombstone Blues" also strikes the deeper note of genuine blues. The song is full of a very Blakean sense that the heroic energies of our civilization are expended in an attempt to suppress its own liveliness. The life that is suppressed in this song is specifically sexual–the "sweet pretty things" squirreled away in their beds, who so interest the narrator. And that's his problem. He can't simply dismiss this world, as he does the world of "Highway 61," because it holds too much of himself and his desire. Intermixed with alienation, then, is a disappointment and loss, and with them the graver, vexed humor characteristic of traditional blues.

This deeper tonality surfaces briefly at the very beginning of the song, as a delicious double-take in the "of course" that concludes the opening line. On the one hand, those words carry a mocking snarl: the "city fathers" really don't need to call out the alarm because their daughters have entombed themselves voluntarily. In this world, as in Blake's "Thel," female sexuality is degraded not by the harlot but by the "hysterical bride," or the life-fearing virgin: Jezebel is a "nun," and Delilah sits "worthlessly alone." But Dylan's "of course" also possesses a bitter backbite, introducing a forlorn ache that runs through the song like a subterranean stream that–apart from the chorus–does not fully surface until the final verse-pair. There this feeling surfaces first in the delightful fantasy-memory of "where Ma Rainey and Beethoven once unwrapped their bedroll" and then in the mysterious "dear lady" Dylan addresses in the final verse.

Who is this lady? No one we know, certainly; indeed, no one Dylan knew before she comes to him at this moment. She is at once an emanation (in the Blakean sense) of Dylan's awakened desire, and its alma mater. She is a "real you," addressed by an imagination that has sloughed off its bondage to the sleeping pretty things, to Jezebel and Delilah, to what Dylan apparently would agree with Blake in calling the "Female Will."

"Female Will," in this context, describes not the character of women but an aspect of male psychology. The vernacular term, I believe, is pussy-whipped. When Dylan discovers his "dear lady," he recovers his own desire, and this recovery of emotional freedom and self-possession is the essence of the blues. But in order to achieve this freedom, he has had to own up to the extent to which he shares the male panic of the "city fathers" he's mocking. The "medicine man" who elbows the socially sanctioned doctor out of the song to talk some sense into the "hysterical bride" is clearly some sort of stand-in for the narrator, but at this point the narrator, who sounds as surprised by the appearance of this charming interloper as we are, can't yet claim him as an alter-ego, for he still has not purged his own latent hysteria.

The key figure who enables him to do so, I believe, is Galileo. Unlike the other historical figures who populate this song, Dylan's Galileo is a most ambivalent fellow. He's a jerk and a fool, but then he is pitted against Delilah, who, in her rancid self-absorption, is worse than a jerk or a fool. And though he is undone by his discovery of it, he has had the wit and the soulfulness to recognize "the geometry of innocence, flesh on the bone," which is as mysteriously sweet and luminous an image of desire as you're ever likely to find. Dylan's song appropriates Galileo's heroic vision while rejecting his male megalomania and its resentments. Unlike the earlier rejections of the city fathers et al, this one necessitates a change in the narrator's own psychology–a change that first precipitates in the not-quite-mock-sympathy expressed, in the next verse, for "brother" Bill's appetite for death. Once he has discovered the enemy within himself, the narrator's ironies are no longer merely at others' expense.

I've insisted on the psychological triumph inherent in the sudden appearance of Dylan's "dear lady," but the tone of this final verse is more uncertain than I've let on. In Dylan's delightfully impudent vision of a new Adam and Eve, Ma Rainey and Beethoven boldly "unwrap their bedroll," but Dylan's greeting of his "dear lady" is almost undone by his anxieties that he lacks the creative wit and nerve to "hold" her. His wistfulness here surely expresses his doubts of other people, but it also expresses the residual self-doubt of a poet-lover whose own mind is still shadowed by its "useless and pointless knowledge" of the human tendency to betray the "geometry of innocence." His final words to her are ambiguously soothing and frightening, caught halfway between a caress and another toss of Galileo's map book.

This sort of tonal ambivalence blossoms in "Desolation Row," a song that I would classify as post-blues. Like "Tombstone Blues," it's comprised of similarly "funny" material, but Dylan's relationship to the world he imagines in "Desolation Row" is fundamentally different. For one thing, Dylan is beyond any need to satirize the "city fathers." He has already evicted them from his psyche, so they appear in their true form as an anonymous and ubiquitous "they," demonic agents beyond all possibility of the "I"-"you" exchange of true human society. The "blind commissioner," who is both one of "them" and "their" vicar, is more pathetic than ridiculous, and when "they" reappear later in the song as "the agents and the superhuman crew," with their grim need to "round up everyone that knows more than they do," they're fearsomely rather than ridiculously pathetic.

Dylan is beyond satire because he begins this song–"As Lady and I look out tonight"–where he ended "Tombstone Blues," with his "dear lady" already by his side. This "Lady" is not a woman but his muse, his desire, and to say that she is by his side is to say that he is already singing his song from Desolation Row. Desolation Row is Dylan's name for the place of desire, the only place, this song insists, from which one person can truly connect with another.

Formally, "Desolation Row" is a traditional ballad, and while Dylan locates himself in it, this is not primarily his story. Rather, it is the story of a bohemian underworld entrapped in "their" world–as an exotic diversion–because it lacks the courage of its convictions. This bohemian life transpires "on" Desolation Row but not in it. The song is very much the story of Dylan's companions; it addresses the same world, albeit in a radically different tone, as "Positively Fourth Street." But he is truly alone, alienated by his existential honesty from his friends–and even, perhaps, from his own ordinary self. I think "Einstein disguised as Robin Hood" is something of a self-portrait. Remember, in 1965-1966, Dylan liked to call himself a "mathematical poet" and joke about being hanged as a thief. So I don't think it is stretching things to see this once renowned electric violinist, "with his memories in a trunk," as a dark alter-ego, a fate that awaits him should he lose his creative nerve.

Dylan's narrative isolation–though explicit only in his concluding dismissal of "your letter yesterday" as "some kind of joke"–first manifests itself, in the narrative's sole dramatic moment, when Cinderella's greeting dissolves into a defensively evasive smile. Cinderella, by all rights, should have been the narrator's soulmate, the human form of his mythical "Lady." To observe that she "seems so easy" is to suggest a self-defeating edge of self-doubt and desperation to her sexual openness. Her response, "it takes one to know one," confirms this, thwarting intimacy by throwing the question back at the questioner. Our final glimpse of her–"sweeping up" (Romeo's mess, presumably)–offers an image both of her authentic self (doing the dirty work makes Cinderella Cinderella) and of her self-betrayal. Sweeping aside the truth of Romeo's childishness–and of her own defeat–is a dishonesty that bars her from Desolation Row.

Things get progressively worse. Cinderella's lie opens the door for everyone to be "making love or else expecting rain": Ophelia, Einstein and his "friend a jealous monk," Dr. Filth and his nurse, and Casanova and his heart-attack machine, and finally–look who's back!–the curfew cops. I don't intend to trace the path by which one thing leads to another–it would be great fun, but there are limits even to pedantry. I only want to emphasize that this sequence of vignettes does have a narrative force to it. Its narrative logic is emotional rather than dramatic, but it does tell a story, the story of how a certain kind of bohemia reinforces the life-denying tyranny it was created to subvert. When the "agents and the superhuman crew" return to restore order, it doesn't come as a surprise. Bohemia collapses in an exhaustion that invites their return.

The most compelling thing about "Desolation Row" is not its cultural analysis, or even the canny psychology of its vivid thumbnail character sketches. The key to the song's power is its tone, a tone hinted at in the "brother Bill" verse of "Tombstone Blues." The denizens of "Desolation Row" are, like the characters who populate "Highway 61 Revisited" and "Tombstone Blues," beyond the pale of direct human encounter. But in this song Dylan does not simply demonize them. Instead, he regards them with an odd blend of moral judgment and protectiveness that is epitomized in Dylan's climactic pun on "lame": "all these people" are both useless squares (despite their bohemian pretensions) and wounded creatures. The narrative both mocks its characters and broods over them mournfully.

Dylan achieves this equivocating tone by the device of "giv[ing] them all another name." The characters' names in this song are not just a narrative short-hand, like the nicknames in "Highway 61 Revisited," nor are they to be taken at face value, like the historical figures in "Tombstone Blues," who are invoked by their proper names to play a role in Dylan's allegorical fantasia. The names in "Desolation Row" function as pseudonyms that both expose the characters to ridicule–we know all about Cinderella, and you're no Cinderella!–and grace them with a certain ennobling pathos. The names in "Desolation Row" function as cover stories that we partly see through and partly take to heart. Of course, this effect is not merely a matter of names. It also accrues from a sleight-of-hand in Dylan's presentation of the scene and props that is unexpectedly Jamesian in its protective reticences. This is what he means, presumably, by "rearrange their faces." I don't know, for instance, just what might be written on the cards kept by Dr. Filth's nurse, but I'm quite sure they don't read "have mercy on his soul." For that matter, I'm also pretty sure that Dr. Filth's grail-like "leather cup" veils a pornographic joke.

The only bohemian figures who appear as themselves are two of bohemia's patron saints, Ezra Pound and T.S. Eliot, "fighting in the captain's tower" of a Titanic that, by this point in the song, is both a bohemian pleasure cruise and "their" ship of state. The difference–between the state and bohemia, between the establishment and the counterculture–no longer matters, and Dylan seems to be holding Pound and Eliot at least partly to blame. "Desolation Row" is a self-consciously Eliotic poem that parodies the imagery of "The Waste Land" from start to finish. It also employs Eliot's (and Pound's) allusive "mythic method,"* toying with but finally refusing what Dylan probably regarded as their use of it for smug satires of the wasteland of modernity.** It does seem to me to be fair to say that "Desolation Row" succeeds in making us feel that Cinderella's failure–or Ophelia's, or Casanova's, or the mermaid-infatuated fishermen's–is *our* loss. That's something "The Waste Land" or "The Love Song of J. Alfred Prufrock" (whose ending is studiously echoed in the Pound & Eliot verse of "Desolation Row") don't seem to care to make us feel about any of their

* For an argument that Dylan derived the distinctive freewheeling insolence of his "mythic method" from the visionary hipster rapper Lord Buckley, see Oliver Trager and David C. Barrett's "Black Cross: Lord Buckley, Joseph S. Newman, and the Bob Dylan Connection" in *On the Tracks* 15, pp. 18-24.

** W. T. Lhamon's gloss on this passage is exactly to the point: "The curse of modernism was its dissociation. Seldom knowing how to work an audience, modern poets seldom had a public. They had, instead, individual readers, individual critics, and greatly delayed responses to their acts. . . . the separation of authors from audiences in modernism doomed it, like the Titanic in Dylan's "Desolation Row" scenario (Stanza 9). In Dylan's song, the captains are aptly named after the modernist poets "Ezra Pound and T. S. Eliot" who fight among themselves forgetting their crew and passengers, forgetting their responsibilities, "while calypso singers laugh at them." Lhamon, "Dylan's Living Lore," *The Telegraph* 37, p. 120.

characters. In fact, it's the sort of feeling from which Eliot and Pound's early poetry often seems designed to distance itself. Dylan's own moral fastidiousness is the lodestone, no doubt, of Eliot's powerful appeal to him–but other aesthetic traditions, including the elegiac mysticism of Beat poetry and the folk ballad, have led him to see Eliot as under-nourishing.

In "Desolation Row," pathos wins out over satire and comedy. You can hear this in the audience reaction to Dylan's debut performance of the song at the Forest Hills concert in late August, 1965–a week before *Highway 61 Revisited* was released. At first, almost every line is greeted with delighted–one is tempted to say smirking–guffaws, but the laughter gradually subsides, disappearing entirely halfway through the song, even though some of Dylan's funniest lines are yet to come. By the time I heard him perform it that year around Thanksgiving in Washington, D.C., we all knew the song by heart: we had absorbed its humor, but its pathos, and its frightfulness, remained. No one was laughing. For better or worse, in the end, "Desolation Row" does not foster a sense of immunity from the grim comedy it depicts. Cinderella was right: "'It takes one to know one,' she smiles."

## II

Where *Bringing It All Back Home* represents a culmination, *Highway 61 Revisited* is a new beginning. It is all raw energy, the first punk explosion. Dylan sounds like he is making his first record, as if he's been waiting all his life for his moment in the sun, and he is ready for it. In a real sense, this is Dylan's first record, insofar as it is his first genuine song cycle, his first collection to offer an interwoven whole that is greater than the sum of its parts. Unlike Dylan's earlier records, *Highway 61 Revisited* is not just an album, a portfolio of recent or representative work; it's an attempt to project a vision in song, his first attempt to tell the whole story.

The whole story that emerges is best described as the result of the interplay between three kinds of songs. The first, which I called the backbone of the LP, are the three mutant talking blues. The last is a trio of songs–"Like a Rolling Stone," "Ballad of a Thin Man," and "Queen Jane Approximately"–that comprise the album's fullest voice, a reinvention of rock 'n' roll as what Allen Ginsberg, describing "Queen Jane," aptly termed "blue invitations." (There should have been a fourth song of this type– "Positively Fourth Street"–but more on that later.)

Then there are three songs that comprise the heart of *Highway 61 Revisited*. They are all three very different from each other, but each of them is a blues, in the mode of what Robert Palmer terms "deep blues," and in each of them the rub is sex.

"From a Buick 6" resembles "Highway 61 Revisited" in the narrator's utter disengagement from the characters in his song. That may seem an absurd thing to say about a first-person narrative, but here it's true. The song's ostensible narrator, the narrative "I," is pretty much a cipher. He may claim that "I got this graveyard woman," but clearly (as in "She Belongs to Me"), she's got him, and, moreover, she does all the work–not only in his life, but in this song. She does everything; things happen to the narrator, mostly as a result of her actions. This "soulful mama" who's "bound" to furnish his death-bed blanket looms increasingly as not just an earth mother but as Mother Nature herself. He is her prisoner ("she keeps me hid" and "brings me bread"), and his prison is his own sexuality, figured here as his potent Buick 6: "when the pipeline is broken" and he's "all cracked up on the highway," she's always there to "sew me up with a thread," and "she keeps this four-ten all loaded with lead."

"She don't make me nervous": the narrator doth protest too much. At one level, of course, she doesn't make him nervous; he's obviously quite comfortable in his sexual prison. But in the irony of this line the narrator's mask drops, and a narrator behind the narrator, an ur-narrator, if you will, briefly shows his face. He is uncomfortable, not with this woman (insofar as she is actually a woman, she is an angel) but with himself, with his own ego. The song's meanness is self-directed: it's the narrator's own passivity, really, that makes his woman seem a nightmare man-eater. The ur-narrator seems about to emerge again at the beginning of the final verse, where, in a classic Dylan move, he addresses directly someone (usually, as here, a woman) he's been talking about. His request for a "steam shovel" and "dump truck"–vehicles for violently altering nature–indicate an attempt, if only unconscious, to break out of his prison. But in asking her for more provisions, he misses the point: "I need a dump truck baby" is not the same as "I'm gonna get me a dump truck baby." His abortive rebellion thus collapses in a now rather transparently anxious celebration of his dependency on her unbounded beneficence ("she brings me everything *and more*" [emphasis added]). The song's final note–the anxious "just like I said"–is the narrator's grim concession of his bondage to the repetitive circle of nature.

The overall effect of this song is finely multivalent. It does celebrate this woman, or this image of woman, without any detectable irony, but it also distances itself from the ostensible narrator and from the terms of his possession of her. Insofar as it does this, it makes the ur-narrator (what Whitman would call the Real Me) feel good, as Dylan has said a blues should. But insofar as it leaves him with the same hapless ego, its work is incomplete. Like "Highway 61 Revisited," the song's power is indistinguishable here from a kind of powerlessness.

"Just Like Tom Thumb's Blues" retraces the same ground, except here Dylan disengages himself not from the pleasures but from the pains of sex. This song is a great and crucial work, but it is also an odd song, one that ends up in a place it never seems to have been heading. It is in some ways two songs in one. The first, third, fourth (a functional bridge), and fifth verses comprise a Blakean vision of sex as an initiation into the world of death. The first verse is a spectacularly nutshelled vision, a dazzling texture of puns ("gravity" and "airs," "hungry" and "mess") whose clairvoyance annihilates the duplicity of punning and yields instead a sense of blind, mute process. The only audible sound is the animal cry emitted when its impassive parade of otherwise perfect anapests briefly bunches into a trochaic squeal on "hungry women." As Dylan says of "Sweet Melinda," "she takes your voice/and leaves you howling at the moon."

Needless to say, it's beyond silliness even to raise the issue of whether "sweet Melinda" is to blame for Dylan's predicament. Like the other women in this song, this "goddess of gloom" is no woman but a mythic creature, a siren-harpy–just as "all the authorities" invoked in the fifth verse are not to be confused with any social establishment. In fact, these impish "authorities" are anti-authorities, the lords of misrule; their cops "don't need you" because, unlike the "city fathers" and the "insurance men" who govern the social world, they don't police reality. Down on "Rue Morgue Avenue" there are no alibis; you're on your own. The reality Dylan encounters in this song is the reality that, elsewhere on this record, the profoundly disordered social order–including the mock-bohemia of "Desolation Row"–has erected itself to exclude. "Tom Thumb's Blues" is an anti-pastoral, a south-of-the-border Easter vacation–known these days as spring break–that turns into a harrowing of hell. When Dylan–having had his fill of reality–announces, with wicked irony, his intention to return for asylum to the Big Apple, he turns the traditional hierarchies of the pastoral on their head: the city, not the country, is the place to go if you want to "get silly."

If that were all there were to it, this would be a profoundly cynical song. The song I have so far summarized would have to be titled something like "Just Like a Lady-Killer's Blues." It would summarize the origins of the psychology of male sexual revenge, whether of the strong-willed or weak-minded variety–Jack the Ripper or Casanova.

The verse I have not yet mentioned–the second–contributes little to this story, except to wallow wonderfully in the pain of it all. But "Tom Thumb's Blues" wouldn't be–and almost certainly wouldn't have become–the song it is without this verse. This song is written in the second person. The "you" it begins with–the "you" of "when you're lost in the rain"–is an interior "you," the "you" we commonly employ as a less formal, more intimate synonym for "one" and whose referent is really "I," the speaker. But the "you" of the second verse ("When you see St. Annie") is clearly another person, a friend–a *missing* friend (since the whole point is that Dylan here has no friends) and thus an imaginary friend. Wallowing in his pain here, Dylan discovers its true source:

loneliness. The pursuit of sex (and whatever other intoxicants his "best friend the doctor" furnishes) is really a pursuit of companionship, and Dylan's failure to find companionship in his adventures has abandoned him to the natural fate of sex, which, like the natural fate of everything, is nihilism: "Angel" becomes a "ghost."

I said that Dylan here discovers the source of his pain, but actually he seems to stumble unconsciously upon it. In any case, Dylan moves forward as if nothing had changed, resuming the voice of the "you" who is really oneself. The suggestion is that Dylan doesn't realize yet that he's looking for a friend and that his failure to find one reflects some flaw in himself. Nonetheless, the pseudo "you" of the succeeding verses is shadowed–at least for the listener–by a poignant sense of a lost companion, of a broken self seeking its completion in a missing other. In the third verse, lines like "you're so careful and kind" and "she takes your voice" flicker ambiguously with a simultaneous sense of companionship and abandonment.

Dylan himself finally notices this motive in the silence that separates the fifth from the final verse, a verse whose meaning turns on a deep sense of personal betrayal. Dylan returns to New York City, it turns out, not to exploit its bohemian safety but to regroup. He returns with his loneliness, a fund of desire he didn't have, or didn't realize he had, when he left. The song ends with a triumphant self-assertion–"I've had enough"–that is made no less triumphant by the realization that what it really means is "I have nothing–nothing that I really want."

"It Takes a Lot to Laugh, It Takes a Train to Cry," the third and finest of the three blues songs on *Highway 61 Revisited*, begins where "Tom Thumb's Blues" leaves off. Dylan now knows what he wants: he wants to get laid–without dying; he wants to "get across," in almost every sense of that phrase you might imagine. Of course, he fails–this is a blues–but he comes away as fully possessed of his own desire as he will ever need to be.

"Train to Cry" almost got derailed. In the original version of the lyric, known as "Phantom Engineer" (the version Dylan sang when he introduced the song during his infamous 1965 Newport Folk Festival performance), Dylan pulls back at key moments from the force of his own feeling, as if to deny that he really has anything to lose should "your train get lost." "Phantom Engineer" is a fine song, a persuasive song–in an important sense, he does have nothing to lose: there will be other trains. But there's also a sense in which he does have something to lose–if only his precious time–and a much more interesting and evocative song was born when he finally admitted it.

"It Takes a Lot to Laugh, It Takes a Train to Cry." The title, I would argue, is a surreal allegory, although its allegorical meaning, like that of the entire song, is both freely improvised and truly inspired. And though what I have to say about it is not similarly inspired, I am going just to wing it. "It Takes a Lot to Laugh, It Takes a Train to Cry" means (among many things) that it takes me (a man) to laugh and you (a woman) to cry. That can mean men laugh, women cry; or a man by himself laughs, but a woman makes him cry. This last seems to me closer to the core of the song–the core that "Phantom Engineer" was anxious to suppress. "Lot" carries the sense both of the biblical Lot (his wife certainly got lost) and "a lot," a large amount that is still implicitly less than "a train," an even larger amount. The title is thus telling us that tears are deeper than laughter but also that women are deeper than men–though, I would caution that this latter truth applies only if you are a man, since its fullest meaning, for Dylan, is always "you" are deeper than "I."

It should also be mentioned that here, as almost everywhere, Dylan reverses the traditional blues symbology in which cars are female and trains male. Cars are relatively rare in Dylan's songs, but like the Buick 6, they are always symbols of male sexual power. (In the blues, where they are usually female, *ownership* of a car is the common symbol of male power.) Dylan's trains–the "freight train moving" of "Simple Twist of Fate" or the "rolling train" that "blows right through me" of "Brownsville Girl"–always seem to be symbols that link female power with the power of his own emotional life, both of which are often fearsomely overwhelming. In the closely related song "I'll Keep It with Mine," a *Highway 61* outtake released on the *Biograph* collection in

1985, the train that "leaves at half past ten" and returns tomorrow "same time again" is an image of some psychic paralysis in the woman that also leaves Dylan ("the conductor") "stuck on the line."

Here Dylan rides a "mail train":

*Well I ride on a mail train baby*
*Can't buy a thrill*
*Well I've been up all night*
*Leanin' on the window sill*
*Well if I die*
*On top of the hill*
*And if I don't make it*
*You know my baby will*

Sly, very sly. At one level, this is very seductive. If you don't listen too closely, or think about it too much, it seems to say: "I've got a tough job, tedious and unrewarding, but I get through it thinking of you, and if things never get better for me, at least you know I'm doing it so things will be better for you." We can imagine it as a note accompanying the singer's enclosed paycheck.

Or something like that. This verse is so thickly figured that you could probably cook up any number of literal plots to fit it. Whatever literalizing fiction we choose, the overt tone is a kind of dutiful cheeriness, a love-sick whistling in the dark. But even on a first listening, its sweetness is edged with more than a whiff of bitterness. "Leanin' on the windowsill," an image that is the stanza's emotional fulcrum, just can't be reduced to "thinking of you." It seems to blend the expectancy of the "raven at my window" in "Love Minus Zero" with the disappointment of the balcony scene that concludes "Absolutely Sweet Marie," where Dylan is left "wondering where you are tonight." This opening verse is pervaded by an obscure–and even deliberately obscured–sense that the singer's "baby" is somehow the cause of his predicament.

This obscurity is cleared up at the end of the song, when the singer refers to "your train." The train he rides, I suggest, is her sexuality, its promises and its pleasures for him. When we re-listen, it sounds less like a love-sick promise and more like a bitter complaint against the disappointments of sex: to "die on top of the hill" so that his "baby" might live is, after all, a fairly direct figure for the male's fabled sexual and biological fate. His complaint is not against this fate (the song's delicious rocking rhythms refuse to deny its pleasures) but against the way his relationship to his "baby" is reduced to the exigencies of that fate.

All this–or something like it–becomes clear, as I said, by the end of the song, when the singer identifies the disappointments of "your train" with the larger fatality of nature ("the wintertime is coming/the windows are filled with frost") and dissociates himself from "your" looming disaster with a very Dylanesque warning. But the heart of this song is its sublime middle verse, a stanza comprised mostly (and for all I know, entirely) of traditional blues lyrics in which the singer makes it quite clear how he wants to "get across"–and what it means to be a "lover" and not a "boss."

Unlike the final verse, this one is very un-Dylanesque, an attempt to arouse your attention not with a warning but with a visionary promise, an offer you might refuse but won't be able to forget:

*Don't the moon look good mama*
*Shinin' through the trees*
*Don't the brakeman look good mama*
*Flagging down the Double E*
*Don't the sun look good*
*Going down over the sea*
*Don't my gal look fine when she's*
*Comin' after me*

I don't suppose it needs to be said that this imagery, especially its verbs, is profoundly, deliciously sexual, but it is also notable that this verse is written in a different kind of language than the rest of the song. It is not allegorical: it does have to be interpreted to be intelligible. The moon, the sun, and the brakeman are all enlisted, as it were, to amplify the sexual thrill openly addressed only in the final line, but the delight we are invited to take in these things is for their own sake as well. Indeed, the delight Dylan takes (and invites you, who may or may not be "his gal," to take) in the sight of his gal "comin' after me" is seen finally as part of a larger eroticized landscape, as but one instance in a universe of interpenetrating natural and human energies. This sense of interpenetration is carried both by each of the four images in themselves and by a structural oscillation between male (sun, brakeman) and female (moon, gal) and between natural (moon, sun) and human (brakeman, gal) images. It's also carried by one of the first instances of Dylan's flair for what might be called prepositional (or quasi-prepositional) redundancy: "going *down over* the sea" and (as he now sings the latter half of the first line) "shinin' *in through* the trees" (emphasis added). In recent years, Dylan has revised, in live performance, that sexually delicious "coming after me" to the more innocent delight of "chasing after me." I've always regretted this revision–I like the way the original torques up the tension between blues raunch and childlike playfulness–but in truth, the change is entirely in keeping with the verse's implicit Jack-and-Jill story.

The edge of excitement in this stanza is that of a man not so much missing his gal as imagining a way of being with her he has never experienced. Sex, as here imagined, is not (merely) a natural transaction or even exchange but a kind of conversation, an ecstatic mutual telling-and-listening that is most powerfully conveyed not in any aspect of imagery but in its rhetorical form: a questioning.

*Highway 61 Revisited* is the album on which Dylan re-invents himself as a great questioner. A question, especially as Dylan learns to use it, proposes a reciprocal regard and wonder–a listening for the listener whose answer questions our questioning–that is ultimately the real answer Dylan's questions are always seeking. Hereafter, the question, along with its variants, often supplements or even supplants figurative language (and other modes of evasion) and negation in Dylan's poetic tool-kit.

The question attains its fullest expression in the quartet of *Highway 61 Revisited* songs in which Dylan re-invents rock 'n' roll: "Didn't you?" and "How does it feel?" "Don't you, Mr. Jones?" "won't you come see me, Queen Jane?" and "Why [then] don't you?" These songs are unimaginable without their questions–indeed, they *are* their questions. But in "Train to Cry" Dylan's questioning arises as if accidentally, as an unsolicited change of mood that turns this song about thwarted intimacy on its head. In the final verse, Dylan emerges a new person, purged of the elegant groveling with which he began the song. He ends with an implicit offer of a renewal of love–on his fierce terms–but the power of this ending lies in his take-it-or-leave-it indifference to "your" response. There is a genuine cruelty in his tone here that–despite Dylan's reputation–is relatively rare in his love songs. He even seems to get off on imagining "when [not if] your train gets lost"–indeed the wondrously seductive rocking rhythm of the *Highway 61 Revisited* recording of this song makes it impossible not to get an erotic charge from what, on the face of it, seems like an erotic disaster.

So what's going on here? Well, here's what I think: The train, remember, is less an image of this woman than of her emotional power over Dylan. He is imagining his release from the thrall of that power, a release that has, in fact, already occurred. When he sings these words, that train already is lost–to him. He possesses his "baby/mama" as an ideal, in his heart and mind. This ideal woman, as we saw, is also imagined as a train (among other things). But the relationship in this ideal between train and brakeman, et al, is mutually sustaining in a way that belies the pretense of love between Dylan and the woman to whom the song is addressed (a woman who, of course, may also be an idealized, or imagined, figure).

This dialectic between an actual "you"–often called "she"–and imagined "you" is central to Dylan's poetry. But usually he attempts to re-fashion "her" in the light of his imagination of "you." That, as I will argue shortly, is rock 'n' roll. "Train to Cry" is a blues, and the aim of the blues is rather more modest, not to mention more plausible, than that of rock 'n' roll. In the blues, the singer's aim is always just to get out of it alive, his spirit intact. Or, to borrow the wryly reductive conceit from "Blood in My Eyes," the Mississippi Sheiks blues Dylan covers on *World Gone Wrong*, a blues singer just wants to get back his "money"–his investment of self in whatever disaster his song addresses.

In "Train to Cry," Dylan gets his money back. The song swallows the visionary eros of its middle verse as a private booty, but not without what feels like a violent inner struggle. The opening lines of the final verse suggest to me a man awakening from a dream, or perhaps moving from one dream to another, from a dream of summer and its transparencies to a nightmare of "wintertime" and "windows...filled with frost." There is a tremendous pathos in the images that open this verse, especially in the archetypal nightmare image of being unable to "get across." These images are full of emotional suggestions and possibilities that Dylan will return to in other songs–I'm thinking especially of "I Dreamed I Saw St. Augustine" and "Senor"–but here he does his best to throttle their pathos. He does this by shouting his refusal to be defeated as a lover to a lover who–as he knows and as we know and as he knows we know–is not listening. But Dylan doesn't care; or maybe it would be better to say, he isn't going to care: he's got his heart's desire (in his heart, where it belongs), and "you" can jolly well fend for yourself in whatever hell it is you're drifting toward. The tone of its finale is triumphantly mean-spirited.

Almost. The final half-line–"when your train gets lost"–is missing a syllable, a lack that always deforms the vocal–"when you-hore train" or "when your traaaiiin" or whatever–in a way that exposes, if only for a moment, the wound in the singer's heart. It's not enough to upset his equilibrium, but it is enough to confirm that his desire, however repossessed, is still a form of hunger.

## III

Bob Dylan did not invent rock 'n' roll, and he wasn't even the first to write rock 'n' roll songs whose lyrics could be usefully described as poetry. But as far as I can tell, he did invent rock 'n' roll poetry. His songs are the first whose words work on us the way rock 'n' roll music works on us.

The term "rock 'n' roll" covers a multitude of sins, and I am here invoking it only in terms of those to which I am committed. What I mean by rock 'n' roll can be defined by listening to the best of Elvis's Sun-era recordings and live performances, and to the recordings of a handful of canonical songs birthed in his wake; "Tutti Frutti," "Whole Lotta Shakin' Goin' On," "Blue Suede Shoes," "Dixie Fried," "Who Do You Love?" "School Days," "Memphis, Tennessee," "Peggy Sue," "Not Fade Away," "Be-Bop-a-Lula," and maybe few others.

Listen to these records, and rock 'n' roll defines itself as a certain wildness, a pursuit of the transcendence found in the moment, in the elusive yet palpable here and now. This is not what we now commonly mean by rock 'n' roll–post-Beatles, post-Stones, post-Byrds, post-Doors, post-everything. The wildness of the earliest rock 'n' roll–what Dylan himself still insists on calling "rockabilly"–is neither a socio-political nor (Camille Paglia notwithstanding) a Dionysian wildness. It is, surprisingly, an Emersonian wildness, or a boyishly Thoreauvian wildness. Rock 'n' roll is all about the excitement of transcendence, a transcendence that takes the form of a revelation. Rock 'n' roll seeks what Walt Whitman would call a "show of things."

Rock 'n' roll's earliest triumphs achieve their effects mostly through their music, especially their voices. Rock 'n' roll is the ecstatic edge in Elvis's voice or the blithe impudence in Chuck Berry's. The words function mostly as a kind of soundtrack or subtitle, a verbal crib to what's going on. But the best of these songs were written by gifted writers, and under the pressure of their pursuit of a rock 'n' roll moment, their lyrics often approach or even attain the character of authentic poetry. And on occasion, that poetry or near-poetry sometimes even assumes a form that amplifies–rather than merely annotates–the rock 'n' roll that spawned it.

Consider Bo Diddley's "Who Do You Love?" This is basically a revved-up blues boast, with the usual blues mix of menace and humor. Except the humor is not really a blues humor; it's a kind of clowning, surprisingly akin to blackface minstrelsy. Moreover, the menace and the clowning don't quite coalesce into a single tone. They are more like the two faces of a coin, discernible alternately but not simultaneously. The song is Bo Diddley's version of Queequeg's tomahawk/peace pipe in *Moby-Dick*: depending on how we choose to take it, the songs strikes our ears either as a fair warning the singer is brandishing or an outlandish capering to provoke and entertain our attention. The result is an oddly disjunctive mix of friendliness and hostility that just might have something to do with rock 'n' roll.

Such a mixture certainly informs the one section of the lyrics that attain the peremptory authority of true poetry. Each verse ends with this couplet.

*Come on baby*
*take a walk with me*
*Eileen, tell me,*
*who do you love?*

These lines still electrify me every time I hear them–no matter who is singing them. In a way that is very Dylanesque, they offer intimacy in the guise of a mugging, an intimacy that blows right past the perfunctory fiction of "Eileen" and grabs each listener–personally–by the back of the head. "Who do you love" here *sounds* like "Show me your money"–but it's a trick question. Refuse to show him your "money," and he'll not only take it anyway, but he'll cut your head off. Show it to him, and you have a fast friend for life.

These double-edged meanings certainly get your attention, but what really makes these lines so potent in their context is the way they rope the listener into the song. One of the new and distinctive features of early rock 'n' roll is the way the singer encourages his listeners to identify with him not as someone who is speaking to (or even speaking for) them, but as someone who is *listening* to (and for) them. Like much of early rock 'n' roll, this song is an invitation to come out and play, to reveal who you love.

It is no accident that much of this rock 'n' roll was, like "Who Do You Love," made by African-Americans addressing, as if for the first time, a national, mostly white audience. The origins of rock 'n' roll are intimately related to the origins of the Civil Rights movement. Bo

Diddley, his song insists, *is* Queequeg. He approaches his listener not as a slave, not even as an ex-slave, but as a free man, of inherent nobility, and he approaches that audience not because he needs it but because, spurred by what Queequeg's creator called an "infinite fraternity of feeling," he finds he wants it. Rock 'n' roll, in this sense, is a democratic art, a gamble that the fraternity of feeling in us is indeed unbounded–whether by race, class, or even gender. What gives a song like Buddy Holly's "Peggy Sue" its irresistible charm, for instance, is the way it is secretly not finally about teenage horniness. It is rather an attempt to persuade a girl to accept an unruly (and admittedly very horny) boy as an equal and fit playmate.

I know, I know. Bo Diddley was just trying to make a hit record. I'm just describing what, from the sound of it, making a hit record was then worth to Bo Diddley. If you saw him in the Chuck Berry documentary, *Hail! Hail! Rock 'n' Roll*, you already know that the whole experience actually undermined whatever faith he may have once had in the "infinite fraternity of feeling" in his fellow Americans. Most of his best songs–"Mona," "Roadrunner," "Bo Diddley"–are in spirit not rock 'n' roll but blues. It's as if the rock 'n' roll bravura of "Who Do You Love?" simply erupted from him, against his better judgment.

Chuck Berry himself, in that same film, expressed great satisfaction with the way his brand of rock 'n' roll had been rewarded–emotionally as well as financially–by the attention of a national audience. But then Chuck Berry is an altogether different sort of Queequeg. Perhaps the slyest intelligence and most devious wit–before Dylan–ever to practice rock 'n' roll, this "brown-eyed handsome man" knew that he had been invited to the party only because he had somehow been mistaken for Uncle Remus. But he also knew that while his white audience thought it needed an Uncle Remus, it really wanted a Martin Luther King, a new Moses to lead it out of Egypt. And, after his own fashion, Berry was perfectly willing and able to play that role.

The premise of his greatest song, "School Days," is that white society–emblemized by public school–is in reality a plantation system, and that rock 'n' roll will set you free. On the one hand, all this means is that life is serious business, and rock 'n' roll offers teenagers, naturally restive under that seriousness, the release of mindless physical fun. Rock 'n' roll is as innocently healthy, and as innocuous, as sports. On the other hand, you don't prompt your listeners to "lay your burden down" and promise to "deliver you from the days of old," as Berry does, without opening your song to more deeply resonant yearnings. Perhaps the seriousness of life is a banal fraud, and perhaps what rock 'n' roll offers is a remission from that *ancien regime* commonly known as the real world, a remission that in his song "Rock 'n' Roll Music" Berry himself calls a "Jubilee."

"School Days" introduces some new poetic moves that prefigure Dylan's own rock 'n' roll poetry. "School Days" is the first memorable rock 'n' roll song written in the second person, a device that, like the direct question, imports the listener into the song. Its greatness, even among Chuck Berry songs, lies in the suppleness with which he gradually intensifies and releases the feelings latent in this point of view. The early verses are a kind of urbane, understated talking blues, and the "you" is both self and other, singer and audience. We don't even stop to think whether this you is Berry's teenage audience or his own remembered childhood (or even an allegory of his adult identity). At this point this connection between singer with audience merely expands the circle of oppression: we're all miserably isolated in the same miserable boat.

The pace quickens with anticipation in the third verse ("soon as three o'clock rolls around"), but the oppressive mood doesn't really lift until the climactic fourth verse:

*Drop the coin right into the slot*
*You're gotta hear somethin' that's really hot*
*With the one you love, you're makin' romance*
*All day long you been wantin' to dance,*
*Feeling the music from head to toe*
*Round and round and round we go*

The primary emotion released here derives from Berry's identification of himself as his listener. It's the ecstasy of experiencing oneself *as* another and yet still as oneself, of being simultaneously speaker and listener, of finding an ego that is both "I" and "you." Thus, the "we" invoked in the final line is only partly the singer's vivid imagining of his listener's togetherness with her dancing partner. It is mainly an aesthetic "we," a freshly minted mutuality that now exists between the singer and his listener and within each of them. This "we" is Berry's trope for the transfiguring thrill his song summons.

The specific form of "we" invoked in that final line is the ultimate divination (and divinity) of rock 'n' roll. It is Dylan's central trope for the presence of God in human life. Here, its emergence seems to catch Berry by surprise, provoking from him an open-hearted psalm of praise from a writer who usually speaks with a glassy coolness:

*Hail, hail rock 'n' roll*
*Deliver us from the days of old*
*Long live rock 'n' roll*
*The beat of the drums, loud and bold*
*Rock, rock, rock 'n' roll*
*The feelin' is here, body and soul.*

Of course, that's not quite how the song actually goes. Berry falters in this final verse, as if backing away from what he has done. After all, he's supposed to be Uncle Remus. In fact, he sings "deliver *me* from the days of old" and "the feeling is *there,* body and soul." These changes don't matter as much in performance as they do on the tongue–mainly because the music is still "here," and "we" are still here, and the cat's been let out of the bag.

But unlike Jerry Lee Lewis, who sang (even if he did not write) "Whole Lot of Shakin' Goin' On" and "Great Balls of Fire," Berry remained cagily circumspect in his claims for what I would call the pentecostal substance of rock 'n' roll. This pentecostalism discloses itself not as a speaking in tongues but as a dancing in circles, as a dancing out of oneself and into the morning. Dancing, in early rock 'n' roll songs, transfigures reality. Pre-Dylan, a climactic "Let's dance," "Let's rock," or some variant is the most common trope in the rock 'n' roll repertoire.

But this is a trope to end all merely verbal tropes, a trope that dissolves mere words in the "round and round" of a dancing body. Not a bad idea, not bad at all, but a better idea would be to have it both ways, to have your poetry and dance it too.

## IV

Bo Diddley and Chuck Berry are not the only important influences on Dylan's rock 'n' roll poetry, and there is more, obviously, to Bo Diddley and Chuck Berry's influence than is revealed in the two songs I discussed. As we are still just beginning to appreciate, Dylan has listened to the entire body of American popular music–rock 'n' roll included–with a more voracious and responsive attention than any mere scholar. But the example of "Who Do You Love?" and "School Days" offers a useful point of departure.

Purely as an aside, I would suggest that while Matt Dillon and/or Dylan Thomas may have provided the material with which Robert Zimmerman renamed himself Bob Dylan, it always seemed clear to me that he was naming himself after Bo Diddley (real name: Elias McDaniel) by adopting a name with the same cadence and structure of consonants and vowels. And like Bo Diddley, Dylan often used his name in his early song titles.

And now back to our regular programming.

To restate my premise: *Highway 61 Revisited* includes three of the four songs that together constitute the first flowering of a specifically rock 'n' roll poetry: "Like a Rolling Stone," "Ballad of a Thin Man," and "Queen Jane Approximately," The fourth song, released only as a single (but later included on the 1967 *Greatest Hits* collection), is "Positively Fourth Street." These four songs could be described as dances; not dance music but dances with their own audiences, kept in motion by the direct question and the second-person address–the two devices we discovered in "Who Do You Love?" and "School Days." In fact, Dylan uses these devices in a way that retains the flavor they had in those songs. The direct question wields an ambivalent hostility/friendliness, and the second-person address establishes a transfiguring translucence. Each of these songs blends, in different mixtures, Bo Diddley ferocity with Chuck Berry cool. They embody a complex of feeling, perception, and imagination that is far richer and more deeply provoking than any of their rock 'n' roll antecedents.

Taken together, these songs also constitute a map of Bob Dylan's rock 'n' roll kingdom. They represent the four kinds of rock 'n' roll song that Dylan is interested in writing. Dylan has never written a rock 'n' roll song that is not a remake, or a revisiting, of one or more of these songs. Rock 'n' roll songs, as I have defined them, are dances with their audience, and Dylan's dances with his audience arise out of two modes of conversation with himself, or what we might call interior dances. One of these interior partners is female (not necessarily a woman), a muse figure, or what Blake would call an emanation. The other is male (not necessarily a man), an antagonistic alter-ego and/or friend. Unless his name is Jesus (or Senor), in Dylan's songs this male figure is almost always a false friend, one who is best understood (for me, anyway) as Dylan's version of the Blakean spectre, as the shadow self cast by the true self's anxieties.

"Like a Rolling Stone" is Dylan's archetypal song of his emanation, and "Ballad of a Thin Man" is his archetypal song of his spectre. ("Thin Man," it only recently occurred to me, is Dylan's trope for a man's shadow.) "Queen Jane Approximately" and "Positively Fourth Street" are Dylan's archetypal songs *to* his emanation and spectre, respectively. The difference arises from the fact that the former songs are written in the second-person, the latter two songs in the first person.

In defining the former two songs the "song of his emanation" and the "song of his spectre," I am deliberately invoking the title of Whitman's "Song of Myself." The analogy first occurred to me when I attended a Dylan concert in 1978 and realized that the two dozen or so individual songs Dylan sang led into and out of each other in very much the same manner–at once associative and narrative–that the 52 sections in Whitman's poem prepare for and succeed each other. The more I thought about this, the more it seemed right–and the more I noticed there was something fundamentally *different* about the way these two primally secretive, devious, and elusive poets show themselves in their poems. Whitman sings of (and finds) others in himself, but Dylan sings of (and finds) himself in others. I said earlier that Dylan kidnaps his listener into his songs, but that is just half the story, perhaps even the lesser half: he opens his mouth at all only because his listener has already kidnapped him. Both Whitman and Dylan are poets of a primordial American lonesomeness, but this lonesomeness is inflected differently in each: for Whitman it is rooted in the insoluble mystery of "myself," and for Dylan in the corresponding mystery of "you."

Thus, while Dylan sounds like he has taken Mother Whitman's poetry to heart, he doesn't at all ever sound like Walt Whitman–except, as on "Gotta Serve Somebody," to parody him. He does, however, sound like this:

> *I'm nobody, who are you?*

In an earlier chapter, I identified Emily Dickinson as Dylan's poetic mother, but in fact she is his poetic father: Dylan draws his material from Whitman, but he draws much of his method from Dickinson. Whitman's nonchalance, his oceanic aplomb, is present in Dylan, but as a point of departure and not as a goal. What Dylan's poetry pursues is not equilibrium but, like Dickinson, surprise. You can hear the difference, I think, in the opening of "Like a Rolling Stone," in the way its pseudo-Whitmanesque lines–long, leisurely, loping–find their resolution not by circling soothingly back upon themselves but by suddenly snapping their tails:

*Once upon a time*
        *you dressed so fine*
*Threw the bums a dime*
        *in your prime*
                *__didn't you?__*
*People'd call*
        *say beware doll*
*You're bound to fall*

*you thought they were all*
***kiddin' you!***
*You used to laugh about*
*everybody that was hanging out*
*Now you don't talk so loud*
*now you don't seem so proud*
*About having to be*
*scrounging*
***for your next meal***

Like the lady said, "I'm nobody–who are you?" The difference between Dickinson and Dylan, in a nutshell, is that where Dickinson seeks surprise, Dylan seeks to *be* an arrow of surprise. Bo Diddley, remember, is a gunslinger.

Once more as an aside. Allen Ginsberg often reported that Dylan had told him that Emily Dickinson was his favorite poet–according to Ginsberg, Dylan's film distribution company, Circuit Films, took its name from Dickinson's line "success in circuit lies." I suspect that Dickinson might be Dylan's favorite poet because he first discovered the power of poetry in reading her. I would guess that, like me and countless others, Dylan was introduced to Dickinson in grade school. I also suspect that, like me, he was fed mainly Dickinson's weaker, cuter poems, with only one or two of the great Dickinson poems–smuggled in under cover of some pious gloss–allowed to assault innocent ears. I'd bet, too, that one of these poems was "I'm nobody, who are you?" His teachers, like mine, probably read the tone of this poem as one of hapless pathos. I believed my teachers and swore off Dickinson as a bore until I rediscovered her in graduate school. But I'll bet anything that little Bobby Zimmerman recognized her caressing Dylanesque snarl right away.

## V

Enough preliminaries. I want to discuss "Like a Rolling Stone" and "Ballad of a Thin Man" as examples of Dylan's two primary genres of rock 'n' roll poetry. The song of the emanation and the song of the spectre, as I have defined them, each has a characteristic form that corresponds to its distinctive subject matter. Each is a variety of what I would call a lyrical dialogue, but in "Like a Rolling Stone" that dialogue takes the dramatically unitary form of a quest romance, and in "Ballad of a Thin Man" it takes the episodic form of a picaresque narrative. The former is an internalized conversational variant of the folk ballad, the latter of the talking blues.

In my opening chapter, I interpreted the drama of "Like a Rolling Stone" in terms of a specific, historically documented crisis in Dylan's relationship with his audience. This is not the only, or even necessarily the best, context in which to understand this song. But it works, and more importantly, it works in part because this type of song always seems to trace the arc of some specific drama, one with a beginning, middle, and end. Indeed, like many types of Dylan lyric, these songs of the emanation have a very distinct three-part architecture, even when they have four or five verses. Often, as in "Like a Rolling Stone," the third verse has a regressive character that creates a sort of structural syncopation. That is, if the basic narrative–as told by the first, second, and fourth verses–can be reduced (for the sake of discussion) to "get high! get higher! get highest!" then the effect of the fourth verse is to make it "get high! get higher! *I said get high!* get highest." The effect is to make the concluding "get highest" seem more intense–and, since we seemed to be going backwards, more surprising. Another sort of structural syncopation, as we shall see, is exhibited by "Queen Jane Approximately," where the second and fourth verses retard the narrative by doubling the verses that precede them.

All songs of this type exhibit both a strongly purposive forward thrust and (usually) a penchant for dilatory tactics. Hmmm, now that sounds familiar! I have been insisting that early rock 'n' roll (that is, before the Rolling Stones) is about dancing and not sex, but it is nonetheless a species of erotica. In fact, it is this very mixture of eroticism and transcendentalist spirituality that made rock 'n' roll such an explosive provocation for its first listeners. This double vision also informs "Like a Rolling Stone," so that "get high" resolves on the one side into "become invisible" and on the other into "be naked." The aim of a song like "Like a Rolling Stone," that is, is to reveal your invisible nakedness, or naked invisibility.

The aim of a song like "Ballad of a Thin Man," on the other hand, is to cast you off like a bad habit. The difference is that the "you" in these songs is what Dylan in another song calls "my twin, the enemy within." It may help to understand the difference between these two second-person forms to look ahead to the *Blonde on Blonde* outtake "She's Your Lover Now," where Dylan addresses both his emanation and his spectre (and in that order) in each verse. One might say that the aim of the songs of the spectre is to purge both the singer and his listener of their false selves, of the inhibition that keeps them merely visible–or, in light of the climactic image of "earphones" in "Thin Man," audible–to each other. If "Like a Rolling Stone" aims to dance its listener into the magic circle of the singer's invisibility, then in "Ballad of a Thin Man" the singer aims to dance himself beyond his listener's corrupted hearing. In the former he is taking off your clothes, in the latter he is removing his own.

On the face of it, I must admit, "Ballad of a Thin Man" is addressed to an entirely external nemesis. If "Mr. Jones" is Dylan's spectre, it is primarily in the sense that he represents the press, the clueless gaggle of idiot questioners who shadowed Dylan's every move in the mid 60s. The song's drama plays itself out as ritual dismantling of Mr. Jones's defenses against his own human nakedness. But I would argue that Dylan's portrait of Mr. Jones arises ultimately from a profound self-knowledge. The emotional center of the song is the question that concludes each verse:

*Something's happening here*
*And you don't know what it is*
*Do You?*
*Mister Jones.*

Mr. Jones doesn't know what's happening, but then neither does Dylan. He is beyond the need to *know* what he is doing, or perhaps more accurately, he is using this song to propel himself beyond that need. The prospect of not knowing what's happening frightens Mr. Jones, but it delights Dylan. Mr. Jones cannot conceive, let alone hear, such delight, and it is in this sense that in singing this line Dylan has placed himself beyond Mr. Jones's hearing–a development Dylan rubs in by impishly suggesting, in the song's final verse, that Mr. Jones "should be made to wear earphones."

As I earlier argued, the mix of love and hatred in the chorus of "Like a Rolling Stone" changes continuously in the course of the song. That is not how "Thin Man" works. There is a sense in which the song is all over at the end of the first verse, by which time Dylan has already attained the two-faced tone–at once vicious roar and ecstatic silence–that is the song's final motive. So why then does he go on–or why do we keep listening. What more is there to be said? The answer has to do with the nature of his antagonist.

At its best, the spectre is that biologically useful coward in all of us that is commonly known as the reality principle. The spectre is that part of us that pays the bills and keeps order, making sure that when tomorrow arrives, we're still here in one piece. He is the reporter in all of us, and the cop, too: "Who is that man?" he asks. "Just stick to the facts, ma'am, *please,* just the facts." The spectre polices reality, the "somebody naked" whose unpoliced nakedness freaks him out by offering him a mirror of his own existential nakedness, "here all alone." But the spectre's always making himself a nuisance by confusing his police blotter with the reality–which, as we all know, is really too much–it is meant to contain. It's relatively easy to shoo the spectre away, when you set your mind to it, but it's damn near impossible to keep him from finding another perch in our spirit from which to caw at us. So you just have to keep scaring him off, and you can only stop when you've found the strength not to notice him.

And that takes several verses. Dylan needs to have a certain amount of fun–and increasingly richer and more terrific fun–before he can call it a day. "Ballad of a Thin Man" and its ilk–"Gotta Serve Somebody" is its best successor–seem to me to be essentially shame-building rituals.

Their aim is to project certain modes of thought and feeling from one's own spirit by ridiculing them. But first you have to identify them, and you do this by following the frightened spectre's picaresque dream-logic. In "Thin Man" Mr. Jones descends precipitously, verse by verse, into in a phantasmagoria whose reality is unpoliceable in increasingly profound and disturbing ways.

The sequence that runs from the geek to the sword-swallower to the one-eyed midget is often interpreted as an allegory of homosexual degradation, but I have two problems with that. First, the self-disgust that Mr. Jones feels here is an emotion that the song seeks to expel: it's a song that seeks to make us ashamed of the narrowness of our sense of shame. And second, Dylan is using the homosexual–or for that matter, the just plain sexual–overtones of the imagery here explore his disgust with his own relationship as a performer to his audience. There is something fundamentally barbaric and mutually exploitative about that relationship, Dylan suggests, and he seems to me to be determined not to try to change that but to *get over it*. For instance, in the sword swallower episode, Mr. Jones seems to be both the exploited audience (the sword swallower is somehow getting off on him) and the exploited performer (it's his throat that is used for someone else's pleasure). But the lyric is written in a way that encourages us to sympathize with the sword swallower's grimly comic view of the proceedings. (Dylan usually also sings the song from that point of view, but not always. In performances of the song during the 1978 world tour he sang–and even acted out–the song from the point of view of Mr. Jones's spooked terror, but the sense of the lyric remained, so that the persona onstage seemed a clueless fool, like the protagonist of a Poe story.)

This three-part nightmare is interrupted, after the first episode, by a bridge and a verse. This is Dylan's first use of a bridge, a structural device he uses to enlarge the vistas of his songs. Here he uses it to introduce implicitly a new understanding of his spectre that opens the way for him eventually–when he's gotten enough off his chest–to end his song:

*You have many contacts*
*out among the lumberjacks*
*To get you facts*
*when someone attacks*
*your imagination*
*But nobody has any respect*
*anyway they already expect*
*You to just give a check*
*to tax-deductible charity*
*organizations*

The tone here is an elegant blend of scorn and indifference, but these lines are animated by a deeper and more surprising mix of pity and relief. Dylan is reassuring Mr. Jones that he really has nothing to be afraid of, since he is finally invulnerable in his own unimaginativeness. Dylan seems to realize that his spectre is a poor puppy dog, after all, one who can never be reached person to person. (As it turns out, he's actually a sad "camel" braving a desert of his own making.) What Dylan seems to realize, finally, is that it's not up to Mr. Jones to "get it," but up to him to ignore Mr. Jones's anxious yelping. Dylan's sense of relief–of release from the necessity of blowing away all of Mr. Jones's defenses–is conveyed rhythmically, by the hammered rhymes that issue in the polysyllabic loosening of "imagination" and "organization." The fact that the polysyllabic "charity" doesn't rhyme with "check" the way "attacks" rhymes with "facts" underscores the extent to which Dylan is reveling in this release.

Anyone who has seen *Eat the Document*, the rarely shown but widely bootlegged cut-up documentary Dylan made of his 1966 European tour, will remember the way the image of him singing "organi-ZA-shuhhhhhhn" cuts away to an image of him yawning at some London street scene. This is perfect. But it's important to remember that this line ends with a bored yawn that is also an orgasmic yawn–something that, to my ears, Dylan himself has edited out of almost all of his post-1966 performances of this song. Most of these performances bore me, because it seems that in them Dylan himself is merely scornful of and bored with Mr. Jones and has forgotten how happy he is not to have to listen to him.

The bridge is followed by a verse that "consoles" Mr. Jones, even giving the little devil his modest due: He knows things, and he knows people who know things, and they know him. (I suppose we must add critic and pundit to cop and reporter in the list of Mr. Jones's functional identities.) There is something to be said for knowing things. Indeed, it seems that Dylan here might be remembering the ways in which knowing things has been useful even to such an adventurer in the unknown as he. It's hard to believe, that is, that the reference to "all of F. Scott Fitzgerald's books" isn't intended as a winking acknowledgment that Dylan might have been inspired by the author of *Babylon Revisited* and *The Great Gatsby*, the latter a book about a poor Minnesota boy who dreamed a big dream that led him to change his name, ditch his past, and set out to make the cosmopolitan riches of New York City his own.

It's important to recognize the softened tone of this verse, but I don't want to exaggerate this element. The song's tone at this juncture is perfectly captured in the concluding sentence of a charmingly batty introduction of the song Dylan offered in Vancouver on March 26, 1966:

> Mr. Jones lives in Lincoln, Nebraska–to prove I don't make these things up–he hangs around the bowling alley there–he also owns the watermill rights–but we don't talk about that when we're in Nebraska–we just let Mr. Jones have his little way.*

Dylan concludes this verse with the climactic image of the song, an image that forcefully insists that, while a lot of knowledge may be a bit of a good thing, if you let yourself get too comfy in the "little way" of your knowing–as Mr. Jones clearly does–you do so at your own peril:

*You're very well read*
*it's well known*
*But something's happening here*

* Bauldle, *The Ghost of Electricity,* p. 24.

*And you don't know what it is*
*Do You?*
*Mister Jones.*

By wrapping himself in the protective covering of what he knows, Mr. Jones has hoisted himself with his own petard: He is thereby "well known," an epithet that I would suggest is the fiercest curse the poet in Dylan can utter. Like Thoreau, Dylan seeks a life that is "undefined in front," and "well known" is an image of damnation as absolute as "a complete unknown" is an image of sanctification.

The final two Mr. Jones-Goes-to-the-Circus episodes have an emotional momentum fueled more by Dylan's delight in his own imaginative freedom than by his disdain for his antagonist. The song's final verse is a post-climactic recapitulation. It begins with the same words as the opening verse–"you walk into the room"–but whereas earlier Dylan's words were saturated with a sense of Mr. Jones's anxiety, in this final verse his spectre is viewed wholly from without, as if under glass or in an exhibit in a psychic zoo. Here Dylan seems to be savoring his sense of having put Mr. Jones in his place and also resigning himself–with palpable disappointment–to the fact that his shadow will never depart. Dylan's wry joke–"there ought to be a law/against you coming around"–is at his own expense: Mr. Jones *is* the law–the appetite for laws and law-abiding–the fly forever buzzing inside our head that we must learn not to let distract us. Perhaps that's why in recent years Dylan has changed the song's ending, replacing "you should be made to wear earphones" to "next time you come around, please telephone." This change–copped, perversely, from Elvis's "Don't Be Cruel"–swaps one good joke for another, and although the new joke is arguably suitable to a verse in which Dylan is measuring his residual vulnerabilities, I still prefer the nasty sting of the original.

"Positively Fourth Street" is the other of Dylan's great rock 'n' roll songs from this period that belongs on this album. It would have made a perfect finale, both as a final commentary on "your letter yesterday" at the end of "Desolation Row" and a sobering counterpoint to the idealized I-you ecstasies of "Like a Rolling Stone."

"Positively Fourth Street," to a certain degree, is simply a more severely demonic version of "Ballad of a Thin Man." Mr. Jones may be "well known" but the false friend Dylan addresses as "you" in "Fourth Street" is seen through with a withering finality as merciless as anything in all of Dylan's work. The song turns repeatedly and fiercely on what "I know" and what "you know," and each step along the way Dylan deploys his lethal knowing to immobilize his erstwhile "friend" in his own falseness.

Immobilize–as in paralyze. "Positively Fourth Street" is one of Dylan's most intellectual lyrics–compared to "Thin Man," it sacrifices imagistic suggestiveness for conceptual penetration. The fulcrum of its thought is one of Dylan's finest rhymes:

*You see me on the street*
*you always act surprised*
*You say how are you, good luck*
*but you don't mean it*
*When you know well as me you'd rather*
*see me paralyzed*
*Why don't you just come out once*
*and scream it*

Dylan's use of "surprised" here doesn't make much sense unless we recognize it as a trope, an appropriation of Emily Dickinson's favorite trope for the vitality of individual being. Here, it means something like "open," "genuine," "inviting life." The prerequisite of "surprise" is ignorance, but Dylan's friend has half-smothered his own vital being, as Dylan in the preceding verse precisely put it, by "[trying] to hide what he don't know to begin with." What we don't know is *all* we have "to begin with." Without it, there are no fresh encounters, no hellos.

This song does not seemed to be addressed to those friends and fans who turned on Dylan when he abandoned folk music for rock 'n' roll. In fact, the friend addressed–always eager "to be on the side that's winning"–sounds more like a sycophantic follower of the new fashion

Dylan was leaving in his wake. But the real issue is not this friend's attitude toward the singer but the essential falseness, the deadness, of either his allegiance or his betrayal. The issue is not which side he is on but rather whether he is really *here* at all. He is just a human spectre, an apparition who (to unpack just part of the wit of the song's justly famous final punch line) can "see" (and be seen) but cannot "be."

Dylan pretty much puts his adversary in his final resting place–but not without a price. The wit of "Positively Fourth Street" is homicidal, but it is suicidal as well. The sound we hear, in the voice the lyric shapes as well as in Dylan's recorded voice, is that of a man who is murdering part of himself. The song's basic meter–an emotionless, largely monosyllabic deadpan–is continuously corrupted by the wounded sobs of the polysyllabic, feminine rhymes that stitch together the front and back end of each verse. Periodically, the lyric's coolly ruthless plain-talk even breaks up on its own:

*No I do not feel that good*
*When I see the heartbreaks you embrace*
*If I was a master thief perhaps*
*I'd rob them*
*And though I know you're dissatisfied*
*with your position and your place*
*Don't you understand that's*
*not my problem*

The singer recovers admirably here: "not my problem" even carries a whiff of the antithetical joy that gives "Ballad of a Thin Man" its fearsome edge. But the dominant emotion here is a much lesser one, the sense of relief that comes when something painful is finally over. In the opening lines of this verse, however, what we hear, almost nakedly, is the pain. And while the singer, with a characteristically Dylanesque back-handedness, professes a smidgen of compassion ("No I do not feel that good to see the heartbreaks you embrace"), what he actually reveals is an emotion much more powerful, and surprising. The "master thief" is one of Dylan's master images, the shamanistic social mask he dons every time he lifts his voice in song. And this image always carries, as it clearly does here, a powerful sense of desire. The emotion that keeps breaking through the executioner's mask in this song is not rage but loss, an almost erotic bafflement and failure: "if I was a master thief." This spectre, whoever he is, and whatever he's shown himself really to be, is someone the singer once thought of as his friend–someone the singer at the very least *liked*. Now he can't like him anymore; that hurts. End of story. It's a simple song, really.

And it's an astonishingly powerful simple song. I would argue it's even more powerful than any song to his emanation–any conventional love song, that is–Dylan has ever written. Why is that? Curious, isn't it? The answer is not just that Dylan is more moved by his betrayal by friends than by his desire for lovers, although that is probably part of it. The song's extraordinary power derives from the sense of finality the song achieves. Dylan is usually a master of endings that evade finality. His farewells–including his kiss-off songs–always either open up new beginnings (as in the discovery of his own "precious time" that concludes "Don't Think Twice") or reveal themselves–finally–to be anti-farewells, last-chance trials by fire whose aim, as in the sublime "It's All Over Now, Baby Blue," is to re-awaken a lapsed lover or friend. But "Positively Fourth Street" is different. Dylan's lost friend is finally lost, an irremediable cipher, and Dylan himself is buoyed by no compensatory gains. The whole experience is a kind of black hole.

It is a black hole into which the very possibility of friendship seems to have disappeared. Think about it. If *Highway 61 Revisited* is Dylan's homage to *Huckleberry Finn*, as I think it is, isn't it odd that in none of the songs does Dylan-as-Huck enjoy the companionship of any Jim, or even Tom Sawyer? (Unless, we want to regard "Positively Fourth Street" as the song Huck *should* have sung to Tom Sawyer. Ah, don't we all wish we could rewrite the damn ending of that book! )

The hero of these songs is utterly friendless. And what makes this even stranger is that on his early records, Dylan's persona was a virtual creature of his sense of friendliness. From the hushed intimacy with which he addresses his "friend" in "Blowin' in the Wind" to the delightfully impudent conversation in which he imagines himself and President Kennedy addressing each other as "My friend Bob" and "My friend John," Dylan's early songs everywhere offer a sense of an invisible, unbounded circle of friendliness–Melville's "infinite fraternity of feeling"–as a counterweight to the visible bleakness of the social order that usually furnishes these songs with their overt subject.

Dylan addresses this issue, as we saw, in "Restless Farewell":

*Oh ev'ry thought that's strung a*
*knot in my mind*
*I might go insane if it*
*couldn't be sprung*
*But it's not to stand naked under*
*unknowin' eyes*
*It's for myself and my friends*
*my stories are sung*

These lines are as true now as they were when Dylan wrote them almost 40 years ago. What's changed is that since 1965 his confidence that a friendly audience is waiting to greet his songs has become, to put it mildly, embattled. The change began to make itself felt on *Bringing It All Back Home,* which was largely about personal spiritual growth in which friends are conspicuous mainly in their absence. By *Highway 61 Revisited,* friends have become a big part of his problem. In different ways, "Just Like Tom Thumb's Blues" and "Desolation Row"–the two major songs on side two–are both about finding yourself spiritually abandoned among friends.

In this light, "Positively Fourth Street" looms as a farewell not just to a particular friend, but to friendship itself. After *Highway 61 Revisited,* Dylan–or the poet in Dylan–seems to have lost faith in friendship, a faith he has never recovered (except, beginning with *Slow Train Coming*, in a highly speculative form in which friendship is the culmination and reward of spiritual fidelity between lovers). After 1965 Dylan's songs are virtually bereft of faith in the redeemability of social (as opposed to erotic) relationships. Friendship, in the ordinary social sense, figures only as the matrix of disappointment, deceit, and betrayal.

On the other hand, while his songs are so impoverished, the music itself is not. About the same time Dylan began to lose imaginative faith in friendship, he began to find work for his friends, as he told an English schoolgirl in *Don't Look Back*, and to make music with a band. Indeed, sometime while he was touring the world in 1965-1966 with a quintet that would later metamorphose into The Band, he even wrote a song that seems to celebrate his good fortune in finding companions in his pursuit of his muse. These "five believers" may "look like men," but in truth "they're just my friends." It's as if true friendship has become an unimaginable thing, something not to be believed in, or trusted, except as an experience, when it's happening, where friends prove each other in honoring each other's living spirit.

"Positively Fourth Street" was a top-10 hit in the fall of 1965, and that fact still surprises me. I suppose people identified with Dylan's cool disdain. I–and many others, I'm sure–have never been able to listen to the song except as if it were being sung to me (or at me), not by me. By seeing through you, the song helps you find and reclaim whatever inside yourself is capable of really listening to anyone. It's an improbable radio hit precisely because it calls to judgment the bad faith with which our social life is commonly conducted, including the once crucial social nexus between rock 'n' roll radio and its audience. "Positively Fourth Street" is the sound of Dylan clearing the air.

"Queen Jane Approximately"–the song Allen Ginsberg reported hearing on the radio in "Wichita Vortex Sutra" but that was never anything near a radio hit–fills the air with a cooling breeze, Ginsberg's "blue invitations." It's the least ambitious of the four *Highway 61 Revisited* songs I've designated as rock 'n' roll, but the song's lightness should not be mistaken for slightness. It's one of Dylan's purest and sweetest love songs.

The title alludes to Lady Jane Grey, the reluctant nine-day teenage queen (Elizabeth I's immediate predecessor) whose life was crushed–literally–by a false social identity forced upon her by her family's ambitions. The figure Dylan addresses–who is both a fictive woman and his own soul–is only "approximately" Queen Jane because she still has a chance to save herself; indeed, it is the burden of the song to realize that chance. The lyric affects–most affectingly–a courtly Elizabethan tone, but its imaginative substance derives from Whitman and Blake. The song is a socialized, psychologized version of Whitman's romance with his soul in "Song of Myself."

The result is a lyrical fairy tale. Our Queen Jane is trapped within the constricting expectations of her family–expectations that are imaged as a kind of surveillance:

*When your mother sends back*
*all your invitations*
*And your father to your sister*
*he explains*
*That you're tired of yourself*
*and all of your relations*
*Won't you come see me, Queen Jane?*
*Won't you come see me, Queen Jane?*

But that's not exactly how it goes, is it? "Relations" (meaning relatives) is the word we would expect, but what Dylan in fact sings is "creations." The point, I think, is that Queen Jane's relations, as she undoubtedly fails to recognize, *are* her creations.

You can take the song's scenario as a slightly allegorized tale about the way a soul can lose the identity she erected in the multiplicity of social relations that identity brings into being. "Queen Jane" has always been widely identified as a song addressed to Joan Baez, and whether or not this is true, it's easy to imagine it as Dylan's response to his feelings about the public identity she had created for herself. Or you can take it–as I prefer–as pure fairy tale, as a psycho-social exploration of what happens to the imagination when it becomes entranced with–and entrenched in–one of its creations. Queen Jane's plight, in this view, could be described as the consequence of failing to heed the warning Dylan offered in the early prose poem, "Advice for Geraldine on Her Miscellaneous Birthday":

*do not create anything, it will be*
*misinterpreted.*
*it will not change. it will follow you*
*the rest of your life*

The anxiety about being "misinterpreted," while undoubtedly sincere, is a red herring. The true burden of this passage is the artist's fear of being trapped–trapped in what he has already created, where he has already been. It's a danger that Dylan has had to confront and master, since, singing his songs night after night, year after year, Dylan must continually revisit his old creations. At his frequent best, he truly re-creates them, so that he sounds like he is making up on the spot words that perfectly realize a new feeling and awareness. At his most perverse, Dylan tears his songs to shreds. Many of Dylan's performances amount to grand refusals, Samson pulling down the pillars of a now alien, idolatrous temple that once housed his spirit. And at his worst, Dylan simply goes through the motions, unable to move, sick of the repetition, clutching faded flowers than no longer belong to him, squandering worlds of possibility out of a debilitating solicitude for a jealous aging muse: "When your mother sends back all your invitations," etc.

"Queen Jane" has a weakness: the middle three verses seem to me to be merely functional. Like the fourth section of "Like a Rolling Stone," they are too threadbare and easily seen through, too nearly reducible to their interpretations. They don't match the inventiveness that characterizes Dylan's best work, the inexhaustible suggestiveness and surprise that make him a great poet. On the other hand, a little dose of greatness, strategically placed, often goes a long way. "Queen Jane Approximately" is like many Dylan songs: its lyrical parade disguises merely noble or even pedestrian middle verses in the borrowed glory of its royal beginning and ending. Dylan rarely sings this song, and I would guess the main reason is that the disguise doesn't altogether work. Listen, for instance, to the passionate 1993 Supper Club performances–four tries in two nights–and you'll notice that Dylan's voice can never find anything, rhymes aside, to light it up as it navigates the song's middle verses.

But the middle verses do advance a plot that works simultaneously on two levels, and in opposite directions. On the most obvious level, the five-verse sequence conducts Jane through the confinements that constitute her world: two verses about her immediate family, two verses about what we might call her courtiers, and a final verse in which she confronts the "bandits" who define her world's borders. The thematic repetitiveness of the first two verse pairs–what I earlier called a kind of structural syncopation–underscores the theme of repetition and the spiritual nausea it induces. This overt plot traces an augmenting degradation and desperation.

But this movement–from the claustrophobic center of her world to its borders–also traces a path of escape, a loosening of her confinement that Jane shows no signs of noticing until the consciousness-shattering double-bind induced by her bandits' outrageous complaint unexpectedly releases a new self-awareness:

*When all the bandits that you turn*
*your other cheek to*
*All lay down their bandannas*
*and complain*
*And you want somebody you don't*
*have to speak to*
*Won't you come see me Queen Jane?*
*Ah won't you come see me Queen Jane?*

The old Jane needed her bandits: their thievery paradoxically maintains the integrity of her world by defining its boundaries. She turns her other cheek to them not in charity but as a haughty sovereign who refuses to be violated even by their violence. Jane's feelings have been mirrored in those of her relations throughout the song, and here, too, the bandits' exasperated surrender seems to reflect the change that is stirring within her. That change announces itself in the penultimate line, and while the lovely conceit of "someone you don't have to speak to" has always gotten the most attention, the song finds its climax in the first half of this line: "and you *want*" (emphasis added). "Somebody you don't have to speak to" is the right conceit here because it is the only imaginable object for Jane's reawakened desire that does not usurp the primacy of her mere desiring, of her freedom to reinvent herself anew.

The reiterated "won't" in the final return of the song's refrain echoes Jane's emergent "want," seeming to nurse it rather than to offer any real satisfaction for it. It's not just that there's something otherworldly in Dylan's invitation; the primary power and appeal of the song, I think, lies in the way the tone of the refrain gradually purges itself of all merely personal desire as the lyric moves through each successive verse. The singer himself is the visionary bandit who finally steals Jane from her doldrums with an invitation that seeks nothing for himself.

In this respect, Dylan's poetic stance in "Queen Jane" isn't as different from that in "Like a Rolling Stone" as it superficially appears. He may have inserted himself into this lyric, but the self he inserted is his poetic self and not his merely human self, or even a fiction of his mortal self. For all its dazzlingly street-wise prescience, the voice that sings the rock 'n' roll songs on *Highway 61 Revisited* is still addressing us from privileged ground, from a high horse. Don't get me wrong; I'm not complaining: this voice is the voice of our best and truest self.

But it's at least interesting to note that the exploration of a more truly personal poetic voice–a voyage that commenced, on *Another Side of Bob Dylan*, with Dylan's discovery of the poetic possibilities of the mysteries of sex–reaches its climax, on *Highway 61 Revisited*, with a series of break-through rock 'n' roll songs whose voice is as sexless as Huckleberry Finn himself.

Quite a feat, but a most problematic one as well. After all, while Huckleberry Finn's voice is presexual, Dylan's initial rock 'n' roll voice is, odd as it may sound, postsexual. Having purged himself (in what I have termed the album's talking blues and blues proper) of both the fear of and the addiction to sex, Dylan's persona finally emerges not as a spiritually healthy adult person but as a rock 'n' roll angel, an almost disembodied mystery tramp who doesn't rule the streets so much as he contains them in his fierce imaginative freedom. This metamorphosis is convincing on its own terms but way too precocious. It feels like we skipped something, and apparently it felt that way to Dylan, too. His next collection of songs, composed just before and after his marriage in November, 1965, explores what it feels like to live, fearlessly and freely, in a sexual body.

# 7

## *Blonde on Blonde I*

### Hamlet Revisited

The songs on *Blonde on Blonde* are tousle-headed beasts. They sound like Dylan looks in contemporaneous photos: gaunt angels of desire shrouded in an electrified and electrifying nimbus.

Their rhetoric is not at all as surreal as legend (and uncomprehending imitators) would have you believe, but their imaginative reach is perpetually catching their listeners by surprise. Let me explain by example. Answer this question without stopping to think: what song contains the line "To live outside the law you must be honest." I'll bet you had to think about it, even though it's one of Dylan's most famous lines. Even if you recognized instantly that it comes from "Absolutely Sweet Marie," I'll bet you can't quickly say what it's doing there, why it's in that particular song. The great lines or images of earlier Dylan songs are inseparable from their songs: if you know the line, you know the song, and vice versa, because in most songwriting great lines recapitulate their songs. That's not the way it works on *Blonde on Blonde*. "To live outside the law" may have been prompted by its context–and may sufficiently serve it–but it also momentarily overwhelms its context. Lines like this are like genies let out of a bottle.

*Blonde on Blonde* is flooded with tropes–lines more than images–that seem–thrillingly–to outrace their context in this way. Dylan seems to have invented this mode of poetic thought for this album–and abandoned it soon after. He has often spoken of trying to recapture this album's "thin wild mercury sound," and he is often accused of imitating it–most notably on its two sibling albums, *Street Legal* (1978) and *Empire Burlesque* (1986). But I can find no evidence that he has even really tried. The poetic line in *Street Legal*, for instance, normally functions as a sort of kamikaze trope, one that by culminating its context seeks to make that context–and itself along with it–disappear into oblivion. The poetic music of *Street Legal* belongs to the god Mercury as magician and healer, as that of *Empire Burlesque* belongs to Mercury as psychopomp, the conductors of souls to the afterlife. *Blonde on Blonde* is governed by Mercury in his brightest, lightest forms, as the fleet-footed trickster or thief. Here he is the "thin, wild" Mercury, and he is present mostly in the music of thought the lyrics project. Their numinous aura is Mercury's signature.

*Blonde on Blonde* may or may not be Dylan's best album, but it is certainly his most outrageous. In many ways it's his most nakedly personal album. Nowhere else is his persona so demythologized and its psychic vulnerabilities so ruthlessly exposed. But it is also his most playfully theatrical. I referred to *Highway 61 Revisited* as Dylan's first attempt to tell the whole story, but *Blonde on Blonde* is not the second. Claustrophobic in its preoccupations, perversely mercurial in its moods, at once vaulting and banal in its poetic strategies ("Shakespeare in the alley")–*Blonde on Blonde* appeals to our attention not as a story but as a show. It's the soundtrack to some unwritten musical–an antic chamber opera, say, composed at Wittenberg by Hamlet, shortly after he has learned of his father's death (and surmised its circumstance) but before he has returned to Elsinore and Mom.

I have called *Street Legal* and *Empire Burlesque* the siblings of *Blonde on Blonde*, and what links them is a poetic psychology that uses a mercurial slipperiness as a defense against a paranoid lucidity. The premise of each album is that "they" are out to get us, and on each album "they" turn out to be enemies within as well as outside the self. The songs on each album are fundamentally shaped by Dylan's bone-deep knowledge that "they" are everywhere, inescapable and undefeatable. Their identity–as well as the mode of evading them–varies from album to album in ways that reflect Dylan's ruling poetic obsession as it shifts from freedom to faithfulness to justice.

## II

The final enemy of our freedom lies in our own bodies. On *Blonde on Blonde* "they" are the singer's hormones–and the ladies who incite them. The album is saturated with a Hamlet-like sexual disgust and horror whose supreme expression is achieved in the great "Visions of Johanna."

*Ain't it just like the night to play*
*tricks when you're trying to be so quiet*
*We sit here stranded though we're all*
*doing our best to deny it*

This opening couplet exercises an extraordinary power of insinuation. Without directly saying it, let alone explaining or justifying it, Dylan somehow communicates an absolute, unappealable nihilism. Part of this results from the way he implicates his listener in his mood, prompting us to recognize what he doesn't have to spell out because we already know it, in fact, have always known it. The "you" he addresses is largely a phantom; these lines register the uneasy quiet of a man talking to himself. But even insofar as this "you" is an actual listener–that is, us–it serves only to remind us that we are really listening not to Dylan but to ourselves, to our own "stranded" spirits. In this context, the "we" invoked is a grimly comic evasion, a pathetic denial of the strandedness "we" are acknowledging "we" deny.

And what are we denying? To be stranded is to be left high and dry on the sands; Dylan's figure is a descendent of Whitman's trope for the catastrophe of birth, "struck from the float forever held in solution."

These opening lines– like the entire song–convey boredom, frustration, confusion, terror, and more, but the underlying emotion is an abject loneliness that the night both mocks and aggravates when it "tricks" us into thinking there's somebody else here.

The night tricks us with sexual promise. As the rest of the song makes clear, the speaker is suffering not from sexual frustration but from sexual pleasure that brings no pleasure, that defrauds ("tricks") the spirit. The "all-night girls" of the second stanza are the night personified, even as they (and the night's tricks) are a reflex of singer's own pulsing desire. As in Poe's "The Tell-Tale Heart," the paranoia that animates "Visions of Johanna" is a projected self-knowledge. Dylan's song never moves beyond the impasse of this opening scenario; the rest of the song, in one sense, is but an exacerbating elaboration that culminates when the singer's desolation becomes its own death song:

*The harmonicas play*
*the skeleton keys and the rain*
*And these visions of Johanna*
*are now all that remain*

End of story.

But wait, there's something wrong here, isn't there? The song I've so far described might be subtitled, "The Love Song of Quentin Compson," the transcendently sophomoric nihilist hero of Faulkner's *The Sound and the Fury*. A sophomore myself when the song was first released, I was appropriately blown away by its nihilistic glamour. But to reduce this song to its nihilism is to account for everything except the life in it. And while "Visions of Johanna" is the supreme expression of the nihilism that underlies the songs on this album, it is also the most sublime realization of the album's fundamental imaginative mode: it dissolves the gravity of life's meanings in Mercurial play.

The song's closing couplet, cited above, is in fact one of Dylan's most powerfully triumphant imaginings, a breakthrough realization that, I suspect, made *Blonde on Blonde* possible. The "skeleton keys" are a *danse macabre*, but they are also the keys to the kingdom, master keys that open the secrets of the "rain," itself one of Dylan's master symbols. Rain in Dylan is always associated with women. But it seems to function as a symbol not of women but of the emotional life, even as he identifies the life of the spirit as the wind, here figured in the harmonica music.

The rain (like the wind) is a psychologically ambivalent symbol in Dylan's songs, mainly because the fertility of the emotional life is first experienced as a flooding that disrupts the boundaries and erodes the contours of established identity. The rain appears in this fearsome aspect in other *Blonde on Blonde* songs, most notably "Just Like a Woman," but "Visions of Johanna" is haunted by a contrary fear of desiccation, of a soulless mating. The "handful of rain" Louise holds is both a promise of relief from this soullessness–an offer of some kind of connection–and a mockery of that promise: rain doesn't come packaged in handfuls! (The fact that "rain" is slang for heroin reinforces this sense of Louise's offer as a fix that won't fix anything. Indeed, Dylan would later build a whole song–"Shot of Love"–out of this conceit.) There is something truly drenching about the rain that falls at the end of "Visions": it is the form in which Johanna remains.

But why do we believe in the magical power of the "skeleton keys" to summon this rain? The answer is that the lyric has been secretly preparing for it all along. The key, as it were, is in a single word: "play." This word reverberates backward through the entire song. It's the long-delayed counterforce to "little boy lost" who "takes himself so seriously," and it illuminates realities that the paranoid little boy (one of the singer's alter-egos) has overlooked. This concluding use of play also prompts a second look at those "ladies" who "play blind man's bluff with the key chain." (And there's that key again!) The first time round, we inevitably hear this use of "play" to mean "toy with." That's what girls do: toy with us boys. The natural history of sex, or love, or life, is that eventually, everyone goes their own way, to separate deaths. In the end, everything we take seriously winds up in the grave. But maybe these ladies, who appear in the next line as "all-night girls [who] whisper of escapades out on the D Train," really are *playing*. Maybe they actually are still "girls" as well as ladies of the night, just as the singer (and his stand-in, the blind man) is still a boy as well as a man, a little boy who has "lost" his capacity for play. And maybe even mother night is really playing tricks with us and not just on us. Maybe the singer just needs to lighten up–it's certainly worth noting that the harmonicas play only after his "conscience explodes." It's as if the final couplet reflects the singer's sudden realization that his investment of spirit is not in the matter of his song but in the playing of it.

There is another strain in the lyric that finds its fruition in the magic of the "skeleton keys." The explosion of the singer's conscience is occasioned by the appearance of the "fiddler," the last in a series of alter-egos who function as emotional tuning forks for each verse. In the first four verses, these alter-egos alternate between images of an ascendant false self (Louise's lover, little boy lost) and images of a crippled true self (the nightwatchman, the primitive wallflower) struggling to regain mastery of the psyche. The series climaxes in the celebrated fourth verse, where the singer finds himself in a museum. The museum–the abode of the muses–symbolizes the "salvation" he has been mistakenly seeking from the absent Johanna, and there is a terrifying sublimity in his discovery that this land of his heart's desire excludes him. (This discovery seems to be the "freeze out" figured in the song's original title.) But, as he has the wit to recognize, there is also something more than faintly risible about it too. The land of his heart's desire, Mona Lisa helps him see, is actually not any object of desire but his heart's own perpetual desiring, "the highway blues."

Mona Lisa's smile is his ticket out of the museum and out into the streets, where he has his life. The tone of comic sublimity this verse achieves releases him from his self-imprisonment, so that in the final verse he is able finally to slough off his false self–his spectre–as the pathetic "peddler" and embrace himself finally as the "fiddler," a figure of capable playfulness. Stepping to the road to write "everything's been returned which was owed," the fiddler dissolves the obscure guilt that had empowered the singer's constricting, puritanical conscience and frees him to play his heart out.

Not that all is suddenly sweetness and light, the body of the song banished like a bad dream. The singer's new freedom doesn't vanquish the dread in the song, but it does open up new possibilities. The night does play tricks on us; that much is certain. It may play tricks together with us. The girls' key is on a chain; there's no escaping that. It may also open a door or two. We know we're doomed; our salvation remains forever unknowable because it exists only where and as we seize it, if we can, in the play of the moment. "Visions of Johanna" concludes with a triumph that testifies to nothing more than the spirit's unaccountable capacity to enjoy itself.

The Mercurial reversal of the song's final couplet comes with the sudden, unexpected release of a fresh discovery. This feeling is crucial to the emotional drama of the song, but it is also something of a deception. That is, the excess of spirit–the joy–that emerges only at the very end of the song's emotional plot has been part of its presentation all along. Indeed, it is this quality that made "Visions of Johanna" an instant legend and accounts for its perennial prominence in short lists of Dylan's best songs. I'm referring to the luminous, *under*-determined expressiveness of lines like "we can hear the night-watchman click his flashlight, ask himself if it's him or them that's really insane," or "Mona Lisa musta had the highway blues, you can tell by the way she smiles," or most famously, "the ghost of electricity howls in the bones of her face." Like all great poetry, these lines beggar explication; here they also render even the most pointed explication beside the point.

For instance, the night watchman, whether real or hallucinated, is pretty obviously a projection of the singer's anxious conscience, and his puzzlement over who's insane is the singer's first, largely still unconscious, inkling that his own conscience might be part of the problem. And had Dylan written, "the night watchman doesn't know if it's him or them who's insane," that would be all there is to be said about this line. But the night watchman "click[s] his flashlight"–an oddly vivid level of detail that itself clicks a poetic flashlight on him–and then engages the singer (and us) with his personality when he "asks himself" what's going on. The final blow to mere gravity of exposition is the insouciant wonder sustained by "really," a vernacular trap-door that, as Dylan often demonstrates, can open almost any locution to the imponderable play of thought.*

It is important to make it clear that I'm not trying to explicate the meaning of the "night watchman" line. Rather, I'm trying to explain a certain *kick* the line gives us that changes our relationship to its meaning. I could proceed to inspect the line about Mona Lisa, or the ghost of electricity, or, for that matter, any other line (or group of lines) in the song and find something similar, but while that would be fun for me, I think it would be tiresome for a reader. The point to be made is that the entire song, like all the songs on *Blonde on Blonde* (albeit in different ways), have such a double affect. There are the grim truths of life, and then there is the kick we get out of living. And if "kick" seems an inadequate term for ultimate worth, then so be it. Liveliness, after all, is its own only justification.

## III

"Visions of Johanna" seems to have been the first *Blonde on Blonde* song that Dylan composed. It was first recorded at the end of November 1965, along with several other new songs that Dylan had mostly abandoned by the time he returned to the studio in February 1966 to begin recording the rest of the album. The abandoned songs, which include the astonishing "She's Your Lover Now," occupy an instructively transitional poetic space between *Highway 61* and *Blonde on Blonde*.

* This "really" is missing from the *Blonde on Blonde* recording. Its first official appearance was in *Writings and Drawings* (the 1973 predecessor of *Lyrics*), but it is not a late addition. In the two circulating recorded versions from November 1965 that I refer to in my text, Dylan sings "asks himself if he's really insane" and "asks himself if it's him that's really insane." The line does not appear exactly as I quote it until sometime in the spring of 1966. It is, for instance, the version Dylan sings at Albert Hall on May 26 that was released on *Biograph*. In the more famous version from Manchester (released on *Live* 1966) he sings "asks himself if it's him or them that should be insane," a clumsy variant that, oddly, is the text printed in the contemporaneous *Blonde on Blonde* songbook.

The first of these songs, "Can You Please Crawl Out Your Window?" was actually composed and first recorded during the *Highway 61* sessions in the summer of 1965. To a large extent, it's merely a flippant rewrite of "Like a Rolling Stone," but there is a crucial new element. Dylan's attention is here equally divided between the Miss Lonely figure and a male figure that can be thought of as her "diplomat," who makes but a passing appearance as a bit player in "Like a Rolling Stone." In fact, the wonderful refrain aside, all the real liveliness of the song inheres in the singer's imaginings of the psychic machinations by which this diplomat keeps his Miss Lonely under his thumb.

This sinister figure doesn't have a name, but let's call him Osmond, the creepy aesthete who holds the American princess Isabel Archer hostage in a false marriage in Henry James's *Portrait of a Lady*. This Osmond, I would suggest, is the singer's alter-ego, the first of many anonymous third-person male alter-egos who will play major roles in scores of Dylan songs from *Blonde on Blonde* onward. His status as an alter-ego is here rather attenuated–he remains throughout a distant third person, and there is none of that uncanny sense of a doubling of self that accompanies Dylan's more fully realized figures of this type. But nonetheless he represents the first move in the new poetic direction Dylan would pursue after *Highway 61*. He is the first step, that is, in Dylan's effort to remove his persona from a visionary pedestal and locate him squarely in the midst of the psychosexual fray that grounds human behavior.

"I Wanna Be Your Lover" backs away from this purpose–the alter-ego figures are gnomes on the periphery, and the singer retains his visionary innocence–but here the Miss Lonely figure, who in "Like a Rolling Stone" and "Can You Please Crawl Out Your Window?" was all terrified helplessness, is suddenly as poisonous as Osmond. In fact, she's so fearsomely poisonous that the singer is driven, it appears, to separate the woman he sees ("hers") from the woman he imagines he wants ("yrs"):

*I wanna be yr lover baby*

*I wanna be your man*
*I wanna be your lover–*
*I don't wanna be hers*
*I wanna be yrs!*

There is only one woman in this fidgety little comedy: the "you" the singer addresses is a protective fiction, a personalizing mirror that safeguards him from the "bullets in [the] eyes" of the Medusa who–in her various guises as "Mona," "Jumping Judy," and "Phaedra"–stands before him.

This scenario gets fuller play in "Tell Me, Momma," a song that Dylan appears never to have recorded in the studio but which led off the electric set during the final leg of the fabled 1966 tour. It's unclear when the song was written–its earliest reported performance is on February 5, 1966–but its poetic character occupies something of a middle ground between "I Wanna Be Your Lover" and the songs on *Blonde on Blonde*, most of which he had yet to record when he debuted this song. What links it to "I Wanna Be Your Lover" is each of the song's three verses' initial couplet or two, which are devoted to establishing this momma's sexual menace:

*Cold black glass don't*
*make no mirr'r,*
*Cold black water don't*
*make no tears.*

Beyond this first one, most of these opening couplets appear to be unfinished–the text printed in *Lyrics* is not only gibberish but not even the gibberish Dylan is singing. Indeed, in all three live versions I have heard–including the one from Manchester, England, on the officially released *Live 1966* CD–Dylan is clearly singing slightly to greatly different words than the *Lyrics* version, only some of which I can make out. My sense is that Dylan knows what he wants to say, but he hasn't quite found the words that will enable him to spit it out with the concentrated, viciously nonchalant humor and barbed venom his voice–words or not–has already found.

In each verse the initial evocation of menace yields, in typically Dylanesque fashion, to direct address. But here, for the first time really, the singer's seductive powers fail him. His appeal for recognition is curdled by a foreknowledge of defeat, metamorphosing from a baffled nostalgia ("Don't you remember making baby love") to a despairing, defiant cry ("But come on, baby, I'm your friend") to a tonality that all but dissolves any residual friendliness in a heartless sadism:

*Everybody sees you on your*
*window ledge.*
*How long's it gonna take for you to*
*get off the edge?*
*You're just gonna make everybody*
*jump and roar*
*Now whatcha wanna go and*
*do that for?*

This is the tone we've been hearing throughout the song in the long, two-part chorus that follows each verse. The song's balance of desire and disdain, of resilient expectation and black despair yields eventually–I'd say right about here, at the end of the third verse–to a sense of something more fundamental, something that makes this song more than just a variant of "Like a Rolling Stone" and its ilk. That something new is impasse of two implacable wills, a face-to-face deadlock, the demonic inversion of ecstatic rock 'n' roll dancing.

As usual in Dylan, this demonism is defined as a triumph of knowing. "I know that you know that I know" here describes a circuit not of intimacy but of predatory will. And when the singer completes this circuit–"I know that you know that I know that *you show*" (emphasis added)–it's as if she's blinked first, and now he's got her. Earlier in the song, this epiphany may have still carried some sense of the possible recovery of a lost intimacy, but here, at the end, it is the cruelest moment in all of Dylan–crueler even than anything the Rolling Stones have ever imagined, because its passion is in no way cut by ironic disdain. Once she blinks, the singer has his way with her, not in love but in hatred, and "this time" round, it is surely his voice that is "tearing up [her] mind."

It's easy to see why "Tell Me Momma" would have appealed to Dylan as the opener for the electric set of the final, British Isles phase of his 1966 tour. It's the perfect tuning fork for his epochal facedowns with his audience. One of Dylan's greatest rock 'n' roll musical compositions, it's also–like the abandoned transitional songs I have been discussing–a kind of anti-rock 'n' roll song, turning the rock 'n' roll dance inside out. The prominence given this song in his 1966 live set suggests to me that Dylan was beginning to lose faith in rock 'n' roll and, subconsciously at least, to sense–before his fabled motorcycle accident a couple months later–that this couldn't go on. He was beginning to recognize his audience as an implacable howling beast, and he was beginning to become what he beheld.

But the motive for a change of direction came, I think, not primarily from his audience but from within himself. *Blonde on Blonde* is not–in the technical, somewhat idiosyncratic sense I have been using–a rock 'n' roll album. Before Dylan wrote the album's songs, he had reached an impasse in his rock 'n' roll songwriting: he seemed unable to come up with anything except songs about psycho-sexual impasses. "Visions of Johanna" broke that impasse and opened a new poetic direction that enabled him to write the rest of the songs on the album. Intriguingly, though, Dylan doesn't seem to have recognized his breakthrough right away. The first recording of "Visions of Johanna," made in November 1965 under its original title "Freeze Out," is sung in the harshly assaultive rock 'n' roll voice he used for "Crawl Out Your Window," an approach that utterly buries what's new about the song. (Indeed, the original title, which emphasizes the sophomoric existential tragedy that shapes the plot, suggests that Dylan thought he had come up with the archetypal song about psycho-sexual impasse and did not yet recognize what was new about it.) Another bootlegged take from this November session is much better, but he still sings as if outside his song, reporting on rather than suffering (and learning to enjoy) its emotional force. It's not until mid-February that he gets it right. It seems as if, in writing this song, Dylan had gotten ahead of himself, and required additional transitional work to catch up.

That final transitional work seems to have been largely accomplished by "She's Your Lover Now." The two bootlegged recordings of this song–one on solo piano and one an electric version made with his touring band (and eventually released on *The Bootleg Series*–were made in January 1966, apparently on the same day.

I will argue that this song represents a dead end–aesthetically as well as morally–that Dylan needed to find a way around, but it is also true that, on its own terms, it is a remarkable invention. Considered solely as an achievement in the rhythmical use of words, it takes your breath away. It employs a marvelously slinky long line that Dylan had been exploring off and on since "Like a Rolling Stone" and that reaches its acme in the opening cadences of "Visions of Johanna." But what Dylan accomplishes here leaves everything before it in the dust. What we hear in the earlier songs is a dancing mind, but here we seem to encounter a dancing body, rhythms shaped by an unconscious liveliness the mind can barely keep itself afloat within. The song's metrical shape is a kind of choreography: the rhythm's steady marching iambs are forever sinking into a dangerous anapestic lassitude, only to right themselves again, fight off seduction with mournful trochaic alarms, regroup, reach occasional stalemates in tottering amphibrachs, yield again to the sensual delights running up their sleeves, snap to and push forward. Consider this example, from the song's third movement:

*You never had to be faithful*
*I never wanted you to grieve*
*Oh why was it so hard for you*
*if you didn't want to be with me just to leave*
*Now you stand here while your*
*fingers going up my sleeve*

The effectiveness of this turns partly on the way the trochaic mournfulness of "faithful" slips into the melting sympathy of the anapestic "you to grieve." And then there's the amazing latter half of the second line, where, after the opening anapest ("if you DID"), the singer heroically iambs his way, as it were, across a six-syllable emotional sinkhole before faltering, slightly but ominously, on "just to LEAVE." And as always with Dylan, the prosodic drama turns on the masterful placement of the caesuras that divide his lines into paired half-lines. The break before "fingers" in the last line transforms "your" from a mere counter to a held breath and shapes the trochaic shudder of "fingers going" that lapses, luxuriously, suicidally, into "up my sleeve," an anapest whose pattern is not the usual unstressed-unstressed-stressed but a delightfully tragicomic stressed-more stressed-really overstressed. If the songs on *Blonde on Blonde*, as I suggested, are the soundtrack to an unwritten musical, then "She's Your Lover Now" is the score to an as yet unchoreographed dance.

A marvel of rhythmic expressiveness, "She's Your Lover Now" also takes Dylan's art of the conversational lyric to a new level–and one he basically abandoned after this song. I've been saying all along that the most original feature of Dylan's poetry is the way he interpolates his listener–real or imagined–as an *active* presence in his songs, incorporating dramatic textures within a lyrical mode. But "She's Your Lover Now" is the first (and possibly only) song in which Dylan explicitly activates two listeners. This is something of a charade, since neither the girl nor the guy who has inherited her seem actually to be listening to the singer. But it is real to the extent that their nonlistening, their unresponsiveness, is a dual goad that drives the lyric forward.

Considered literally, the scenario this song explores is quite bizarre. It's the story of a guy trying to get a girl to explain why she doesn't like him anymore–even as the girl tries mightily to jump his bones ("fingers going up my sleeve"). Meanwhile another guy–the singer's usurper in the girl's affections–sucks it all up. This makes no sense unless we realize that there are really just two people–but four personae–in the song. There's the singer and his girl. But the singer (though at first he doesn't seem to know it) is addressing a part, or aspect, of the girl that can't hear him, even as he fights off that aspect of the girl–*her* spectre–that his spectre, who figures here as the singer's merely sexual self, laps up.

None of the songs on *Blonde on Blonde* overtly represent such a doubled internal listening, but I think it is implicitly present in many of its songs, especially those addressed to a female figure. As I shall attempt to show in discussing these songs, the singer's movement through them cannot be fully accounted for–as it can, for instance, in "Like a Rolling Stone"–as his response to her imagined listening to him. On *Blonde on Blonde*, his moves are also shaped by his response to an invisible male alter-ego, a spectre who is to the singer as the singer's mere literal words are to what he is really saying. "Someone else is speaking with my mouth/I'm listening only to my heart," Dylan sings in the 1983 *Infidels* song "I and I." That someone else is his spectre, a figure who first appears as an occult presence in Dylan's songs on *Blonde on Blonde*.

"She's Your Lover Now" does not introduce this shadow–he already appeared briefly in "It's Alright Ma" and "Ballad of a Thin Man" is addressed directly to him–but it does introduce him in a new light. In those earlier songs, the spectre is a backsliding tendency within the singer; here he is an ever-present doppelgaenger. Where once he was conceived as a state of mind one might set aside, or hold in abeyance, now he is revealed to be an uninvited guest who won't leave–and steals your girl to boot!

Of course, this means that the singer steals his girl from himself. The discovery of how that can be–and what it means–is what this song is all about. And there's a suggestion that this story would be the same were the perspective reversed: the spectre "kiss[es] her on the cheek every time she gives a speech," smothering in flattery whatever impulse she might have to communicate. The working title of this song was "Just a Little Glass of Water," which seems to be an allusion to the traditional blues line about asking for water and being given gasoline. That's what happens here, apparently to both the singer and his girl: their attempts to slake an essentially spiritual thirst for companionship succeed only in setting both of them aflame.

The subjugation–central to the song–of the spiritual by the sexual is figured largely as a corruption of gesture and speech. The spectre's essential perversity is revealed in one of Dylan's most sublimely resonant jokes: "And you, you just sit around and ask for ashtrays/can't you reach?" The spectre uses speech to get the material world moved around in his service, but not to move, or reach, another spirit. As his kisses reduce spirit to body, his words reduce speech to its ashes. That's why the singer will later observe, disdainfully, that this spectre really has "nothing" to "say."

The imagery Dylan weaves into the fabric of this basic opposition is richly suggestive, and he develops it with a vernacular grace that preludes the astonishing throwaway rhetoric of *Blonde on Blonde*. But I don't intend to follow that out here. I want to examine what the song does with its scenario.

The structure of this song–the shape of this particular dance–is unusual, if not unique, in Dylan's work. As Dylan himself told Paul Zollo in the 1991 *SongTalk* interview, his usual approach in composing a song is to improvise his way out of the mess he got himself into by starting it:

> There are ways you can get out of whatever you've gotten into. You want to get out of it. It's bad enough getting into it. But the thing to do as soon as you get into it is realize you *must get out of it*. And unless you get out of it quickly and effortlessly, . . . it will just drag you down. You could be spending years writing the same song, telling the same story, doing the same thing. . . . There's a bunch of ways you can get out of that. You can *make* yourself get out of it by changing key. . . . And see if that brings you any place. More times than not, that will take you down the road. You don't want to be on a *collision course*. But that will take you down the road. Somewhere.*

I can't imagine any better account of the motive and method of Dylan's songwriting. His songs feel as if they evolved this way: they open with some uncovering of trouble, anxiety, desire, which they move to quiet or appease. And as they move along, they continually surprise themselves–and us–in the ways that initial disquiet worsens or abates as it modulates into various interim forms, finding some final form of release

* Paul Zollo, "Bob Dylan: The SongTalk Interview," p. 37.

or ease or mastery or triumph or truce that frees the singer from his song.

That's pointedly not what happens here. The singer disappears into a song that holds him under its spell. The structure of this song has little, if any, flavor of improvisation. It is composed of four movements, each of which is composed of exactly the same four gestures enacted in the same prosodic sequence: a quatrain, a triplet, a couplet, and a triplet. It goes like this: the singer first addresses his girl, invoking some shared experience or sense of things that establishes their intimacy. Then he addresses her again to complain that she has betrayed that intimacy. Then he turns to her new lover to see if he might be of any help. Then he announces, "I give up" and bequeaths the problem to the other guy. He goes through this little four-part charade four times, and although each movement evinces an increasing panic and desperation, the main feeling is of redundancy, of going round in circles, of being trapped in some neo-Beckettian (i.e., very funny) circle of hell.

The song's final movement does articulate a genuine breakthrough in understanding, but the singer's realization of his plight merely entrenches it. The language and imagery in this section is completely over the top, but the effect is exactly opposite that of similar rhetoric on *Blonde on Blonde*. Instead of a kick of liveliness, we hear a death cry, or as Dylan unforgettably puts it:

*My voice is really warm*
*it's just that it ain't got no form*
*It's just like a dead man's last*
*pistol shot, baby*

The singer's realization that his voice is a formless warmth is a concession that this scene is too much for him, that his spiritual demands, fundamentally incommensurable with this sexual dynamic, have, as it were, infantilized him. His "last pistol shot" is an anti-ejaculation, the spirit's refusal of the world into which it has been born.

As he disappears–or perhaps one should say as he evaporates into a pure spirit who haunts a scene he can neither alter nor escape–he catches an ambiguous glimpse of a correspondent spiritual terror in the girl he is leaving behind:

*Oh your mouth used to be so naked*
*and your eyes used to be so blue*
*Your hurts used to be so nameless*
*and your tears used to be so few*
*Your eyes cry "Wolf," while your mouth*
*cries "I'm not afraid of animals like you"*

Are those eyes crying "wolf" in terror of the sexually predatory world into which her consciousness has been born–a world they confront in the appetitive leer of the singer's spectre, who, after all, on the literal level, is the singer? Or is that intimation only a false promise, a "crying wolf" in the proverbial sense? Are the intimations of a fellow human spirit, that is, merely one of the baubles with which she, herself a she-wolf, ensnares him? Indeed, now that you mention it, is his own innocence–the voice that purrs this song–merely a self-deluding dodge?

The song ends without resolving this ambiguity. Indeed, the officially released version of this song abruptly crashes to a halt when he stumbles on the last line of this verse. He mistakenly sings "your mouth cries 'wolf,'" and stops. It somehow makes a better ending than the anticlimactic redundancy of the final two verses, in which Dylan casts one last withering glance at the useless turd that is his spectre–and who, remember, is all of himself that remains fully *in* the world–and melodramatically takes his (unavailing) leave. By ending in mid-sentence, however accidentally, Dylan leaves us with a much more powerful–and apt–sense of a consciousness that collapses under the augmenting weight of its own alienation.

## IV

The similarities between "She's Your Lover Now" and "One of Us Must Know (Sooner or Later)" have often been remarked upon–indeed, Paul Cable* and others have suggested Dylan left the former off *Blonde on*

* Cable, *Bob Dylan: His Unreleased Recordings*, p. 75.

*Blonde* because it had too much in common with the latter. My own sense is that "Sooner or Later"–which Dylan first recorded just four days after "She's Your Lover Now"–is essentially a rewrite of "She's Your Lover Now," a second-go at a lyrical-dramatic theme that wouldn't let go of Dylan's imagination. And this time, his song takes him somewhere he's never been before, a place that opens a whole new world of poetic possibilities.

"Sooner of Later" is, to my mind, one of Dylan's greatest songs. If I had to select a dozen Dylan songs for a "Best of" CD, this would be one of them. *Blonde on Blonde* has one other song that belongs on such a CD–"Visions of Johanna"–and two others–"Absolutely Sweet Marie" and "Just Like a Woman"–it would be painful to have to leave off. Although it surprises me to hear myself saying it, I think "Sooner or Later" is the best of the lot. What I mean, I suppose, is that although I can't even write a passably decent song, I can imagine myself having written "Visions of Johanna" or "Absolutely Sweet Marie" or "Just Like a Woman." I can't imagine myself writing "Sooner of Later," even after listening to it–on the stereo and in my head–hundreds of times over the course of more than three decades. Imagine writing it? Hell, I'm not even sure I can yet even imagine listening to it.

Imagining listening to it is one definition of criticism, and since that's what I'm practicing here, I'll give it my best shot. Let's take it from the top:

*I didn't mean*
*to treat you so bad*
*You shouldn't take it so*
*personal*
*I didn't mean*
*to make you so sad*
*You just happened to be*
*there that's all*

This is the same world as "She's Your Lover Now," the same scenario, but Dylan's poetic voice is profoundly changed. The first thing we notice about that voice is its astonishing self-possession, an elegant humor and poised wit that is downright enviable.

And the wit of these lines is also provokingly, outrageously transcendental. Consider the situation: the singer is addressing someone who feels romantically, if not sexually, abused by him. And what does he say? Well, he says a lot of things. First, "I didn't mean"–ok, that's an apology. But what didn't he mean? To treat you bad and make you sad? No, he didn't mean to treat you "so" bad and make you "so" sad? What does this mean? That he wanted to hurt her just a little? And why?–to get back at her? to get her attention? Or maybe he didn't really want to hurt her at all, but he did want to do something–say have his way with her–that he knew would hurt a little and that he wanted more than he wanted not to hurt her? How about all of the above? and maybe more that I haven't the wit to remember? Or how about we just acknowledge how niftily and persuasively those two lines–the first and the third–conjure the precise emotional temperature of a familiar, perhaps universal, romantic muddle?

I called the wit of this transcendental, but before explaining what I mean by that, let's first note something crucially new for Dylan in these lines. In admitting that he did what he didn't–but partly did!–mean to do, notice he says I did it–not *him,* that guy sitting over there, my evil twin, some guy I never wanted to be but somehow can't quite shake. No: *I* did it. The "I" who didn't mean it nonetheless did it. Same guy, same persona. This is a big change. Dylan has finally gotten his transcendental personality off its high horse–without abandoning the transcendentalism. Dylan's persona has never–well, almost never–concealed the contradictions in his psyche from the story his songs tell, but for the first time he's going to try to embody those contradictions in the voice that does the telling. Maybe this will carry him beyond the impasse of that contradiction.

And make no mistake about it, the voice we hear here is the transcendental Dylan talking, the mystery tramp. Just look at the second and fourth lines.

*You shouldn't take it so*
*personal . . .*

*You just happened to be*
*there that's all . . .*

Don't take it personal? I suppose you could take this as adding insult to injury, or as a cad's cynical snarl. But while the singer may take a certain devilish delight in the sting of that plausible misunderstanding of his meaning, the whole song makes it clear that that's not what he is saying.

I would offer two glosses on the disdain Dylan here expresses for the merely "personal." One is the biblical commonplace (e.g., Romans 2:11) that "there is no respect of persons with God," and the other is Gatsby's grand dismissal of the emotional reality of Daisy's love for her husband: "It's just personal." Both these usages of the word, like Dylan's here, rely on the understanding that the "personal"–what we ordinarily think of as our identity–is merely a mask we wear, a clothing of our nakedness. Thus, while the singer is not seeking–or trying to justify–anonymous sex, he is anonymously seeking the anonymity in "you." *I'm nobody, who are you?**

The fourth line recapitulates this thought, but in even more rudely–and challengingly–impersonal terms. The dismissive "happened to be there" is a blithely transcendental existentialism. It implies that since our spiritual interactions with each other transcend the personal histories that led us into each other's company, those merely personal identities can have no claim on our real connections to each other. In short, the singer seems to be rebuking the girl for harboring personal expectations toward him. This is certainly harsh–a transcendentally harsh spiritual ideal–and the singer seems to know that. Remember, he says you shouldn't take it "so" personal–an acknowledgement that our persons–and the pains and pleasures they haplessly endure–are never entirely left behind in the transcended dust.

But the language here triumphs not so much by its concessions to

* Or, as Dylan later told Jonathan Cott, "Deep in our souls we have no past. I don't think we have a past, any more than we have a name." Cott, "Standing Naked,"*Rolling Stone*, p. 44.

the mundane as by the force with which it makes our transcendental yearnings seem real, even off-hand. Part of this is due to the unpretentious resonance in this context of words like "happened" and "be" and "all"–and part of it is in what I would call the prosodic gestures these two lines make. The whiff of disdain attached to the word "personal" derives from the way its first syllable interrupts an otherwise unsullied iambic purr with an exasperated PFUI! The fourth line is a series of rolling amphibrachs that turns on the placement of "there," which tries to assert itself as a stressed syllable but is swallowed up as both as the final (unstressed) syllable of the second amphibrach and the first (unstressed) syllable of the third. The metrical plight of this tiny word seems to enact the impermanence and insubstantiality of the moment in which "you" and "I," equally impermanent and insubstantial in our impersonated identities, encountered each other. And as we listen to this, and hear ourselves characterized this way–well, we either yelp in pain or we disengage our real selves from those impersonations and recover our anonymities. *You're invisible now!*

At this stage of the song, I suspect we do both, with the pain and attendant bewilderment holding the upper hand. Things will be different by the end of the song, when Dylan concludes the final verse with what may be the most powerfully ecstatic line he has ever written–a line at once dizzying in its emotional complexity and irresistible in its wild grace: "I never really meant to do you any harm." The question is: how does he get from here to there?

To answer that, we need to step back from the song and observe it as a whole. It has three verses, each followed by the same chorus. As in "She's Your Lover Now," each of the verses has a similar structure, but unlike "She's Your Lover Now," here there is a definite sense of moving forward, of discovery and change.

The verse structure here is in two parts. The first part is a complaint (albeit in the first verse it's sort of masked as an apology), and the second is a remembered vignette. Each of the vignettes presents an ambivalent image of wounding and being wounded, and they culminate in increasingly revelatory insights:

*I didn't know that you were saying good bye for g*
*I didn't realize how young you were . . .*
*I never really meant to do you any harm . . .*

The final insight brings the song full circle because it is also an apology-complaint. Finally, there is the chorus to consider:

*Sooner or later*
*one of us must know*
*That you just did what you were*
*supposed to do*
*Sooner or later*
*one of us must know*
*That I really did try to get*
*close to you*

This is fairly straightforward. "Supposed to do"/"Close to you" recapitulates the dichotomy between the merely personal and the transcendentally anonymous–to use my own terminology–that is central to the song, and they do so in ways that enrich the concepts. "Supposed to do" is a wonderful way of identifying the merely personal, insofar as it lumps together both what the world expects of you and what you might expect of yourself, and dismisses them as equally suppositional, both forms of the "foolish consistency" that Emerson famously dismissed as the "hobgoblin of little minds." Our concern for our reputation with ourselves is as vain as a concern with our reputation before the world. And "close to you" is a modest yet evocative definition of the transcendental urge that drives his efforts to connect with her.

What gives pause in this chorus is its opening line. My sense is that most listeners hear it as sarcasm. That is, they hear "Sooner or later, [the] one of us [who does not already know] will know." Or in simple words, "Eventually you'll get it, babe." But that's never made sense to me, partly because as sarcasm it's lame, but mainly because it doesn't fit the spirit of the verses.

So (humor me) let's take the first line of the chorus at face value. That means, *neither* of "us" now knows that I was sincere and that you screwed up. How is that possible, especially since "one" of us is now expressing that very knowledge? Hmmm. That's as far as I got–"hmmm"–for many years, until one morning I woke up with an answer. Not *the* answer, but an answer, one that works, in the sense that it opens up the song to me–the lyric, that is–in a way that matches the feeling of the performance recorded for *Blonde on Blonde*. (Dylan rarely performs this song live, and I've never heard a live version that gives any hint that this is a great song. Curious.)

And a strange answer it is that my dreaming mind came up with. The best way to explain it is to describe an imaginary performance of the song. Let's imagine it's a song from that chamber opera by Hamlet I mentioned earlier–not a conceit I ever expected to revisit–and let's imagine it as a duet, one sung by Dylan and, hmmm, how about Lucinda Williams? Now this is the important part: Dylan sings the first four lines of the first verse, Lucinda the second four, and Dylan sings the chorus. Lucinda then takes the first four lines of the second verse, Dylan the second four, and Lucinda the chorus. Now, Lucinda sings the first two lines of the third verse, Dylan the next two, Lucinda the next two, and Dylan the final two. And they harmonize on the final chorus together. Got it? OK, now listen to *that* performance a couple of times or so, in your head, and then meet me in the next paragraph. Oh, one more thing: you can mix the parts of the duet in other ways, too, if you like. It doesn't matter.

See what I mean? It works. And it works because it is the *same person* who is both baffling and baffled, bewildering and bewildered. The miracle of this song is that even though it is really performed as a solo vocal, it manages to convey a sense of two mutually baffling souls who nonetheless hang onto a sense of that time, "sooner or later," when each "one of us" will "know" the other, beyond supposition. "One of us" may have started out as but an oblique way of saying "you," but by the end of the song the emphasis falls on some yet unexperienced but intensely imagined sense of "us," of we two.

"Sooner or Later" does not accomplish this simply by a three-fold iteration of its opening scenario. Where each successive movement of

"She's Your Lover Now" is just one more turn of the screw, this song keeps breaking open new cognitive and emotional ground. It starts to do that with the second half of the first verse. The tone of this vignette is ambivalent. It could be apologetic (or defensive), as if the singer were saying, "Hey, if I knew you were leaving for good, I wouldn't have let you leave alone, without me." But the tone is also palpably wounded–"How could you leave without me?" He's taking it personal (or she is, if you're listening to the duet version), and this generates some sympathy for the just dismissed realm of the personal: he (or she) is taking it personal because it's as a person–not as pure spirit–that he/she encounters her/him.

This song is, among other things, a meditation on reading. Like Whitman's "Whoever You Are Now Holding Me in Hand," it not about reading books but about how people–lovers particularly–learn how to read each other. The texture of the lyric is a dazzling, dizzying knit of verbs of knowing, seeing, saying, hearing, thinking, and realizing, and even more so, of *not* knowing, *not* seeing, *not* saying, etc. And it uses this vocabulary to tell what turns out to be a delightful, and delightfully simple, boy-meets-girl, boy-loses-girl, boy-gets-girl-back fable. Except here it goes more like this: boy thinks he knows girl, something she does raises a doubt in his mind, nothing she can show him (i.e. nothing he can see) can repair that doubt, he goes blind as his world goes blank, he hears her (voice), and he takes her (word).

The crucial moment in the song occurs in the opening quatrain of the third verse, which appears to repeat, but with a deeper understanding, the opening quatrain of the second verse:

*I couldn't see*
*when it started snowing*
*Your voice was all*
*that I heard*
*I couldn't see*
*where we were going*
*But you said you knew and I*
*took your word*

When he says "your voice was all that I heard," he doesn't mean he didn't hear anything else. He means he finally heard not her words, her meanings but–as if for the first time–her voice, and he realized it was a voice he was listening to, and that it is a voice he has been listening for. And that realization enables him to stop trying to decide whether he could "believe" her words–as he tried and failed to do in the previous verse–but to take her "word," as a token of that voice, and respond to it. There is no certainty in love; there is only the life it engenders. We are meant to hear the final quatrain, I would suggest, as an outrageously transcendental post-coital cooing, a celebration of a wholly vocalized (not verbalized) body of love:

> *And then you told me later as I*
> *apologized*
> *That you were just kidding me you weren't really*
> *from the farm*
> *And I told you as you*
> *clawed out my eyes*
> *That I never really meant to do you*
> *any harm*

The last line–with its paradoxical profession of innocent harm–draws some of its authority from the way it echoes her "kidding"–we're both kids again, just pulling each other's hair for fun–and from the fact that the singer utters it even as his own eyes are being gouged out. This latter image picks up the repeated cries of "I couldn't see," assimilates that epistemological crisis with the depredations of sex, and redeems both as harrowings of hell that prepare us to listen to what Whitman, addressing his soul in a similar moment of ecstatic erotic violation, called "the lull [and] and hum of your valved voice."

As I mentioned, the last lines of each verse register increasingly revelatory insights, and these, in turn, register transformations in the singer's sense of both who he is and who the woman is he is addressing. The first verse ends with "goodbye for good," a locution that evokes the sorrows both of temporality and of morality that shadow all personal experience. At the end of the second verse, when he realizes "how young you were," the singer recovers a sense of her (and of himself) outside of time, unadulterated by experience. He discovers in both of them the freshet of desire that engenders time, experience, and personality–a Real You and Real Me that remains, as Whitman has it, "altogether untouched." The shock of this recognition releases the visionary realizations of the final verse and its profession of a recovered innocence (literally, harmlessness and unharmedness) that nonetheless absorbs the realities of experience in its midst. The singer does not say "I never did you any harm" or even "I never meant to do you any harm" but, in an archetypally American idiom that manages to have its cake and eat it too, "I never *really* meant to do you any harm." Time, experience, personae (including sexual personae) are reduced to, and enjoyed as, forms of frolic, modes of dress-up.

I know, this is silly. Of course it is. The final chorus could be sung, or simply imagined, as a blissful duet, but even then, the bliss remains prospective, an imagining–which keeps alive our awareness of the mournful solo voice (or twin solos) singing these words. The singer does not actually have his cake and eat it, too. Maybe no one ever does. But he does *imagine* it. And its fineness as an imagining is that it has run the gauntlet of what he knows from experience and not just survived but been refreshed in the process. That's one of the things art does; it's certainly what Dylan's best songs regularly do: stop time, if only to enable him, and us, to recover the infant "inspiration behind the inspiration" and start it all over again, from scratch.

## V

The other great lyrical poem on *Blonde on Blonde* is "Just Like a Woman," a song that feels like it was composed shortly after "Sooner of Later," in the close aftermath of that song's imaginative discoveries. It's one of Dylan's favorite songs–he performs it all the time–and one of his most popular songs. But, from what I can tell, it's also one of his most misunderstood songs. So let me announce straight off how I hear it. It's about a man and woman who have been mutually bruised by their romantic engagement with each other. The lyric records the man's effort to persuade the woman to recognize that she is, after all, still an unbreakable "little girl"–in the process of which effort he summons the nerve to recover, without actually coming out and saying it, the broken but equally unbreakable little boy in his own voice.

There is only one image in Dylan's poetry that is sacred, that is really real. That is the child, the boy and/or girl we forever carry inside us, and that carries us forward in spirit. His "little girl" may suggest Blake, but I think it comes from Emily Dickinson, for whom "little girl" is a favorite trope of her own paradoxical powers.

The meaning of "little girl" is the key to Dylan's song–and the main source, as far as I can tell, of what I see as the common misunderstanding of the song. The song's chorus works two ways, one nasty and one sweet. The nasty voice is the one everybody seems to hear. If we were to translate it into movie dialogue, it would go something like this:

> Yeah, sure, she takes just like a woman, and she sure aches just like a woman–I'll give her that. And she even makes love just like a woman. No doubt. But you know what, the bitch breaks down just like a damn little girl.

In this version, being a woman is cool; being a little girl is not, and the conversation the chorus conducts–with the singer's male buddies, with himself–is a part of an adult sexual battle he's trying to win. But the adult swagger with which "Just Like a Woman" commences gradually transmutes into a child-like vulnerability. This movement is the opposite of regression; it traces the singer's recovery, as leverage by which to master the banalities of adulthood, of the resilient child at the core of his being. And the change in his voice is accompanied by a change in his awareness of her:

> Yes, she takes just like a woman, and she aches just like they all do. What is it with women, anyway? And she even makes love just like every other damn woman. But you know, when she breaks up suddenly there's this amazing little girl.

In the end, we realize that when a woman "breaks like a little girl," she is breaking open and breaking free. Or as Dylan himself later observed, commenting directly on this line: "That's the child in everyone that has to be confronted."* "Just Like a Woman" is a lullaby for adults, an attempt to put to sleep the man or woman we think we are required to be, so that the child may awaken.

It begins, however, in the insomnia of adult vigilance:

*Nobody feels any pain*
*tonight as I stand inside the rain*
*Everybody knows*
*that baby's got new clothes*
*But lately I see*
*her ribbons and her bows*
*Have fallen*
*from her curls*

"Nobody feels" but "everybody knows." This opening evokes a public setting, a party perhaps, where all inwardness is masked behind personae on parade. All is gossip and bitchiness. But we soon discover there are only two people here, and we are forced to realize that even in the so-called privacy of we two alone, a person remains a public construct, a masquerade, a self-regarding version of "everybody." The singer here immediately treats us to an impressive display of his own personal power, when he begins to muse–to whoever might be listening–over changes he has "lately" observed in "baby"'s appearance. The tone is a deliciously nasty mixture of disinterested cruelty and erotic fascination. He's putting her in her place and enjoying her. A boss persona!

But there's other mischief afoot here. "Nobody feels any pain" is also transparently ironic, even without addition of the image, at once poignant and indelibly comic, of the singer "stand[ing] inside the rain." Standing still and upright in the midst of the torrent of his own emotional life, this voice is alienated from its own persona. In its deepest register, it is the voice of a "nobody" who feels any and every pain, a

---

* Jonathan Cott, "Standing Naked," *Rolling Stone*, p. 41.

hidden self who intuits this man and this woman's mutual weariness with their own and the other's predatory sexual personae. This undercurrent of awareness suggests yet another, if only unconscious motive behind his merciless needling of her: maybe he can shame his "baby" to come out from behind her pretenses and play.

In this opening verse, these two attitudes of voice–the one masterfully glib, the other secreting extreme discomfort–coexist in a menacingly charged tension. The chorus, which I think we imagine as a kind of private musing, resolves this dissociation to the extent that it gives direct voice to the singer's awareness of pain, his own as well as hers. Part of what this chorus expresses is the ambivalent mixture of pleasure and pain in sexual love. The list of what she does "just like a woman" is a litany of resentments and of gratitudes that are impossible to sort, one from the other. One reason I suspect Dylan likes singing this song is that the chorus–by the way it elicits varying emotional colorings from his voice–offers him a chance to discover how, on any given night, he feels about sex, women, and whatever sense of life and of himself grows out of or informs those feelings. But it seems to me that the first time round, the emotional awareness carried by the final line of the chorus–"but she breaks just like a little girl"–is still fundamentally muffled. All we hear, so far, is bewilderment, resentment, and even disdain.

Of course, Dylan doesn't have to sing it that way, and in fact I've heard him sing this song so that, from the very first chorus, the words "like a little girl" are infused with a heartbreaking delicacy and sense of wonder. On *Blonde on Blonde*, however, the chorus is sung–all three times–in a provoking deadpan that requires us to let the feelings carried by the verses inform their tonality. In any case, the second verse opens with a move that seems to arise from the exasperated tone I hear in the first invocation of the "little girl."

"Queen Mary" is a somewhat enigmatic figure, but I've always associated her with other *Blonde on Blonde* females–like the Queen of Spades in "I Want You" and Mona or even Ruthie in "Memphis Blues Again"–who seem to function both as sexual mentors and as a quasimaternal refuge from the bewilderments of sex. The singer's decision to "go see" her is announced in a tone that is both snotty and plaintive. The remainder of the second verse fails to move me in any direction at all; it doesn't seem to have a tone. Our sense of the singer's personality is displaced by clumsily impersonal poetic manipulations. "Nobody has to guess" is weirdly arch, but it seems intended to evoke something like the gossipy guessing people engage in about whether a woman might be "blessed"–with love, or even with a pregnancy. The word "blessed" itself seems to come out of nowhere, unless it's prompted, proleptically, by "your long-time curse," a particularly resonant image, mentioned in the bridge, evoking not just the mutual enmity between men and women but the loss of Eden as well.

The point here seems to be that "baby" won't be fulfilled–and redeemed–as a woman until she recognizes the vanity of "her fog, her amphetamine, and her pearls." But what would it mean for her to see that she is "like all the rest?" Who are all the rest? Does this mean she's not such a babe, after all, or that being a babe doesn't lift her above the universal condition of womanhood? And if, so, what does it mean to be "just like a woman?" At this point in the song, I'd have to say, not much! When the chorus comes round this time, the titular phrase itself sounds very much like a curse, and the culminating "just like a little girl" oddly wistful, as if offering some relief–for him more than for her–from baffling woman.

This tone seems to cast the singer into a reverie that takes the form of a bridge. It's the most seductively lyrical and the most visionary bridge Dylan has ever written, and it radically changes the song. However, this is less a bridge–a device that both spans the musical and lyrical gap between verses and provides a vantage point outside their topography–than a tunnel. It whisks the singer back to the beginning of the song, back to the pain and the rain, to re-trace the same ground, but this time from a little lower layer of his consciousness:

*It was raining from the first*
*And I was dying there of thirst*
*So I came in here*

*And your long time curse hurts*
*But what's worse*
*Is this pain in here*
*I can't stay in here*
*Ain't it clear . . .*

The poetry of this mimes the primal urgency and release of sexual intercourse, but it also mimes birth. "From the first" is aboriginal, the "raining" invoked is the waters of generation that lure the singer, a hungry spirit, into the "world" (as he will later identify her) from his desiccated nowhere. The mystery of sex recapitulates the mystery of birth, of origins, and indeed, for the singer, the former is nearly swamped by the latter. The "long time curse" evoked here is not just erotic enmity; it is what Dylan would later call "the pain of birth" (in "Gonna Change My Way of Thinking"). The singer sympathizes with that pain–psychological as well as physical, a lover's as well as a mother's. But he claims priority for his own pain–the pain of incipient suffocation–in a mother's womb, in a lover's arms. The singer emerges from the bridge not a changed man but a rejuvenated boy.

The bridge insists on change, and it enacts a change that, in the final verse, is implicitly revealed to be part of the unaltering rhythm of change–an oscillation between appetite and apathy, between anxiety and ease, between coming and going–that constitutes the singer's creaturely self. The bridge itself is exquisite, but this final verse–which the bridge makes possible–is what lifts this song to a level of greatness. Its greatness is a mastery of tone–an imperturbable poise between renunciation and supplication that I suspect most *Blonde on Blonde* fans recognize as the album's signature mode. But here we seem to hear that tone as it finds itself for the first time. "Ain't it clear," the singer asks,

*That I just can't fit*
*Yes I believe it's time for us to quit*
*When we meet again*
*introduced as friends*
*Please do''t let on*

*that you knew me when*
*I was hungry*
*and it was your world*

The verse opens with an assertion of independence that undercuts its severity with its surprising invocation of "us." The switch to direct address actually began in the middle of the bridge–where the "you" invoked seems to materialize directly out of the emotionally ambivalent intimacy of the imagery–but even if we noticed this, I think we are still surprised to hear it carried forward in the final verse. There is something aboriginal as well, I think, about this "us," and about this "you" who constitutes "us" by completing the circuit of "I" and "you." It's not just that without "you," "I" am incomplete but that without "you" as interlocutor, "I" split apart, into the "hungry" boy I "was" (and will be again) and the well nourished, not-hungry boy I am now.

He asks her to keep his hunger a secret (the exact locution, "don't let on," suggests the singer's persona owes a lot to Huckleberry Finn). I suppose we can hear this as a request not to humiliate him by making his neediness public. But I don't hear it that way. I think at this point in the song we've left the public party behind us. When the singer imagines some future in which they will be "introduced as friends," I think we are meant to imagine them being introduced not only *to* each other but also *by* each other. The burden of this verse, in any case, is to establish how they are going to treat each other, and how they will keep each other as a secret between themselves. This verse is best heard not (or not only) as a "goodbye" but as a "goodnight." The singer is asking her for mercy–don't lord it over me!–just as, implicitly, he is offering her mercy–in this final verse anyway–by keeping to himself his knowledge of how her "world" goes to seed whenever he has not "lately" "blessed" it with the attention through which that world is realized. But there is something Jamesian in these imagined reticences, in they way they raise to consciousness realities that if mentioned openly would overwhelm consciousness. By the end of this verse, the singer is (imagining) having his cake and eating it too: they are man and woman but also boy and girl, friends *and* lovers, companionable predators of each other.

The final chorus carries the full thrill of this. By changing "she" to "you" the singer subsumes his irreducibly ambivalent–and irreducibly enlivening–love-hate for "her" within what is an essentially transcendental conversation with "you." Or maybe that's redundant: Conversation for Dylan *is* transcendental. Conversation is joy, is hilaritas, is eternal delight. He never tires of it, pitching the ball of life back and forth, like playing catch. It is child's play, which is why it's even better when you're playing catch with Dad, or, as here–sort of–with Mom.

Yeah, I suppose I'm getting a bit fanciful here, although I'd argue that mine is a flight of fancy that has resonance within Dylan's work. The simplest way to make my point would be to say that there is always in Dylan a fruitful and instructive tension between what he is talking to "you" about and the fact that he is talking with and (imagining) listening to "you" at all. It's the tension between the flesh and the spirit.

## VI

*Blonde on Blonde* is a collection of songs about women. That statement will do, as long as it is understood that "women" here is a figure of speech, a metonymy for the perplexities and incitements of sex for a young poet. This doesn't mean that the women in these songs are mere allegories, but it may explain why the album's aesthetic favors women of the bitchier variety. The songs I have so far discussed–"Visions of Johanna," "One of Us Must Know (Sooner or Later)," and "Just Like a Woman"–strike me as the cream of the crop. My own favorite poetry is one that enacts a journey of imaginative and spiritual discovery, or self-discovery, and these songs do that with a concentrated power and grace that, for my money, is hard to beat.

*Blonde on Blonde* contains eleven other songs, which I would divide into two groups. There are seven other "songs about woman" that are best understood, I think, as improvised performances of self–in other words, as throwaways–and I discuss them in the next chapter. I conclude this chapter with a discussion of four songs that constitute the backbone of *Blonde on Blonde*–its imaginative armature, if you will. Three of them are not "songs about women," even though one of those is the album's only unambivalent love song. Instead, they place the hazards of sex in a larger context, a context that is at once cosmic and socio-political. These three songs are "Rainy Day Women #12 & #35" (the album's opening song) "Stuck Inside of Mobile with the Memphis Blues Again," and "Sad-Eyed Lady of the Lowlands" (the final song). The fourth song, "Pledging My Time" (the album's second song), is the only one of the album's "songs about women" in which the singer is still bereft of the inner resources–the power of play, and specifically the poetic power of conversational play–that he brings, in one fashion or another, to his encounters with women in all the other songs. "Pledging My Time" is a blues–one of several Dylan blues rooted in Robert Johnson's magnificent "Come On in My Kitchen"–and it's the most dispirited blues Dylan ever composed. Its humor suffices merely to register an unflagging astonishment at his own misfortune. As such, it affords a superb transition between "Rainy Day Women," a song that hilariously celebrates spiritual misfortune as our common lot, and "Visions of Johanna," a song that records and celebrates the singer's recovery of the youthful poet within himself.

"Rainy Day Women" is a title made for Dylan, a poet for whom rain and women are virtually synonymous. Of course, the song has nothing–directly–to do with women. "Rainy Day Woman" is apparently a slang term for marijuana; among other things, it's a song about pot: "Everybody must get stoned." But it's primarily a song about paranoia, and its cure. The song's verses are a litany of the ways in which "they" will "stone" you, and the refrain offers the consolation that we need not "feel so all alone" since "Everybody must get stoned." The celebration of pot is an unacknowledged double entendre, an in-group password. On the surface, then, the lyric is exactly what it's always been heard as, the quintessential 60s counterculture ditty: the world is out to get us, but we're all in this together–and so (whispering) let's smoke a joint and enjoy each other's company.

"Rainy Day Women" is one of Dylan's most cherished simplicities, but I think it's even simpler–and much more unsettling–than has been recognized. There is no double entendre: smoking pot is just one more way in which "they" stone us, one more way in which we–who are our own worst "they"–happily and haplessly stone ourselves. "They," in the last analysis, are the demons of desire. To "get stoned" is to become an adult, to lose the innocence in which (to cobble together images from the song's verses), "young and able," we "try to be so good," happily "alone" at "home," sitting "at the breakfast table." To get stoned is to be inundated by the most universal of mind-altering substances, our own hormones. Or as Dylan memorably puts it in "Pledging My Time," "I got a poison headache/but I feel alright."

The song's Everyboy figure is a defenseless innocent, but his innocence is also innocuous, a tedious banality itching for its own demise. When his persecutors find him, he is already restively "walkin' on the floor" and "walkin' to the door." Riding in his car, playing his guitar, or trying to make a buck, he is tempting fate, looking for ways to lose his precious innocence. "Rainy Day Women" is Dylan's version of the myth of the fortunate fall. "Everybody *must* get stoned" both announces a common fate and makes a universal promise. Everybody gets to come to the party.

But what promise does the party of life itself hold? "Rainy Day Women" is deliciously ambiguous on this matter, its tone at once celebratory and elegiac. This issue is more fully confronted in "Memphis Blues Again," a song that concludes by translating this ambiguity into one of Dylan's most resonant aphorisms:

*And here I sit so patiently*
*waiting to find out what price*
*You have to pay to get out of*
*going through all these things twice*

Life is good, perhaps, but once is apparently enough. The fact that the song concludes rather than opens with this realization reflects a quality that sets it apart from other *Blonde on Blonde* songs. The singer is oddly dispirited; he sounds like he has lost–or has not yet found–his Mercurial zip. Paradoxically *"stuck* inside of *Mobile"* (emphasis added), he is going nowhere fast, a divine child, trapped in the womb-tomb of time, whose plaintive cries to "mama" serve merely to expose his vulnerability. Mobile here is not the city in Alabama but a state of being–the fact that Dylan sings it as "inside-a Mobile" makes it easy to imagine him trapped inside a mobile sculpture or an (auto)mobile–and the Memphis invoked here is not Tennesseean but Egyptian, a necropolis where time has metamorphosed into spellbound geometries and the motion of life is reduced to a shiver of electrons. It is this final Memphian vision that provokes the singer's wondering, quoted above, about the price of release:

*The bricks lay on Grand Street*
*where the neon madmen climb*
*They all fall there so perfectly*
*it all seems so well timed*

The "neon madmen" are the last in a series of figures invoked who seem to represent the universal demons, or Gnostic archons, who appeared in "Rainy Day Women" as simply "they." (In "Pledging My Time," this role is played by the impish "hobo.") In the first verse, the "ragman," who "draws circles up and down the block," is something of a prison builder and, like the "neon madmen," a self-imprisoner. The "railroad men" in the third verse and the "rainman" in the seventh are both sinister mind-benders. The figures in the middle three verses–"grandpa," "the senator," and "the TV preacher"–are less visionary, more mundane figures of oppressive (and self-oppressing) power. (The truth is that the song would be better off without these three verses; only grandpa's antics have any power to arrest the imagination. Indeed, Dylan himself usually skips most or all of these verses when performing the song these days.)

That leaves two figures unaccounted for, Shakespeare (who appears in the second verse) and Ruthie (who makes her appearance in the eighth). (Mona, who "tries to warn" the singer about the railroad men, is something of a pre-Ruthie.) Shakespeare and Ruthie are transcendent figures–images, respectively, of the singer's true self and his true desire. And he is, apparently, alienated from both of them because he has lost his voice. The song is full of images of voicelessness–most memorably in the singer's confession that the mixture of "Texas medicine" and "railroad gin" has "strangled up my mind." The narrative projects human experience as eerily muted, and while the singer apparently sees himself as a lone voice in this dumb show, his voice fails him when it counts. The episodes with Shakespeare and Ruthie are mirror images of the same failure of imagination and nerve. His failure to connect with his own deepest identity ("Shakespeare . . . in the alley") prevents him from finding out whether the French girl has talked, and when Ruthie gives her voice to him, he falls silent, allowing her delightful promise to dissolve back into the "honky-tonk lagoon" from which it materialized.

End of story? Not on your life. There's something funny going on in this song. The singer is merely *playing* dumb. How do we know this? That's hard to say. Maybe it's the sly playfulness in the way he addresses Mona ("Oh, I didn't know that!") and Ruthie "(Aw come on now"). The affect is all wrong–if we assume the singer is as he behaves. The singer hasn't lost his Mercurial zip after all; he's just disguising it. The voice we hear as we attend this song really is that of Shakespeare in the alley, joyously playing the fool in "his pointed shoes and his bells," entertaining us–and himself–by re-enacting a terrible fate from which–by means of the very voice in which he plays out his charade–he has already liberated his own imagination. "Memphis Blues Again" is a mock surrender to a cruel mother nature–a Sphinx who would strangle him in his prime. The song's chorus sounds bleak only if we detach it from the song's narrative voice–and if we ignore the way he taunts "mama" with his devilish "really":

*Oh Mama can this*
*really be the end*
*To be stuck inside of Mobile*
*with the Memphis Blues again?*

He appeals to "mama" as a protector, but, like the "ladies [who] treat me kindly," she is really the guardian of the prison-world from which, paradoxically, he both never can escape and has already escaped.

In "Sad-Eyed Lady of the Lowlands," the singer offers this hard-won imaginative liberty to his beloved, who is immured in a prison-world governed by an anonymous and ubiquitous "they." By all rights, this should have been a great song, and at times it sounds like one, but it's not. For me, anyway, it remains a fascinating failure.

The problem, I think, is that Dylan–not the singer, but the guy who wrote this song–falsifies his "sad-eyed lady" by idealizing her. The song's title gives the lie to the singer's manner of addressing her: he treats her as if she has her being *in* but not *of* the Lowlands, the valley of death in which and of which all mortal beings exist. This sad-eyed lady is treated as a Madonna, an Immaculate Conception, who is inwardly untouched by corruption and mortality. She alone–in this song and on this album–is, to borrow the terminology of "Rainy Day Women," unstoned.

This is not true, and Dylan surely knows that, but, for whatever reason, he does not allow this awareness to be absorbed in his address to his lady. So it gets displaced. It appears partly in the difficulty Dylan has with the final lines of each of the song's ten quatrains. These lines come in five rhyming pairs, each pair separated by the chorus, and they are all variants of "who among them could think he could fuck with you?" They are the least impressive element in the song–by a long shot. The worst of them seem manufactured by formula, and the best of them are merely lame. It's known that when recording this song Dylan kept his musicians waiting around for hours while he reworked the lyrics to this song, and my guess is that he was mainly fiddling with these stanza-ending lines. He was trying to make them right, but he couldn't, because were he to let his imagination work freely on them, he would have had to imagine what *she* was doing, and feeling, while they were messing with her. Some of this knowledge comes through anyway. In the latter verses, "Who among them could think" becomes "who among them do you think," and the line that is published as "How could they ever ever

[sic] persuade you" is sung as "How could they ever have persuaded you." It's as if he knows she was inwardly seduced by the world she also rises above, and he wants her to deny it for him, or at least allow him not to see that. But then, where does he think the "child of the hoodlum wrapped up in [her] arms" came from? A Virgin birth?

The Sad-Eyed Lady's complicity in the ethos of the Lowlands becomes even more powerfully, and disturbingly, clear in the singer's descriptions of her. There is a profound disjunction between the affect that attaches to these descriptions and the affect that attaches to the act of describing. The woman he describes is a Mona Lisa, a glamorous enigma, a seductive dumb show. She is not just in and of the Lowlands; she *is* the Lowlands, the goddess of mortality and mutability. In one sense, then, she is incorruptible, immune to "their" violations–not because she is spiritually pure but because she is Mother Nature. She outlasts her despoilments.

I think this is the image of the Sad-Eyed Lady that seeps through the singer's courtship of her, but you'll never notice that as long as you listen to the singer's voice. I'm not referring here to Dylan's remarkable recorded vocal–a series of furry purrs–but to the song's poetic voice. That is, even on my tongue, and in my tuneless throat, the sound of this voice is that of an impossible intimacy. The series of litanies ("with your . . .) with which the singer addresses his lady are framed not as evocations of her image but as invocations of her presence, or better, of her attention.

The poetry of these litanies is unique in Dylan in that they have absolutely no cumulative power, no implicit narrative force. In this they are utterly unlike the "with your eyes" litany in Ginsberg's "Kaddish" that undoubtedly inspired Dylan's song. Where Ginsberg's litany expands to incorporate and constitute a veritable cosmos, Dylan's lines succeed each other like a series of flashes in the dark, a series of soundings of a provocative silence that swallows each of them in turn:

*With your mercury mouth*
*in the missionary times*
*And your eyes like smoke*

*and your prayers like rhymes*
*And your silver cross*
*and your voice like chimes*

There is something curiously self-blinding about these lines: they refuse to sustain the mental movie that visionary poetry ordinarily engenders. Each successive image strikes the mind first not as a fresh revelation but as a blotting-out of what preceded it. It's as if vision is being sacrificed on the altar of a self-purifying voice. It is as if the singer is trying to create a purely vocal lair into which to entice the attention of this resolutely mute sad-eyed lady. It's as if he's "Shakespeare in the alley," trying to get the French girl to talk.

Except he's not in the alley. He's back where we found him on *Highway 61 Revisited*, in the visionary highlands of his imagination. Imagine how differently the song would sing had Dylan, in the questioning lines that conclude each quatrain, said "I" where he says "they," so that "Who among them do they think could bury you?" would become something like "How could I think I could bury you?" or even "How could you think I could bury you?" Such a change would have given the relationship between the singer and his lady a flavor of mutual complicity–flavor that every other love song on *Blonde on Blonde* possesses, in spades! Such a change, in short, would have imbued that relationship with a candor, tension, and humor that would have brought the song's potent contradictions into consciousness and opened a door onto a real future.

Such a change would have made the verses worthy of the song's magnificent chorus:

*Sad-eyed lady of the*
*lowlands*
*Where the sad-eyed prophet says*
*that no man comes*
*My warehouse eyes*
*my Arabian drums*
*Should I leave them by your gate*
*or sad-eyed lady should I wait?*

I'll be honest. I rarely choose to listen to this song, and when I do, it's only to be able to listen to this chorus, which, to my ears, is one of Dylan's finest creations. It does require the verses to illuminate its meanings–"warehouse eyes" and "Arabian drums," for instance, are the lyric's shelves of images and its libidinously pulsing voice, respectively–but for me anyway, despite their many local splendors, the verses are too tedious to command steady attention.

On the other hand, just as I am finishing this, what should arrive in my mail but an issue of the Rolling Tomes newsletter *Series of Dreams* that includes a reprint of an article in which several respected singer-songwriters name their favorite Dylan song. There I discover that Tom Waits has chosen "Sad-Eyed Lady of the Lowlands," about which he has this to say:

> "Sad-Eyed Lady of the Lowlands" is a grand song. It is like Beowulf and 'it takes me to the meadow.' The song can make you leave home, work on the railroad, or marry a gypsy. I think of a drifter around a fire with a tin cup under a bridge remembering a woman's hair. The song is a dream, a riddle, and a prayer.*

What gives me pause, here, is that Waits clearly hears the same song I hear; "a dream, a riddle, a prayer" pretty much nutshells what I've been belaboring for some time now. But while this song works for Tom Waits, it doesn't work for me. Being Tom Waits, he's more likely than I am–by a large stretch–to know how this song sings–what it's like, emotionally and imaginatively, to inhabit it as a singer. I suspect it simply doesn't bother him–not even enough really to notice, perhaps–that the singer remains stubbornly, perversely clueless about a large part of the meaning and affect of his own song. Maybe it shouldn't bother me either. But it does.

---

* From an unidentified article by *Los Angeles Times* music critic Robert Hilburn excerpted in *Series of Dreams* 70, p.5.

# 8

# *Blonde on Blonde II*

## Hermes Reborn

> The closest I ever got to the sound I hear in my mind was on *Blonde On Blonde*. It's that thin, that wild mercury sound. It's metallic and bright gold, with whatever that conjures up. That's my particular sound.*

These are probably the most famous words Dylan has ever spoken about his music. I quote them here in full to reiterate my contention that the spirit of Mercury informs the poetry of *Blonde on Blonde* at least as much as the music. The moral of the story–as represented in the group of seven songs I discussed in the previous chapter–could be summed up (Harry Smith-style) thus: "Mercurial Zip Cures Hamlet Complex!" But it is in the album's remaining seven songs that Mercury really comes into his own. No ailments remaining to cure–or no serious ones, anyway–he is free simply to play. These songs are radically different from the seven songs I have already considered, and the difference is, at least in the first analysis, a loss of intensity, a reduction in power. There are no sublimities in these songs, no revelations of an augmenting consciousness, no sense they are carrying us past barriers of

* Rosenbaum, "The *Playboy* Interview," p. 69.

guilt and inhibition and habit to the limits of what can be known or felt or said. If they can be said to test the limits of anything–and at their best, they surely do–it might best be defined as the limits of what a free spirit can get away with.

In my own appropriation of classical mythology, Mercury unbound is Hermes, his Greek precursor. Each is valued both for the purposes they serve and for themselves, but Mercury–no doubt precisely because he a Roman imagining–seems to come down to us primarily as a service provider, whether as messenger of the gods or as god of healing. With Hermes, on the other hand, the services he provides seem always overshadowed by the tricksy panache with which he provides them. Hermes is the entertaining one, and so from here on out, Hermes shall be our guide.

These songs–for convenience, I'll refer to them as the Hermetic seven–are central to our experience of *Blonde on Blonde*. They are its most distinctive creations, the songs that prompted my fancy of the album as the soundtrack of some unproduced chamber opera. The other, perhaps greater, songs on *Blonde on Blonde* are its soliloquies and its intimate duets. The Hermetic seven, in a way that has no precedent and few successors in Dylan's work, take place on a social stage, in front of an implied or felt fictional audience. Even though the singer continues to speak only to the lady, or series of ladies, who arouse and baffle him, he sings with a consciousness–which he often cruelly exploits–of what *others* might think. The singer in these songs is an actor, too, a self-conscious persona addressing his lady–however rudely or impudently–as a lady, as a self-consciously social being.

The exuberant theatricality of the Hermetic seven is doubtless linked to their most striking imaginative quality, their incorrigible and always surprising playfulness. The "little boy lost" who "takes himself so seriously" has found himself again. Just listen to this couplet from "Most Likely You Go Your Way (and I'll Go Mine)":

*You say my kisses*
*are not like his*

*But this time I'm not gonna tell you*
*why that is.*

We should not be misled by this superb impertinence into surmising that the singer actually knows "why that is." He doesn't seem to know very much at all about this girl who "lies" and tells "stories you know I believe are true." Indeed, his despair at ever knowing her is the reason he's sending her on her way, and the thought of the deficiencies of his kisses–whether through his failure or hers hardly matters–clearly still stings. (And what I call the theatricality of these songs is evident in the way this is felt not just as an erotic wounding but also an insult to the singer's reputation.) The second line is pure gesture, repartee, tossing the ball back into her court. Such a gesture bids not to resolve the ordeal of sex, nor even to dissolve it, but to enclose it within a higher order of play.

This sort of gesture pervades the Hermetic seven: "I Want You," "Absolutely Sweet Marie," "Obviously Five Believers," "Fourth Time Around," "Leopard-Skin Pillbox Hat," "Temporary Like Achilles," and "You Go Your Way." Their peculiar emotional tone–a blend of bitter resignation and insouciant verve–lends the entire album a bright, bracing buoyancy that eventually infects our sense even of those other songs in which playful equanimity is more of a dimly felt aspiration or unconscious asset. Oddly, the breezy élan of these songs seems strengthened by something that ought to undermine it. These songs may celebrate the triumph of play over nature, but–with the likely exception of "I Want You"–the singer never really finds the playmate he is looking for. The ladies never toss the ball back; indeed, few of these songs seem even to leave open the possibility that the particular lady addressed might eventually yield to and collude with the singer's playful spirit.

So why doesn't this pragmatic failure lend these songs a more somber coloring? The short answer is that the singer doesn't let it. These songs invariably take the form of an augmenting playfulness that paradoxically is not deterred by the lady's stubborn unplayfulness, but feeds on it. By the end of the song the lady is usually reduced or nearly reduced, emotionally, to little more than a straw woman to the singer's conviction that, as he puts it in "You Go Your Way," "it can't be this way everywhere."

And then there's this to consider: the ladies in the songs might not respond to the singer's playfulness, but the ladies–and the men–in his audience sure do. When *Blonde on Blonde* was playing on turntables across the country in the summer of 1966, Dylan was the sexiest man in the world, and one who had made sexiness seem sexier than anyone–even Elvis–had previously imagined it could be. And the singer in these songs seems to know all this, and to feed on that, too.

## II

"You Go Your Way" is the flimsiest of the Hermetic seven, but for that reason it offers the simplest illustration of their characteristic imaginative choreography. In the first verse the singer confronts his lover with her betrayal of her promises to him, and in the second he confronts her with the banality of her alibis. He concludes the first verse by saying he's giving up–a decision the chorus amplifies–but he concludes the second verse with something more delightfully Dylanesque:

*Sometimes it gets*
*so hard to care,*
*It can't be this way*
*ev'rywhere.*

But, of course, there is no reason it couldn't "be this way everywhere." The singer's exasperated cry is a spontaneous act of imagination, almost involuntary, a prompting of unsatisfied desire that changes him and his song. What follows next is a bridge in which he sloughs off his accusatory self as the "judge" who's "badly built" and "walks on stilts," a menacing figure whom he gallantly, playfully warns his lover to "watch out" for. The third and final verse, then, is an attempt to create another ground–located somewhere in that generously imagined "ev'rywhere"–in which to meet her. When, in the final verse, he confronts her attempts to provoke his jealousy with the fine evasion about his kisses, we realize that while he still wants her, he's found, in his recovery of playfulness, the inner ground from which he can truly afford to let her "pass." In its final turning, the chorus no longer sounds so cocksure–because it no longer needs to–about which one of them is being "left behind." This all goes by so quickly, and the singer's bitterness, even at the beginning, is so lightly worn, that we do not perceive this little drama as reflecting any deep change in him. It's only his manner that changes, as if it simply takes him a couple verses to find a manner that suits his spirit.

"You Go Your Way" is the only kiss-off song among the Hermetic seven, but it is characteristic because it's a comedy of manners that resolves itself in a provokingly complacent tone of self-sufficient expectancy. It's a tone similar to the tone of the blues yet decisively different: the sense of freshened desire is erected not upon a recognition of loss but upon a narcissism, an implied autoeroticism even, that is Whitmanesque in its charismatic verve.

"Obviously Five Believers" takes its verse form (and music) from a traditional blues, although neither of the two earlier versions in which I am familiar with it–Memphis Minnie's great "Me and My Chauffeur Blues" and Chuck Berry's "I Want to Be Your Driver"–are especially bluesy in mood. Dylan's song plays at being a blues. The first verse, a plea (uttered "early in the morning") for his absent love to "come home," ends with the admission that "I could make it without you/If I just didn't feel so all alone." That sounds promising as a blues premise, and indeed the singer seems to play it that way when, in the second verse, he promises not to let his absent lover down and pleas with her to do the same. The "please don't" with which the verse concludes strikes an authentic blues note, but the first part of that final line–"I can [let you down] if you can [let me down], honey"–couches the song's incipient blues plangency not in the wicked humor intrinsic to the blues but in a puckish playfulness. Unlike the blues, where everything is at risk, the mode of this song convinces us that the singer is somehow invulnerable. He'll be hurt if she lets him down, but, crucially, the hurt won't really hurt.

This Hermetic playfulness fully emerges in the next three verses, verses whose figurings are so elliptical in relation to what they figure (and to each other) as to be pragmatically free of their own meanings. Their chief effect is to make light of their meanings even as they faithfully disclose them. Dylan may not be simply winging it in these verses, but he sounds like he is, and that illusion–if that's all it is–is his triumph.

What he's making light of is precisely what's bringing the singer and his lover down: his sexual needs ("my black dog barking") and her sexual anxieties ("your mama's moaning"). The extraordinary–and climactic–fifth verse both raises the sense of sexual menace to a fever pitch–the shape-shifting singer here figures as a kind of one-man gang bang–yet defuses any sense of real menace with hints that the whole thing is just children playing dress-up:

*Fifteen jugglers*
*Fifteen jugglers*
    *Five believers*
    *Five believers*
        *All dressed like men*
*Tell your mama not to worry*
    *Because they're all*
        *Just my friend*

To characterize the "fifteen jugglers" and "five believers" as images of the singer's imaginative and erotic shape-shifting is, I think, plausible enough. Any interpretation will have to proceed more or less along these lines. But the important point to be made here is that no interpretation, however plausible or even inescapable, can ever really touch, let alone somewhat domesticate–as interpretations of poetic figures usually can–the wild surprise of the little scene this verse conjures.

I still believe that this image–the "five believers" who are "just my friend"–originates from Dylan's tumultuous onstage comradeship with the Hawks (later the Band), so that the lover addressed is, at some level, also his faithless audience. I believe this even though it's not at all evident what this might have to do with the context of the song we're listening to. The Hermetic seven–indeed, as I have earlier observed, the songs on *Blonde on Blonde* generally–abound in figures and gestures that escape any strict accountability to their context. These songs seethe with energies that seem to urge us to view all contexts as modes of masquerade–the versatile forms of playing dress-up–and to mock our persistent moral or critical concerns with coherence-in-context as a tedious neurosis.

But, to return to my own critical task, however we attempt to place this image, it's clear that, accompanied so delightfully by his gang of friends, the singer is in some important sense no longer "so all alone." Or maybe he never was; or maybe we just weren't listening closely enough to what he said. When the song ends with a reprise of the opening verse, we are more likely to notice that the singer is not "alone" or even "so alone" but "so *all* alone." "All" turns "alone" on its head, so that "all alone" suggests not an emptiness but a fullness, a paradoxical narcissistic ecstasy. This sense of the phrase–like the suggestion of replenishment contained in its setting "early in the morning"–is largely a hidden potential in the first verse, but by the time we hear it again–after passing through the outrageous epiphany of the five believers–it is all but inescapable.

It's worth noting here that we have encountered this before. "Rainy Day Women" consoles us with the assurance that we need *not* "feel so all alone," but that assurance is also a measure of what, in getting "stoned," we stand to lose: a primal narcissistic complacency that, in "Obviously Five Believers," the singer playfully restores to himself.

Two of the Hermetic seven, "Leopard Skin Pillbox Hat" and "Temporary Like Achilles," are primarily self-lacerating in their playfulness, and in both songs the self-lacerations are connected with a fear of women that is essentially indistinguishable from the singer's fear of his own psychic androgyny. The image of the "five believers" as merely "dressed" like men suggests, primarily, that they are more properly understood as something like visionary boys, or demon children, but, especially in a context so narcissistically charged, the possibility hovers that they are not (or not only) male but (also) female.

This possibility is taken up directly in "Leopard Skin Pillbox Hat," surely one of Dylan's funniest songs. I have to admit that while I loved this song when I first heard it, I quickly tired of it–it seemed to reduce too completely to its jokes. And I never enjoyed listening to Dylan's many revivals of the song in performance, which have invariably sounded like tedious parodies of "It Takes a Lot to Laugh." That all changed in November 2000, when I heard Dylan sing it at Hill Auditorium in Ann Arbor. I realized I had been mishearing it completely, though I also think Dylan had never before sung it so truly.

What I suddenly realized is that the girl–and the singer's calumnious scorn for her–is a red herring. Yes, she does appear to be a bit of a slut–but not near as much of a slut as the singer himself longs to be. The crucial emotional forces in this song are the singer's horniness and his fear of where that horniness is taking him. This fear is decidedly not a fear of moral degradation; it is a fear of being unmanned. The hat itself–always a mark of masculine show in Dylan–is a provoking symbol of her theft of male initiative and aggression. The singer is both charmed and appalled by this–and even more appalled by what his submission to its charm says about him. His fantasy that her hat "balances on [her] head just like a mattress balances on a bottle of wine" is infinitely delicious, suggesting as it does a sexual world turned upside down. (It is even more delightful when we remember that a pillbox hat, almost uniquely among ladies' hats, is too small and tight-fitting to create problems of balance. The singer's fears are delusional, born of cramped notions of what it means to be a man.) Similarly, the singer's proposal to trump her hat "with my belt wrapped around my head" betrays a near hysterical anxiety of psychic castration, of being reduced to that part of himself below his belt.

The song's finest moment comes in the penultimate verse, when the singer contemplates his cuckolding by his own doctor. After scurrilously observing that he knows about this because she "forgot to close the garage door," the singer concludes with an observation about himself that surely gives him pause:

*You know, I don't mind him cheatin' on me*
*but I sure wish he'd take that off his head*
*Your brand new leopard-skin pill-box hat*

It is a mistake, I think, to hear in this only an augmentation of the fears that have up to now largely shaped this song. Surely, the singer is also charmed, as we are, by the doctor's reciprocating wit in a gesture that both reclaims male prerogative (he's wearing the hat) and actively affirms, if you will, the bigendered nature (it's a girlie hat) of sexual experience. Why didn't I think of that?, the singer must wonder. Certainly that's the suggestion of the final verse, where he acknowledges that what her "new boyfriend . . . really loves you for" is not her "money" but her "brand new leopard skin pillbox hat." Who is that new boyfriend, in spirit if not in fact, but the singer himself, at once chastened and liberated by a fuller self-awareness? It seems that the doctor knew what he was doing after all!

"Temporary Like Achilles" is rather more subdued–occult, one is tempted to say–in its humor than "Pillbox Hat," but despite its somber coloring, it is playful–and wholly at ease in its playfulness–in a way that clearly sets it apart from its genuinely troubled twin "Sooner or Later." (Like "Sooner or Later," "Achilles" is a palpable descendent of "She's Your Lover Now," in both its thematic preoccupations and formal properties, including its reiterating stanzaic structure and its rhythms.) This song rehearses a familiar (Dylanwise) complex of male sexual anxiety and bewilderment, but there are some crucial differences from what we have heard before.

First, here the sense of emotionally empty sexual fulfillment is presented in a way that makes it seem not fearsome but uncannily charming, almost comic even. The song is structured so that its narrative is carried in the opening couplet of each of its four verse quatrains; the third line is a question prompted by the singer's sense of where he is, and the fourth line–a refrain–questions (and in the last two verses, declares) where his "honey" is. There is also a bridge, between the second and third verses. Listen, then, to the opening couplets of the first three verses:

*Standing in your window honey*
*Yes I've been here before*
*Feeling so harmless*
*I'm looking at your second door . . .*

*Kneelin' 'neath your ceiling*
*Yes I guess I'll be here for a while*
*I'm trying to read your portrait but*
*I'm helpless like a rich man's child . . .*

*Well I rush into your hallway*
*Lean against your velvet door*
*I watch upon your scorpion*
*Who crawls across your circus floor . . .*

This sequence seems to trace alterations in the singer's relationship–physical or psychic or maybe both–to a "honey" whose physical and/or psychic presence we come to identify, in turn, with her window, ceiling, and hallway, not to mention her second and velvet doors and circus floor! It's the story of a breaking-and-entering that is also a rape. Or rather, it's the story of a man whose experience of sex is to appear to himself as a rapist. And yet he *feels* "harmless," a profession of innocence that also, darkly, hints at an underlying sense of impotence. This suggestion is taken up in the second verse in the marvelous image of his "helpless" rapture before her riddling portrait. The singer is thus both breaking-and-entering and being lured into a trap, both aggressor and victim. This double vision climaxes in the startling image of "your scorpion," a figure that is at once male and female, aggressor and defense, possessor and possessed.

This seems to me a reasonable digest of the song's narrative plot, but this plot is a subordinate element in the song. Each verse is structured so that this apparitional trauma, in which the singer seems dissociated from his own experience, gives way, in the final lines, to a voice that is fully vested with personality. It is a personality that is full of a superb self-confidence about how much its proffered "loving" is worth, a personality that, as we hear in the third lines of the first three verses, is successively impudent ("How come you don't send me no regards?"), indignant ("How come you send someone out to have me barred?"), and insolent ("Just what do you think you have to guard?"). This personality also occasionally leaks into the apparitional sections of each verse, as in his observations, expressed with a fine blend of exasperation and bemusement, that he has been here before and will be here for awhile. It asserts itself even more crucially in two of the lyric's most decisive figures, the "rich man's child" and the marvelously odd locution "watch upon." The latter palpably replaces something like "gazed upon," which would express the stunned fascination of a consciousness wholly absorbed by its own experience with an expression that implies a consciousness that keeps a watchful eye upon something outside itself. Its very oddity seems proleptically to break the spell held over him by what the singer is about to see, and that effect is more decisive than whatever semantic value we might decide it so oddly carries.

This personality also asserts itself as a poet (or, if you will, songwriter) in the final verse, a verse in which it casts off its apparitional psyche, its troubled sexual self, as the figure of Achilles:

*Achilles is in your alleyway*
*he don't want me here he does brag*
*He's pointing to the sky*
*and he's hungry like a man in drag*

To me this is the finest couplet in the song; indeed, one of the most delicious moments on *Blonde on Blonde*. "Achilles in your alleyway" is Dylan's final judgment on the "little boy lost" in him. He is the human form of the "scorpion," a figure whose sexual ambivalence is made explicit here. Achilles, a "man in drag," is the "temporary" glory of the phallus as hermaphroditic homunculus, as pussy-whipped dick. Bristling with anxieties and resentments, he's nonetheless a figure more of pathos than of menace. You could even say the little fellow is kinda cute. Even Blake never scorched male genital pride with more compact decisiveness.

The singer's personality is indicated by the quite contrary figure of the "rich man's child." This image is invoked as a figure of helplessness, but it also augurs an immunity to harm that's anchored in a primal narcissism, the natural endowment of psychic self-sufficiency that funds the singer's resilient élan. It is in this Hermetic sense that he is a "rich man's child": a child of the gods, a divine child. His inability to read her portrait is finally of no more consequence or concern to him than his inability to fathom–that is to see *himself* in–the self-portrait his song sketches. He can't read her or his mere psyche because the psyche, being merely natural, does not speak the spirit's Hermetic language. The song's bridge, which intervenes between the second and third verses, turns his inability to "read" her into a joke. Her hardness toward him is reduced to various forms–the unresponsiveness of "stone," the caustic and/or ensnaring properties of "lime," or the simple impenetrability of "solid rock"–of inhuman nature.

What does it mean to reduce her obduracy to a joke, or to concede, as the singer does at the beginning of the bridge, that he is a "poor fool in his prime" for expecting more? One thing it surely means is that the singer regards human nature as irredeemably selfish. In this the singer is one with his creator, who, in the much later *Infidels* song "I and I," grimly locates our lives "in creation where one's nature neither honors nor forgives." But to reduce this hard truth to a harmless joke also suggests that the singer has something else, some alternate knowledge, up his sleeve. Our nature may be corrupt, but–but what?–our spirit, or our soul, is not? Maybe. Dylan may or may not want to put it that way; I have no idea. But I do know that he believes in the purity of song, in the generosity of the human voice. The singer's personality is necessarily his voice, and the joking bridge, indeed the entire song, is undertaken as if part of an incipient conversation with, or a calling to, a "honey" whose answering voice he may never hear, but which he is plainly soliciting. "Yes I know you can hear me walk," he sings in the bridge, thereby acknowledging he knows he is trapped (or that she knows she is trapped–it hardly matters) as he skulks toward her "velvet door." But she can also hear him *talk,* as they sit facing each other, the scorpion rising between them, exchanging pleasantries about how weird they both are.

Or maybe the pleasantries aren't truly exchanged; maybe she never responds. It doesn't seem to be that important. The singer, in his truest guise as singer, is a "rich man's child," a narcissist. He "wants" her "loving" (and "loving" here, I firmly believe, is a trope for an answering voice, something to listen to) but he does not need it. This lyric is in love with the sound of its own voice–a truth that Dylan's recorded performance deliciously corroborates. The singer wants love from another voice, but lacking that, to quote a later song, he'll just give himself "a good talking to." That's from the same *Blood on the Tracks* song–"You're Gonna Make Me Lonesome When You Go"–that figures love as "crickets talking back and forth in rhyme." "You're Gonna Make Me Lonesome" is a sweet pastoral; "Achilles" is a seriocomic sadomasochistic nightmare. The difference between crickets and scorpions is merely one of mood.

## III

"Fourth Time Around" covers similar psychic ground but in an entirely different mode. It is primarily a narrative drama, a song whose lyrical tenor is diffused as an accent of the storytelling–at least until the final verse. And unlike in "Temporary Like Achilles," this narrative–one of Dylan's most inspired dreamsongs–engages us on its own terms, perhaps because the singer manages to be simultaneously absorbed in and disengaged from his own experience. The split in his identity–between psyche and spirit, between body and voice, between experience and innocence, or what you will–is not healed, but it is pacified.

The story the song tells is, once again, familiar; indeed, we suspect this is the same couple we encountered in "Achilles," or in any number of *Blonde on Blonde* songs. But because it is presented dramatically, it is the only one of these songs in which *she* gets to talk and in which we are able to watch and listen to the singer interact with her. What we learn is something we have probably suspected about most of the women in these songs: she feels just as strangled by sex as the singer does. This couple seems to enjoy sex with each other–and they may even be fairly said to like each other–but they clearly do not enjoy each other. Their intimacy is uneasily overheated, possessed of a brittle edginess that gives the narrative the feeling of a succession of emotional splinters:

*When she said, "Don't waste*
*your words, they're just lies,"*
*I cried she was deaf.*
*And she worked on my face*
*until breaking my eyes,*
*then said, "What else you got left?"*
*It was then that I*
*got up to leave*
*but she said, "Don't forget,*
*"Everybody must*
*give something back*
*for something they get."*

There is something ambiguous, or ambivalent, or maybe just simply enigmatic about everything said and done here: the lovers' responses to each other seem to be at once aggressive moves in a sexual game and efforts to resist their conscription into the contest. Does she tell him not to waste his words in order to gain mastery over him–or simply to evade his efforts to master her? His initial response is even more ambiguous. Does he weep because she is deaf, or does he cry aloud (to her) that she is deaf? And whatever he does, in what spirit does he do it? As a ploy (even possibly a masochistic, submissive ploy) or in protest of a situation that requires him to parry her ploy with his own?

One could ask these questions about each movement in the ambiguously sexualized give-and-take that constitutes the first four of the song's five verses. Both the singer and his lover go round and round trying at once to outmaneuver the other and to arrest this vicious circling.

To summarize it in this way, however, makes the song sound like a dramatized distillation of "She's Your Lover Now," but that's not at all how it sounds–even before we get to the punch line (the final verse). The whole thing is rendered with such variety, verve, and cunning agility that we're never tempted to identify with the lovers' pain and we're not even all that sure about their own relationship to their pain. There is something not so much charming as charmed about this little drama. It's something of a fairy tale, especially when the singer finally relents to her admonition that he must "give something back":

*So I forced*
*my hands in my pockets*
*and felt with my thumbs*
*And gallantly handed her*
*my very*
*last piece of gum*

Like just about every other image in this song, the gum functions on two levels, both within the game of love–as a mocking and/or self-mocking gift–and, more strikingly, as a kind of amulet, a protective time-out from the game itself. The claim of gallantry, somewhat surprisingly, prevails over the various ironies that beset it from every corner. Indeed, a kind of gallantry pervades the whole song, principally in the circumspection with which its language clothes the sheer raunchiness of the story. But a sense of gallantry also hovers uncertainly over the vicious circle of the lovers' engagement with each other. The nasty sexual merry-go-round is repeatedly arrested in the course of the song, and it is restarted, or so it seems, not by the psychodynamics of sex (though that quickly takes over once it is restarted) but by a resiliently respectful openness to the other.

This sense of things–one that shockingly turns the whole song inside out–emerges openly in the final verse, though we are given some warning of it when, while awaiting the return of his shirt, the singer finds himself trying to "make sense/out of that picture of you in your wheelchair that leaned up against//her Jamaican rum." The woman addressed here is, in a familiar turn, the woman talked about in the rest of the song. Or we might put it this way: "she" is "you-in-your-wheelchair," where the wheelchair is Dylan's witty figure for the sexual body. The "picture," unlike the "portrait" in "Temporary Like Achilles," does not strike me as an actual painting or photograph; it seems here rather to be a vision that dawns upon the singer as he waits for her to retrieve his shirt. More importantly, unlike in "Just Like a Woman," the singer's discovery of "you" does not come at the end of his song, as a promise of transcendence or ecstasy, but in its midst, as a sobering conundrum: how can "you" be here if "she" is still around? It's like seeing Superman and Clark Kent in the same room; it's not supposed to happen this way!

But of course, this is how it does happen. The transcendental lyricism of "Just Like a Woman" may be truer to our desires, or even to our intuitions of what's really real, but the comedy of "Fourth Time Around" is certainly truer to our experience, where we never encounter "you" but always "you-in-your-wheelchair," or on bad days–like the one the singer (and his lover) seems to be having–just "your wheelchair." The singer himself seems to be struck by this realization, as–apparently forgetting that he is attempting to leave–he requests some of that "rum." What follows is one of the most attractively enigmatic passages in all of Dylan. I'm going to pass over this in relative silence, not because I have nothing to say but because I can't find anything to say that does not make me feel like a fool for trying to say anything. Let me observe only that it is significant–obscurely significant, absurdly significant, both within and outside the game–that her attempt to talk to him with a mouth full of gum is what does her in, and that there is something maddeningly ambiguous about our final image of her collapsing in a paroxysm–of agony? of orgasmic ecstasy? or both–onto the floor, as there is in our final image of him, having covered her up, rummaging through her drawer (or drawers) for souvenirs.

The song's final verse emerges as precisely that, a souvenir, an invention of memory. I don't think we are to imagine the singer addressing his lover in the actual flesh; his listener here is as ghostly a "you" as Dylan's singer has ever found. He is addressing her, as it were, as she sleeps (on the floor!). There is a recovery of the transcendental lyricism of "Just Like a Woman" in all this, but there remains, to put it mildly, considerable comedy, and some pathos as well. His sweet talk in this verse, which reads as a somewhat barbed valentine, depends for its effect upon the quixotic possibility that she might be listening for it–or have already heard it–in her dreams.

And what does he have to say? Well, for my money, this song's final verse is the most bracingly pungent and persuasive valentine I have ever heard:

*And when I was through*
*I filled up my shoe*
*and brought it to you*
*And you, you took me in*
*you loved me then*
*you never wasted time*
*And I, I never took much*
*I never asked for your crutch*
*now don't ask for mine*

This "crutch" is clearly a further trope of the wheelchair (partly by way of being a transparent pun on "crotch"). There is a fine, gallantly shared duplicity in his closing claim that he "never asked for her crutch": he's never asked her to give up her sexuality, but, of course, he asks her "for some" (to borrow another gallant euphemism from the previous verse) all the time–and he expects the same in return. It's in this sense that his seemingly outrageous claim that "I never took much" must be understood: the love he has taken from her takes nothing away from her, i.e., does not diminish her in any way. It's a transcendental economy altogether different from the mutually diminishing takings that seem to characterize these lovers' exchanges in the song's earlier verses. (There is also a gallant duplicity in his earlier acknowledgement that she "took him in": she gave him shelter and she deceived him, or, more simply, she sheltered him in the web of sexual illusion by which she entrapped him.)

What matters here, however, is not so much what is said as the gesture the singer makes in saying it. I still vividly remember the impression this final verse made on me, in the summer of 1966, when I listened to *Blonde on Blonde* constantly. I was mostly puzzled as to what Dylan might possibly be saying (wheelchair?? crutch?? say what?!), but this final verse both delighted and mystified me as some sort of sleight-of-voice: with it the song seemed not so much to conclude as to vanish into silence. Right up until the very last word, there had seemed to be still so much more ground to be covered, but suddenly, with that last word, there is nothing more that needs to be said. How cool!

To an extent, this effect is merely a by-product of the ethic of mutual restraint the final lines announce. Those lines effectively consign to silence the reality of mutual sexual predation that, up to that point, had been the subject of this song. The gallantry is in the withholding, and what is withheld is precisely that deadlocked moral willfulness–"I know that you know"–out of which the entire *Blonde on Blonde* song cycle seems to have originated. But this effect also partly depends on the force of a single line–"you never wasted time"–a line whose claim, and promise, is at once so unassuming and so immense. Indeed, I'd hazard the claim that it is the highest form of ethical praise Dylan can imagine. One might even say that the effect I am drawing attention to–of seeming to overfill and underexpend space and time–is the singer's grateful tribute to love received.

Oh, one final thing. This is not the half of it. Everything I've said about this song so far is just the first (or at most the first and second) time around. "You never wasted time" carries us back, with considerable shock of recognition, to the opening words of the song: "She said, "Don't waste your words." Hmmm! Maybe we heard it wrong. Maybe these words aren't spoken as part of erotic warfare or in protest of that warfare but with kindness, a patient and playful wake-up call to an overheated lover who doesn't quite get it. "My love," remember, "speaks like silence." Maybe she wishes you would too–and knows you can and even want to.

Once we listen to the song from this perspective, its tonality begins to dissolve into sheer possibility. "She worked on my face until breaking my eyes": it sounds horrible, until you consider that the eye–and the egocentric imperium it maintains–has always been a sinister figure in Dylan's poetry. And while our sense of the woman's possible sweetness initially makes the singer sound simply clueless, perhaps he rises to the occasion. "I tapped on her drum, I asked her how come?" Hmmm–foreplay? You tell me. In any case, this time round when we reach the final verse, we experience a change in perspective but not the same initial jarring change in tone.

So where does this leave us? We don't know. Love is nasty, love is sweet; now you see it, now you don't. You probably had to be there to know for sure. But then again, to borrow a Faulknerian conceit, if we had been there, we probably couldn't have seen it–in all its ambiguity and obscurity–as we do now. And what's more, Dylan–if not his singer–is completely at ease with this state of affairs, bemused by it even. ("I accept chaos. I'm not sure whether it accepts me.")

"Fourth Time Around" is as sophisticated a song–in form and in vision–as Dylan has ever written. Frank Sinatra could have sung it–and learned something from the experience. Not bad for a song that reputedly got its start in life as a mere parody of John Lennon's "Norwegian Wood!"

"I Want You," on the other hand, has no truck with sophistication. Its mode is most directly identified in its bridge, where the singer announces his refusal to allow any awareness to shape or shadow his inerrant desire:

*Now all my fathers*
*they've gone down*
*True love they've*
*been without it*
*But all their daughters*
*put me down*
*'Cause I don't*
*think about it*

This might sound merely flippant–it certainly aims for that tone–but it is in truth a very precise formulation of a fundamental component of Dylan's ethic. The singer's flippancy is built on a sharp contrast between being ("been without") and thinking ("think about") that is central to the entire song. What matters, it is implied, is what we do–how we live–and not when we think about it. It is also implied that "thinking about" things can become a substitute for–or at least get seriously in the way of–experiencing them, and, conversely, that acting on our desires can cure the impasses of thought. (Or as Dylan would put it three years–and several psychic light-years–later, "No matter what you think about it/you just can't do without it.")

Our singer has taken all this to heart and is going for broke, hurtling himself gloriously forward on the wings of his desire and shedding, as his voice cuts through the aether, every psychic blocking agent that has hidden him from himself:

*The guilty undertaker sighs*
*the lonesome organ grinder cries*
*The silver saxophones say I*
*should refuse you*
*The cracked bells and washed out horns*
*blow into my face with scorn*
*But it's not that way I wasn't born*
*to lose you*

This iconic cartoon is both brightly suggestive and exuberantly obvious, and its obviousness is crucial to the exhilaration this verse conveys. The joy is in seeing these assorted bogeymen flushed out into the empty air.

The second verse–which turns the song's attention from interior to external blocking agents, commences in the same spirit:

*The drunken politician leaps*
*upon the street where mothers weep*
*And the saviors who are fast asleep*
*they wait for you*
*And I wait for them to interrupt*

*me drinking from my broken cup*
*And ask me to open up*
*the gate for you*

This runs along with a wonderful glibness through the image of the sleeping saviors waiting for "you"–an image that imbues "you" with an imaginative power and beauty that is at least the equal of the singer's apocalyptic desire. The singer quickly counters her attractiveness with his devilishly casual self-image as something approaching the saviors' savior. On the other hand, the self-aggrandizing one-upmanship of the singer's fantasies is tempered rather severely by the sober realism of the "broken cup" from which he drinks.

The element of fantasy in all this is not central. Fantasy here is but the penumbra of clarified desire, and it is on that latter note that this verse firmly and decisively concludes: to "open up the gate"–or more precisely, to wait for the right moment to do so–is the essence of that desire. (This image is central to the entire album; it appears–with the same rhyme on "wait" and "gate"–in the chorus of "Sad-Eyed Lady of the Lowlands" and in a diffused form throughout "Absolutely Sweet Marie.") It is an image that is both baldly sexual and gallantly indeterminate: her "gate" is whatever portal from which she deigns to emerge. This second verse strikes me as at once the sweetest and the ballsiest erotic advance Dylan has ever sung.

The song reaches its climax in the third verse. (The fourth–which Dylan rarely sings–is no more than a satyric postlude.) The lyric turns from a visionary to a dramatic mode, as the singer addresses "you," via the usual Dylanesque trope, indirectly, in the dual guise–as mastering dominatrix ("Queen of Spades") and mastered plaything ("my chambermaid")–of her sexual body.

There may, as I contend, be no sublimities in this suite of songs, but their playfulness does engender several shocks of recognition, and the two sharpest jolts in all seven of them–for my money–occur successively in this verse. The first is the singer's observation that his queen-chambermaid "knows that I'm not afraid/to look at her." The underlying conceit here is that she is a Medusa, one he masters with the very fearlessness of his gaze. Yet mastery is not really the dominant tone here; indeed, this is one of the few images, anywhere in Dylan, where the mastering gaze is not demonic and where–not coincidentally–there is a strong sense of the vulnerability of vision, of the eye's inability to avoid what is there to be seen. The singer's mastery of the situation is the obverse of his acceptance of what he sees, and so, in the last analysis, a self-mastery rather than a mastery of her.

This line tells us not only that he is "not afraid" but also that she "knows" this. But "she," remember, is "you," the lover the song is wooing, and with this little detail "you" enter the song, in your own person, for the first time. We seem to catch a glimpse of the being behind or within the eyes that lets the singer know that she "knows." This hint is magnificently realized in the succeeding lines, where we learn that

*She is good to me*
*and there's nothing she doesn't see*
*She knows where I'd like to be*
*but it doesn't matter*

The initial couplet is the mirror image of the singer's claim that he is "not afraid to look at her," and the effect of that mirroring is to require us to see that if he is Perseus to her Medusa, then (from her point of view) she is Beauty to his Beast.

The larger effect of this climax is dazzlingly two-faced. On the one hand, there is an emergent sense of a confronting "I-and-you" (or even "I-and-I" or "you-and-you") couple that lurks about the semi-tame "he-and-she" beast whose mating ritual we are overhearing. I say "semi-tame" because, whatever more it may be, the singer's stance here is an assertion of the prerogatives of lust. He is going to have her, for better or for worse–"for better" in this case being "where I'd like to be," which is with "you," who may or not be a mirage, a mere overdraft on "her." The complexity of the singer's vision here recalls, even as it expands and clarifies, the chorus of that earlier Medusa vision, "I Wanna Be Your Lover": "I dont wanna be hers/I wanna be yrs!"

More importantly, when the singer insists on "where I'd like to be," he throws cold water on that emergent sense of a meeting here and now of "I" and "you." The tone Dylan achieves here could be described as a more tough-minded–some might say mean-spirited–version of the vulnerably tender mood of Whitman's finer short love lyrics, especially "Whoever You Are Now Holding Me in Hand" and "The Terrible Doubt of Appearances." Dylan's tough-mindedness enables him to insist on the paradoxical invulnerability of desire, its immunity to either dissatisfaction or satisfaction. The lyric proper concludes on this very note, with the outrageous (and outrageously punning) recognition that "it doesn't matter." Desire is the claim that the spirit makes on life; but it neither alters the exigencies of life–which here are the exigencies of lust–nor is reducible to them.

If indeed it exists. "It doesn't matter" is recklessly multivalent. It raises the possibility that the spirituality of desire is merely a ruse, a fictive covering, the canniest of all seduction ploys. I think Dylan senses this, and the satyric final verse is his way of laughing in the face of our and perhaps his own doubts. (And yes, by "his" I mean Dylan's; the songwriter, not the singer, seems in charge here.) "I want you"–the words–either carry a Hermetic resonance, or they are purely demonic. You make the call.

## IV

That leaves "Absolutely Sweet Marie," and this is definitely a case of saving the best for last. It's not just the best of the minor songs on *Blonde on Blonde*, but it's possibly the best of all of Dylan's minor songs. In part that is because it contains some of the most exuberantly seductive poetry Dylan has written. The lyric is the voice of Hermes at his most insolently playful.

Although, like many other Dylan songs, it is often mistaken as merely a put-down, "Sweet Marie" has its primary impact as a comically implacable come-on. Its seamless blend of gallantry and impudence–in its deliciously limber-jointed rhythms and its insinuating imagery and diction–is positively awe-inspiring. I mean, just listen to this:

*Your railroad gate*
*you know I just can't jump it*
*Sometimes it gets so*
*hard you see*
*I'm just sitting here*
*beating on my trumpet*
*With all these promises you*
*left for me*
*But where you are tonight*
*Sweet Marie*

I hate to spoil the splendor of this by attempting to parse its meanings, but I've discovered that many of my friends are surprised by what I hear in this, so I guess I'd better. The "gate," here as in "I Want You" and the chorus of "Sad-Eyed Lady of the Lowlands," is a trope for access to the woman–a figure you should take as spiritually and as pornographically as you can imagine–and it's a "railroad" gate for reasons I have discussed elsewhere: the train is Dylan's master trope for the power and promise he finds in women. In the second half of this line, "just can't" is strategically ambivalent: it expresses both a frustrated inability to overcome the barriers Marie has set up and a gallant refusal to take her by force. The second line, by virtue of the audacious pun on "hard," transmutes this doubleness into an uneasy stalemate between plaint and menace. The aura of gallantry is considerably tarnished, however, by the narcissistic–hell, onanistic–line that follows. The "trumpet" is the singer's instrument of access to Marie–again, a figure with spiritual and pornographic dimensions. Both his frustration and his resourcefulness are figured in the fact that we find him "beating on" it–not the way to make music with a trumpet, though we are free, I suppose, to think of that instrument, so employed, as what the singer in "Sad-Eyed Lady of the Lowlands" meant by his "Arabian drums."

In any event, all this serves primarily to set up the fourth line, a punch line whose suggestion of disappointment and loss is all but overwhelmed by an outrageous sense of deeper satisfactions. This latter tone is conveyed largely through little touches of diction and of rhythm. "*These* promises" carries a sense of present possession that "the promises" would not and that "those promises" would deny, and "all these" deepens the suggestion of fullness. And the placement of the caesura isolates the syntax of "you left for me" and forces us to hear it as the claim of a gift received, as if her promises, like so many porn magazines scattered around him, have been transmuted into the props of his self-delighting desire.

On the other hand, the singer still genuinely–and desiringly–wonders "where you are tonight, Sweet Marie." We never doubt this, even as we never doubt his self-sufficiency. This improbable, provoking mix–of generosity and narcissism, of gallantry and impudence–gives this lyric its flavor and charm. Indeed, I would suggest that this stance–an aggressive variant, perhaps by way of Miss Dickinson, of Whitman's characteristic tone–is Dylan's singular contribution to the Hermetic personality. That is, "Absolutely Sweet Marie" is arguably the most Dylanesque of all of Dylan's love songs.

Or, at least parts of it are. If "Sweet Marie" tempts us to take it as a major song–by which I mean a song that contains and is not contained by even the strongest interpretations–that is largely because it does not adhere to a single mode or stance. The middle verses occupy emotional and imaginative ground that's much closer to the baffled, wounded world of the album's major songs than to the charmed playground of its minor songs. This versatility of mode stems, I think, from the fact that "Sweet Marie" engages "you," its listener who is called Marie, more deeply and more seriously than any of the other Hermetic songs.

These middle verses are all complaint, but their plaintiveness is all but swallowed up in and dissolved by the singer's buoyant self-sufficiency. The charmed playground prevails in the Hermetic discontinuities of the lyric's narrative premises from verse to verse and of each verse's resolving trope. The second verse, for instance, finds the singer recalling when he "waited for" Marie, "half sick" with love (or lust), inside the "frozen traffic" of her indifference to his affections. The knockout punch–she kept him waiting even though "you knew I had some/other place to be"–both deepens the pathos of all this and blows it away with the promise implied by that "other place." And since that "other place" is with Marie, or more precisely, a place he hopes to get to when with Marie–that's why he wants her–it is a promise thrown out here for Marie as well as for himself.

In the next verse, the image of the singer as lovesick inside the frozen traffic is transmogrified into the image of him receiving Marie's gifts from inside the "penitentiary." The gifts are "six white horses," an image that in blues tradition is usually associated with death and funerals, but here I think they are the same "six white horses" that will bring her "comin' round the mountain" in the nursery rhyme, a song Dylan recorded with the Band during the Basement Tapes sessions. They are, that is, emblems of the promise of sex, so that their funereal connotations are not, especially on *this* album, out of place after all. (The fact that "horse" is a slang term for heroin is also not unfortuitous.) I say the horses symbolize the promise of sex, but in fact, here they represent the betrayal of those promises. In ways that are extremely difficult to pin down, this opening couplet powerfully evokes a sense of having been had, perhaps for the simple reason that he remains unliberated from the penitentiary even after he has received them, perhaps because the horses are merely "delivered" and not presented. It's as if the long-awaited lover wasn't in the coach or wagon when it finally came around the mountain!

What, one may justifiably ask, is really going on here? What are we talking about? Well, there are no doubt several ways of answering that question, of novelizing the story this lyric is telling in its own Hermetic fashion. No one such novelization can claim any objective superiority over any other, but we need to be able to come up with some plausible answer, if only to maintain some connection to the world of the song. My own view is that what's going on here is what seems to be going on throughout *Blonde on Blonde*: the singer is complaining that he got the promised sex but not the promise of it, the flower but not its bloom.

He's played the game, done his part, and gotten his reward–but at the same time has been cheated of it. You can play by the rules, it seems, and still not play fair.

But that is famously *not* what he says. He doesn't say, "To live by the law, apparently you don't have to be honest." No, he leaps to its obverse, again thrown out as a liberating promise to himself and to Marie alike, adding, with breathtakingly insolent charm, "You know you always say that you agree." The singer knows full well that Marie and his song's larger audience have probably never even conceived this thought before hearing it from him just now.* This line–"To live outside the law you must be honest" opens (Hermetically) a door not only in this song but in all of our experience.

The singer, at this moment in his song, has broken jail and loosed all the bonds, dancing beneath the sky with both hands waving free. It seems to me that right here Dylan's singer, in his poetic identity, is as free as anywhere in any Dylan song, before or since. It's entirely apt then that he pauses right here to interpolate, as a bridge, his most thrillingly divine Hermetic gambit:

*I don't know how it happened*
*But the riverboat captain*
*He knows my fate*
*But everybody else*
*Even yourself*
*They're just gonna have to wait*

The "riverboat captain" I take to be Dylan's domestication of the Greek Charon, the mythic ferryman who conveys the dead across the river Styx to Hades. (And don't ask me how *he* found his way here.) So, yes,

---

* Well, you might have heard something like it. This line–"to live outside the law you must be honest"–is an early instance, it appears, of Dylan's penchant for filching lines from old movies. "When you live outside the law, you have to eliminate dishonesty"–a line from the obscure 1958 crime drama *The Lineup*–says the same thing as Dylan's reworking, but it lacks its resonant force and barbed panache. Dylan turns a poetic thought into poetry.

the singer concedes, the common human fate awaits me too, and the riverboat captain, with his uncanny knowledge of me, will make sure I don't escape or even forget that fate. But meanwhile, the rest of you can't get to me by playing upon my mortality. Fear of death, that is, will in no way compromise the freedom of my life. This bridge is the finest poetic expression I know of that illusion of immortality that is the blessing of youth.

This bridge also performs its function within the song, as an assurance to Marie (and perhaps to himself) that the singer's desire won't be undone by her betrayals. Thus, in the next verse all plaintiveness is dissolved within a charmed comedy, one in which the singer's imprisoning lust is now figured both as the "fever" he keeps "down in my pockets," and as the "Persian drunkard" who "follows" but does not lead him to Marie's still locked abode. All this Chaplinesquerie is clearly meant to seduce Marie with its charm, and it's hard to imagine her not tossing the key down to him from her window.

And perhaps she does. The final verse seems to be sung from the vantage point of a renewed intimacy. Its tone is a bit spoiled, for me at least, by the churlish opening couplet, a backward glance at the time spent in jail, a time when Marie proved to be "bad company." Or maybe what bothers me is just the comparatively clumsy writing, the only fly in the song's otherwise resplendent lyrical ointment. In any case, this couplet has a definite "that was then" flavor that is balanced by the "this is now" with which the final couplet presents us:

*And now I stand here looking at your*
*yellow railroad*
*In the ruins of*
*your balcony*

This certainly makes up for whatever might be wrong with the preceding couplet! Marie, we seem to discover here, is a blonde, and the image of her "yellow railroad" blends her attractiveness and her erotic power in a figure that, when Dylan was asked to comment upon it, provoked him to offer that "there's something about my lyrics that just have a gallantry to them." Dylan says the figure may have been suggested to him by the sight of railroad ties glinting with sunlight,* but his comment seems to address the gallantry in naming something this way, bestowing upon it a gift of beauty. My own emphasis, as with similar moves throughout this song, is on the gallantry of its use in this context, on the way it restores a broken sense of promise. This is even more richly the case with the succeeding line. The "ruins of [her] balcony" is a euphemism for Marie deflowered. But her balcony, while in ruins of a sort, is not altogether gone, either. Its virginal aura, in her lover's gallant perception, still attends her. And this time, when the refrain comes round for a final turn, the singer does not just ask but admits to "wonderin'" where Marie is tonight, and this time it sounds like he actually anticipates a response of some sort.

And one last thing. Why "Marie?" I think I know: she's a grown-up version of the little girl Chuck Berry is trying to get back to in "Memphis, Tennessee" except this time it's the singer who has "hurry-home drops" in his eyes.

V

It's amazing how things turn out sometimes, isn't it? I began my discussion of *Blonde on Blonde* by calling it Dylan's most nakedly personal album and by observing that nowhere else is his persona so demythologized and its psychic vulnerabilities so ruthlessly exposed. But by the time we get to the bottom of it all, that persona reveals itself as some sort of demigod. And this album is not even the first in which I have promised that we would see Dylan dismount what I think I called his transcendental high horse. Well, this transcendental cat appears to possess the proverbial nine lives–and maybe more!

And though it's taken me an astonishing long while, what I have had to say about *Blonde on Blonde* merely scratches the surface of what I have come to call its Hermetic slipperiness. Before letting it go, though,

* Paul Zollo, "Bob Dylan: The SongTalk Interview," p. 37-39.

I want to draw attention to another aspect of that Hermetic splendor, and one which probably has more to do with its revered status among Dylan's fans than any other.

In my discussion of the playfulness in the language of "Visions of Johanna," I examined in some detail the line about the night watchman. Well, when I chose that line as if a randomly chosen example, I must confess I was cheating. I chose that line, unconsciously but with what I now recognize as a cunning evasiveness, because the figure of the night watchman is comparatively easy to explain. We know how he belongs in the song and we recognize him from our own experience. In this, the night watchman is like comparable figures in earlier Dylan songs–Cinderella, Miss Lonely's diplomat, Baby Blue's orphan, etc. We take them rather readily, and without having much to think about it, as allegories, as figures for something we already know or have heard about from real life. These are often things that we didn't have a handy name for before Dylan furnished one–that's one reason we treasure these figures so–but we recognize them. They live outside the song.

That's not always the case on *Blonde on Blonde*. For instance, I had no difficulty placing Ruthie in the symbolic economy of "Memphis Blues Again," but I didn't have much to say about Ruthie herself, did I? How do we place her in the economy of our own imagination? I don't think we do, or if we do, those placings prove to be very unstable. I have come up with an explanation of that sort for Ruthie before, but I'll be damned if I can remember what it was I came up with or, right this moment anyway, come up with it again. And that happens all the time to me in thinking about this album, and only this album. These songs possess a wonderful immunity, while we are listening to them, to violation by any ideas we might have had about them. I find it a lot easier to place myself or people I know in terms of Ruthie than to place Ruthie in terms of anything I know from life. Same thing with Mona Lisa's highway blues, and the ghost of electricity, and even that damn fish truck–not to mention the divine Johanna, who metamorphoses, in the course of the song, from the obscure focus of the singer's anxieties into the radiant source and guardian of his visions of freedom. Louise and

Johanna are the Magdalene and Mary of a prophetic tradition of which "Visions of Johanna," we might fancy, is the only surviving liturgical text.

These figures are not allegorical symbols. They are myths. They create the possibility of talking and thinking about the realities they show forth. And though the term gets thrown around by critics a lot, even by those who are using it in its proper sense, you don't actually encounter mythmaking in poetry all that much. Sure, there's a lot of mythopoeic revisionism–potent stuff in its own right–but poets just don't go around coining myths, let alone coining them as if incidentally, without seeming to give it much thought or ballyhoo. And when you do encounter it, and encounter it lying all around as if mere throwaway, it kinda just knocks your socks off in a way nothing else in your aesthetic experience really can.

And this quality of imaginative intensity and freshness often shows itself in such unassuming guises. Consider the little boy lost (a myth filched from Blake) who "takes himself so seriously." If you attend those words carelessly, you'll translate it as "too seriously." Lighten up, kid–that's the message. But "so seriously" does not mean "too seriously." In fact, little boy lost takes himself with exactly the right degree of seriousness, given the circumstances. That's his problem! He is too merely a creature of his pathetically all-too-human circumstances. And while this is true, that is not what "so seriously" says either. What does it say, you ask? Well, dear reader, 25,000 or so words later, I'll finally give you a break. You tell me.

And whatever you do, don't take it so seriously!

# 9

## *John Wesley Harding*

### The Comeback to End All Comebacks

It's a familiar tale. Bob Dylan returned home at the end of May 1966 from the maelstrom of his world tour, and in late July he suffered a motorcycle crash that, while serious enough on its own terms, he quickly deployed as a cover for a greater crash of his creative will. And he disappeared–perhaps permanently, as we all worried at the time. By early 1967 he was beginning to recover his creative energies in a series of informal sessions with his old band–itself on the verge of discovering its own identity as The Band–sessions that we now know as the Basement Tapes. But we didn't know anything about that then.

No, the first we heard again from our prodigal minstrel boy was at the tail end of 1967, when *John Wesley Harding* was released. "You can always come back, but you can't come back all the way," Dylan tells us on his most recent comeback album, *Love and Theft*. *John Wesley Harding* was his first comeback, and it still remains, after all these years, his most surprising. Taking his cue from the comically enigmatic parable Dylan supplied as liner notes, critic John Landau famously termed the Dylan who returned to us on this album a "moderate man."*

---

* John Landau, "John Wesley Harding," in McGregor, *A Retrospective*, p. 248-263.

Never mind if Landau is right or not. If, before the release of this record, you had asked anyone–anyone in the world–what sort of man this Dylan guy is, "moderate man" is decidedly not one of the answers you would have ever heard. It would have been insanely inapt. The Dylan who shows up on this record performs the most astonishingly abrupt about-face in the history of–well, I don't know how broadly to cast my net here, but it's a lot wider than the mere history of rock 'n' roll.

The change strikes us immediately in the music–the electric rock 'n' roll band has been ditched for an acoustic ensemble dominated by Dylan's guitar and harmonica–and in the song forms, which abandon the experimental baroque expansiveness of *Blonde on Blonde* for short, simple, folk-flavored ballads with no novelty and little variety of form. Eight of its twelve songs are composed of three quatrains, six of which even use the same *aabb* rhyme scheme. (Actually, the stanza Dylan uses can be conceived either as quatrains composed of fourteeners or octets in common meter.) A ninth–"The Ballad of Frankie Lee and Judas Priest"–is the proverbial exception that proves the rule, a tale of self-indulgent craziness, in eleven quatrains, that shows that, on this album anyway, self-indulgent craziness gets you nowhere. A tenth–"Dear Landlord"–differs only in filling the prevailing *aabb* rhyme scheme with a looser metric. The other two–the last two songs on the album–are genuine exceptions that I will take up later.

These formal reversals signal deeper imaginative reversals. While the songs on *Blonde on Blonde* assume the form of theatrical epiphanies of the singer's Hermetic freedom, the songs on *John Wesley Harding*–the last two again excepted–take the form of narrated parables about the treacheries of self-reliance–parables toward which the singer's attitude is variously troubled, and often simply enigmatic. Listen, for instance, to the album's opening verse:

*John Wesley Harding*
*was a friend to the poor*
*He traveled with a*
*gun in every hand*

*All along this countryside*
*he opened many a door*
*But he was never known to*
*hurt an honest man*

And so on, for two more stanzas, and then for eleven more songs. The spendthrift figurative grandeur and rhythmic pizzazz of *Blonde on Blonde* give way here to a plainness of diction and modesty of gait that is more than merely ascetic. There is an unmistakable purgatorial air to the proceedings, one that, to run ahead briefly, makes the singer of the last two songs–"I'll Be Your Baby Tonight" and "Down Along the Cove"–sound like a man who's just been released from jail.

One way to get at the source of this purgatorial flavor is to note that the singer's relationship to what he is singing is deeply ironic–even if we don't know that Dylan's John Wesley Harding is based on a meaner-than-dirt Texas gunslinger who once allegedly killed a man for snoring–and whose name was Hardin.* The entire narrative is a series of transparently dubious personal judgments, a tissue of dodges or evasions or wishful thinkings or spin doctorings or, as Michael Gray was the first to point out, perhaps outright lies. The singer here is no less a poet than the singer on *Blonde on Blonde*, but he is a most discomforting and discomforted poet. It's almost as if he sings plain so as not to call attention, even his own, to himself.

We better start calling this singer the persona, since the actual singer–the guy whose voice we hear on the record and who in fact wrote this song–is largely hidden, another persona altogether, even if the persona in his song may represent some part of him. Our persona, then, takes great pains, as Gray noted,** to maintain for Harding an immaculate reputation as a folk hero, an American Robin Hood. He lives outside the law, but he does only good. I don't share Gray's con-

* A brief biography at famoustexans.com concludes by noting that "Despite his killing of over thirty people, Hardin had a reputation as a gentleman among those who knew him, and he always claimed he never killed anyone who didn't need killing." That sure sounds like Dylan's man!

** *Song and Dance Man III*, pp. 33-35.

viction that the main thrust of this transparent mythmaking is to call into question the validity of our (or anyone else's) cultural myths. To be sure, it does that, but I don't think the main focus of the song is the culture–a largely folk culture, in fact–that perpetrates these myths upon itself. I think Dylan's interest is on the man who is mythologized.

Listening to the song, we not only notice the element of self-deception in myth, we also imagine how all this must feel to the outlaw for whom the myth affords a kind of protection and even impunity. In short, we can hear the song as a tale with which the folk community entertains itself, or as a tale with which Harding comforts himself. Further, we need to imagine that Harding believes, or wants to believe his own myth–perhaps justifiably. This song, that is, is an effort–made by someone who should know–to show what it is like, and what it takes, and what it means, to live as a hero-villain outside the law, and to do so in good faith.

And what is it like? Well, stressful is one word that leaps to mind. Pick almost any line–"no charge against him could be proved." OK. Imagine that. Imagine that Harding is secretly guilty of these unnamed but numerous charges, or imagine him utterly innocent. It makes no matter. They'll always be there, the old charges, and there are surely more where they came from, and it's only a matter of time before someone figures out, guilty or not, how to prove them, maybe even how to prove them to the satisfaction of Harding himself, who had perhaps all along thought himself innocent. Hell, it's only a matter of time before Harding turns himself in just to get it over with. Maybe that's one reason this song is so short: by the fifth verse or so, he'd have to shoot himself! If this is a song Harding is singing to himself, a fantasy of his own epitaph, then apparently even he feels he hasn't got much longer. Perhaps the song is an allegory meant to explain why the 1966 world tour–an outlaw-on-the-run saga if there ever was one–just could not go on.

But it's not just that either. We are all, in our best moments, however rare they may be, outlaws on the run, if only from the compromises of our own lives. Harding's plight, in many smaller ways, is also ours. My own favorite line–"And soon the situation there was all but straightened out"–resonates in an especially pungent way with the good-enough-for-government-work flimsiness that often passes for a clean conscience, even as, looked at the other way round, it eloquently expresses the residue of enigma we find when we do conscientiously examine the moral consequences of our actions.

Or consider this line: "He was never known to hurt an honest man." This does not quite claim that he never hurt an honest man; it's just that if he has, no one has heard of it. But there's more. If we imagine this as a line Harding sings to himself, and if we imagine him singing it in good faith, then we can imagine that for him the words that would suddenly italicize themselves would be not (or not only) "never known" but "honest man." What is an "honest" man anyway, and who gets to make the call? Who validates your belief that the people you treated badly–let alone, as we are to imagine Harding having done, shot dead–had it coming? That's what the law is for, isn't it? But the law is no help to an unreconstructed outlaw when he's having his doubts about himself. "To live outside the law you must be honest," Dylan blithely sang less than two years earlier. Now he's showing us that you must also do something very much like play God with the people in your life. "He was never known to make a foolish move," the song ends, but by this point we know that he knows–and the folks who would celebrate him also know–that there is very little about his moral status that anyone can really be sure about. Little beyond his name, that is, which he knows, even if we don't, was Hardin, not Harding!

By the end of the song, that is, both Harding and his mythmakers are audibly losing whatever faith in his self-reliant verve the song may have started with. And while Dylan, in composing and singing this song, has clearly regained his own self-reliant verve, here, he deploys it against itself, or at least against its own mythology.

Something analogous happens in "The Wicked Messenger," a sort of companion song to "Harding" (they share the same variant rhyme scheme, *abab)* that exhibits similar complexities of perspective. Here the singer does appear to be identical with the narrative persona, but his narrative does engage the points of view of the messenger and his audience–another folk community of sorts–in subtle and shifty ways.

The "wicked messenger," himself an extremely odd fellow, is the antithesis of the outlaw Harding; he is rather the archetypal *inlaw,* a lackey and a flatterer incapable of honest speech. He also has a "mind that multiplied the smallest matter," a splendidly pithy formulation of the make-work trivialization of the stuff of life that often seems to be modus operandi of organized society.

By the end of the first verse this messenger looms as an especially toxic figure, a paragon of wickedness, and we are likely to assume, I think, that the townsfolk perceive this urbane weasel "from Eli" more or less as the narrator asks us to. But it is useful to note that this is an assumption we make. The narrative is deeply enigmatic, even riddling. Does the messenger's thumb gesture successfully identify "who had sent for him," and does he ever learn what message he is to deliver, or to whom?

So it is not at all clear what the messenger is doing taking up quarters, when the second verse opens, "behind the assembly hall." Waiting for his instructions? And where is it that he is "oftentimes" seen "returning" from? Nothing is clear, but there is a creepy sense that he has infested the town, and is up to no good. But then, most surprisingly,

*Until one day he just appeared*
*with a note in his hand which read,*
*"The soles of my feet, I*
*swear they're burning."*

If this is his message, at last delivered, it is not at all what we expected. It is preposterously out of character. It sounds like something the outlaw John Wesley Harding might have cried out once the comforting spell of his song had shattered–or very much like something the outlaw Bob Dylan had recently cried out in the then unreleased Basement Tapes song "This Wheel's on Fire." What are we to make of this? Is he delivering someone else's message, or his own? When he "answered with his thumb," who did he point to? Himself? It's beginning to seem that way. The "wicked" messenger is beginning, in fact, to seem a lot like one of the self-confounding grotesques in Sherwood Anderson's *Winesburg, Ohio*. It's as if all along he has been nursing in his soul a prophetic impulse for which his glibness of tongue has been both an inept preparation and an unconscious, compulsive evasion. It is notable, too, that he can still express this prophetic impulse only in a written note. His tongue is still hostage to flattery. Perhaps we are to understand that his release from that spell depends on how his message is received.

If so, he is out of luck. His apocalyptic message does prove uncannily prophetic: the leaves begin to fall, the seas to part. We can take this in any number of ways, but for me, it is a simple index of the rending effect these words have on an audience in no way prepared to hear of it: this message blows their cover. The townsfolk, unsurprisingly, are not amused and quickly confront him with their displeasure:

*And he was told but these few words,*
*which opened up his heart,*
*"If ye cannot bring good news, then*
*don't bring any."*

This is grim, as bleakly chilling a satire as Dylan has ever managed. The messenger's heart–his natural fellow-feeling–horribly betrays him, so that, just like many of Anderson's grotesques, his emergent imagination sinks obligingly back into oblivion. What they are saying to him, unconsciously to be sure, is "resume your flattery of us–just don't be so oily about it. It makes us uneasy, as if you were making fun of us."

"John Wesley Harding" and "The Wicked Messenger" are the first and the last in the sequence of ten songs that comprises the main body of *John Wesley Harding*, an album that, like none before it and few (if any) since, Dylan seems to have composed as a unified suite of songs. Interestingly, it was the first (and maybe still the only) time he wrote the lyrics first, without music. In my own experience listening to it, it is also the first Dylan album on which the songs conspire with each other, as if they are taking turns having a go at the same underlying preoccupation. (I find a similar sort of thing on *Slow Train Coming* and *Oh Mercy,* Dylan's two other purgatorial albums.)

I would suggest that the persistent concern that ripples kaleidoscopically through these songs has to do with the limits of self-reliance as guarantor of individual freedom. The thrust of the album is to purge from self-reliance any sense of mere willfulness, so that self reliance is validated only insofar as it is experienced as a surrender to an inner prompting that I call the spirit. A willful self-reliance is represented by John Wesley Harding and his mythologizers, but the surrender to the spirit is merely parodied by the "wicked" messenger's submission to the will of the townsfolk. This much is orthodox Emersonianism. But as we shall see, on this album Dylan shies away from embracing even a genuine self-reliance, which he seems to identify with the spirit of prophecy. The album's deepest critique of the Emersonian tradition of self-reliance is made against its facile democratization. Self-reliance, Dylan seems to be telling us, is not for everyone. And even for the chosen few–like himself–it is not for all times.

## II

"John Wesley Harding" is followed by two dream songs, the first ("As I Went Out One Morning") drawing upon American historical mythology and the other ("I Dreamed I Saw St. Augustine") drawing upon a Biblical ethos. The former is entirely a dream, or dream vision, one that is steeped in the sense of anxiety and foreboding with which "John Wesley Harding" ended. It is also unique, as far as I can tell, among Dylan's songs in that it is an allegory of ideas and not an allegory anchored directly in experience. In short, it sounds like a tale out of Hawthorne rather than Melville.

The story is a simple one: the singer, breathing "the air around Tom Paine's," spies a damsel walking in chains. His offer to help her quickly turns into his resistance of her attempt to seduce his heart. At this point "Tom Paine himself" comes running toward them, shouting at her to desist, and as she lets go her grip on the singer's arm, Paine arrives in time to apologize for her behavior. The terms of the allegory seem transparent enough: Paine, the radical pamphleteer of the American

Revolution, is the spirit of independence–what Emerson would later teach us to call self-reliance–and the damsel is Miss Liberty, the soul of freedom. The singer we can call Young Goodman Bob.

So what does this story tell us? That's hard to say–mainly, I find, because it's hard to know exactly what it means for Miss Liberty to be in chains. What was her transgression, and against whom? What I do know is that the song turns uncanny each time it comes to the resolving cadence of the third line of a verse. The first instance occurs when Goodman Bob offers his help:

*I offered her my hand*
*she took me by the arm*

The turnabout from the first to the second half of this line causes a shudder every time I hear it. "My hand" is only vaguely physical; he probably just means "I offered her a hand"–i.e., made some vague offer of help. I think what happens is that she accepts his offer, but her acceptance entails more than he bargained for. Taking him by the arm initiates an intimacy he had not foreseen, and the fact that she "took" him at all challenges his initiative and threatens his mastery of the situation. His conclusion–"that very instant"–that "she meant to do me harm" seems rather precipitous, even delusional.

The second verse turns on another action by Miss Liberty. Having been ordered to "depart from me this moment" and having been summarily warned that she has "no choice" in the matter, she puts herself at her master's mercy:

*"I beg you sir," she pleaded*
*from the corners of her mouth*

Now, I don't know what it means to speak from the "corners" (as opposed to "corner") of one's mouth. But I do know that Goodman Bob is noticing the corners of her mouth as she speaks–perhaps she's smiling. Unlike his own ("I told her with my voice") hers is a voice that is embodied in ways he can't help but notice and be drawn to. This verse concludes not with his moralizing containment of her but with the seductive sound of her offer to accept him–"secretly," no less–and escape with him to the south.

No doubt this is why Tom Paine "himself" suddenly appears, hurrying toward them from across the field. Goodman Bob seems to be wavering in his independence. Miss Liberty knows better than to disobey Mr. Independence; she responds–immediately it seems–to his command that she "yield":

*As she was letting go her grip*
***up** Tom Paine did run*

The emphasis is added: "up" is the most disturbingly uncanny word in the song: It's as if he arrives so abruptly–he's "up" before he "runs" up–as to make it seem that he's always been there, so that the breach of his absence is no longer imaginable. That seems to be the effect he is seeking, anyway. His appearance on the scene in this fashion evokes both a barely concealed panic and a frightfully peremptory mastery–something Goodman Bob has been seeking all along. Paine's mastery of Miss Liberty is meant, I suspect, to awaken our memories of all the suppressions of liberty throughout American history and expose them as the heritage of that religiously independent male will that has always seen itself as the guardian of liberty. Paine's concluding apology to Goodman Bob–"I'm sorry for what she's done"–is positively Blakean in its grisly hypocrisy.

And how does Young Goodman Bob himself feel about all this? We don't know–he disappeared from his own song for good back there while still absorbed in the corners of her mouth–but I suspect he feels as anxiously troubled as the listener does. In any case, such a mood certainly suffuses the next song, a dream that this time the singer presents as a dream, one he will seek to master.

Dylan's St. Augustine does not appear to be too deeply implicated in the 4th- and 5th-century bishop of Hippo. He is simply a figure of impressive spiritual power. The singer's dream, set to the tune of the labor song "Joe Hill," identifies him as a figure of compassion ("blanket underneath his arm") and spiritual wealth ("coat of solid gold") who searches for lost souls. But otherwise he is most unsaintly in his demeanor, "tearing through these quarters in the utmost misery." It's not his misery that seems out of place so much as his violent "tearing." He seems more lion than saint, and more roaring angel than either.

St. Augustine's speech to the people of the world is a most remarkable imagining. In a nutshell, he tells them–"with a voice without restraint"–that although their generation has no "martyr" of its own, don't worry, live your lives, you haven't been abandoned ("not alone"). The implication, I think, is that Augustine is offering himself as their "martyr" in making this speech. A martyr, in its original sense, is one who bears witness to the truths of spirit and soul, and who does so come hell or high water, even unto death. The fundamental truth to which St. Augustine here bears witness is contained in the magnificent terms in which he addresses his people: "ye gifted Kings and Queens," and it is to this visionary sense of themselves that he calls upon them to "Arise! Arise!"

The singer, however, is not consoled.

*I dreamed I saw St. Augustine*
*alive with fiery breath*
*And I dreamed I was there amongst the ones*
*that put him out to death*
*Oh, I awoke in anger*
*so alone and terrified*
*I put my fingers against the glass*
*and bowed my head and cried*

The opening line recapitulates the second verse, in terms ("fiery breath") that hint that St. Augustine is the prophetic voice–a voice that by suppressing in himself the singer has helped martyr, in the ordinary sense of the word: "put him out to death." The word "out" in "put him out to death" suggests that Augustine's death is a kind of banishment, which accords with the condition of ghostly exile, "tearing through these quarters," in which he enters the song. This voice, it needs to be noted, is more than the voice of Tom Paine, of independent self-reliance, though it certainly subsumes self-reliance. But it also includes dimensions represented in that visionary democracy of ordinary people as "Kings and Queens" that take us back to Dylan's first song, with its sweet sense of the struggling community the lost and the found, of the "princes, and paupers, and peasants, and kings," who make up this "funny old world."

The singer awakens from his dream "in anger," presumably at his own self-betrayal, and "alone and terrified," because in his self-betrayal he has exiled himself from the comfort of Augustine's blessing and can hear only the "fiery breath." But "alone and terrified" is also an apt response to his sense of what it might cost to reclaim that prophetic voice. The song ends uncertainly and ambiguously. The singer "bows his head" not in prayer but in tears. But "and cried" also echoes the voice in which Augustine "cried" his blessing. Perhaps the lion in him is stirring, perhaps not.

"All Along the Watchtower" arises out of this ambiguity. This song is, far and away, the best song on John Wesley Harding, and it's one of Dylan's most potent creations. The song's first two verses are cast as a conversation between "the joker" and "the thief," characters who emanate from a deeper level of the imagination than those we encounter elsewhere on the album. There is something merely provisional about John Wesley Harding, Tom Paine and Miss Liberty, St. Augustine, the wicked messenger, and all the others. They seem to have been created simply to serve the purposes of their song, in part by *limiting* its attention to the matter at hand. "All Along the Watchtower" may have started out the same way–one often has the sense that Dylan stumbles onto his finest imaginings–but there is nothing provisional about its central figures. They are primal beings, figures of myth, central figures in what, if we were ever moved to sketch it out, we would discover to be Dylan's own myth of what he later called "the war against the spirit." One could write an entire book on this matter, and since I'm not about to–not yet anyway–let me just propose that the joker and the thief are Dylan's names, respectively, for the profane and the sacred aspects of trickster, the mythic master of limits and boundaries. The difference between these two figures, here and throughout Dylan's work, is that the joker merely evades limits; the thief finds ways to render them permeable.

In the opening verse of "Watchtower," the joker superbly articulates the undercurrent of feeling that has been gathering through the album's first three songs, a sense of the beleaguredness of the imaginative spirit in the world it inhabits. In a way that reverberates fundamentally with our sense of the moods of John Wesley Harding, Young Goodman Bob, and the St. Augustine's prodigal son, the joker is looking for "someway outta here," and he sounds stumped, and more than a little desperate. Yet, before collapsing into silence, he provides, by way of defining the "here" he is looking for "someway outta," this unsurpassable definition of what's wrong with the society we all live in:

*Businessmen they drink my wine*
*Plowmen dig my earth*
*None of them along the line*
*Know what any of it is worth*

The first two lines sum up the grievance of sentimental socialism; the latter two–the ones that matter–have yet to find a political sponsor and probably never will.* The joker's desperation is indeed warranted.

The thief's response, which occupies the second verse, nonetheless reduces the joker's complaint to monkey chatter.

*No reason to get excited*
*The thief he kindly spoke*

* In fact, the second line subtly initiates the transition between these two ideas. This line may sound at first like a mere variation on the idea of the first line--the bosses or landlords confiscate the fruits of my labor--but that reading doesn't hold up under close inspection. The "plowmen" are laborers, too, after all, working in all likelihood for the same bosses. The key word here is "dig," an odd verb for the action of a plow, which is usually said to "cut" a furrow. The sense, I think, is that the plowmen's labor is not cultivating but somehow abusing and degrading "my earth." The most depressing thought then--one that makes this quatrain a proverb about the plight of those living under runaway capitalism--is not that we don't get our fair share but that no one, including our exploiters, accomplishes or acquires anything of real value.

*There are many here among us*
*Who feel that life is but a joke*
*But you and I we've been through that*
*And this is not our fate*
*So let us not talk falsely now*
*The hour is getting late*

The sublimity–and the art–of this verse cannot, to my mind anyway, be overstated. To get a bearing on it, it might help to recognize that this verse is "Ballad of a Thin Man" revisited: the authentic imagination is putting its anxious spectre in its place. The difference, of course, is the kindness with which this is accomplished–and we don't really need the singer to tell us "he kindly spoke" to hear that kindness for ourselves. The thief is doing his best to bring the joker along, to help him prepare himself for the apocalyptic moment–the moment that *is* "our fate"–toward which the lateness of the hour is taking them. The thief says all the right things here, but more importantly he says those things in a voice that carries a gospel authority. And I mean that literally. The thief is Jesus, not theologically but poetically: the voice-print is identical.

The final verse is a glorious dodge of the oncoming moment of truth. Dylan has said that this verse comes first in the chronology of his tale, and while that is not inevitably the way you have to look at it–I have always imagined it to be simultaneous with the opening two-verse conversation–he certainly could have begun the song with it. But that would have severely weakened the lyric. The power of this final verse depends in great part on the immanence throughout it of that final moment toward which the hour is rushing.

The princes are keeping watch, anxious not so much that the moment of truth will bring dire things but that they will have to face any moment of truth at all. Perhaps they are afraid of losing "their women" and their suggestively "barefoot" servants. Barefootedness in Dylan is an emblem of vision, but vision is not the service the princes are likely to request from their servants. Theirs is a time-serving world, and they are unprepared to see themselves or be seen under the aspect of eternity. The growling wildcat and howling wind they hear in the near distance are emblems of the voice of prophecy. The princes's world *is* going to end soon, but only in the Blakean sense, in being submitted to a prophetic uncovering of the realities obscured, to borrow an image from "St. Augustine," by the "glass" of time.

The thief is not merely ready for this apocalypse; he is the agent of it. What about the joker? Hard to say. The joker, among other things, is the mortal part of Dylan's imagination, the voice we merely hear, while the thief is the immortal part, the voice we imagine listening to, the voice we must steal from the song. On *John Wesley Harding*, the joker in Dylan sings the song's final couplet in a deadpan: we don't know if he's teasing us or if he is uncertain in his own heart whether he is part of the rising wind or merely one of the beings it will soon howl down upon. In concert–and Dylan has performed this song as often as any in his repertoire–he almost always leaves no doubt that if he is not the living form of that wind, he's at least its ever-ready evangelist.

One of many remarkable aspects of this most remarkable song is that it manages to keep itself so short. The conversation between the joker and the thief is precisely the sort of imaginative premise that generates Dylan's longest songs. Perhaps that explains why Dylan indulges himself in the bravura eleven-verse nonsense of "The Ballad of Frankie Lee and Judas Priest," a song whose title characters are parodies of the joker and the thief, respectively. Judas Priest–the name itself being a commonplace curse-word euphemism for Jesus Christ–is a most impressively canny Mephistopheles; he seems to have emerged from the darker corners of Melville's *The Confidence-Man*. But Frankie Lee is an even cannier vision of a certain nameless American archetype, a fool for the main chance who is afflicted with a bad conscience that only makes things worse.

There's no point in tracing how Dylan both persuasively works out the details of this all-too-predictable tale and manages to keep it surprising along the way, but I want to draw attention to a couple of things.

The first is that, unlike the four songs that precede it, this tale has little of mystery or enigma about it. Indeed, except for "The Wicked Messenger," the rhetoric of all the remaining songs on the album is as plain as the nose on your face, their meanings hidden in broad daylight. There is a freshening clarity of moral vision in these songs, as if some spiritual cloud has just lifted, that is a major part of their affect. The moral tag that Dylan adds for the final verse is thus more than normally superfluous, and its superfluity here is itself the joke.

And that brings up the other thing to be said about this song. The tale the song relates may itself be grimly humorous, but its telling is simply funny, and its jokiness grows broader, cornier even (especially in the rhymes), as it goes along. The effect is to emphasize the distance between the singer and the spiritual psychology that drives his tale forward, as if it were a tale about an alien species. The contradictory blend of this aesthetic distance with the canny insider's knowledge with which Frankie Lee's psychology is represented accounts for the song's distinctive flavor, a kind of giddy relief over its own recently recovered moral sanity. The "little neighbor boy"–who I take to be identical with the "stranger" who delivers the message that launches Frankie Lee on his fatal journey–is perhaps best seen as a self-portrait that the singer, "his guilt so well concealed," inserts as a concession to his own residual moral dubiousness.

## III

The next four songs comprise a mini-suite of their own. All of them seem to arise from the singer's renewed moral self-confidence, which we find persuasive in large part because it finds both good and evil within and outside himself. For the first time on this album, the singer sounds like he belongs to–and feels comfortable belonging to–a human community.

For instance, "The Drifter's Escape" is a Kafka parody set in a demonic social and legal order that would sacrifice the drifter to its desperate need to purge guilt from its midst. But the judge, the jury, and the crowd shouting for "more" serve here merely to represent the singer's sense of his own path not taken. What catches our attention are two things, the initial one being the drifter himself, the first character on the album who feels to me like a real person–real, that is, to the singer, and not just an aspect of the singer's sense of himself. And this first person we meet turns out to be a pretty compelling everyman: he knows he's guilty of something, though he's not sure what–and has no reason to believe he's guilty as charged–and he acknowledges that he is weak and needs help. And while the drifter is not merely an aspect of the singer, surely the singer recognizes–as we do–himself in the drifter. This everyman is a fellow man, and the main thrust of the song seems to be to release the freshness of that feeling of humankindness, as if something just discovered. The other thing that catches our attention is that surprising couple, "the attendant and the nurse." Their instinctive outrage at the "cursed jury" strikes a note we haven't heard in Dylan's songs since–well, let's say since "Chimes of Freedom." The attendant and the nurse, however belatedly and ineffectually, apparently share the singer's sense of human kinship. For the first time in years, let alone on this album, the singer in a Dylan song does not feel so terribly alone in the moral company of his fellows. And while God may or may not have heard and been surprised by all this, the singer–who is the god of his own song–sure does. Who do you think sent the lightning that "struck the courthouse out of shape?"

"I Am a Lonesome Hobo" feels like a companion to "The Drifter's Escape." The hobo here is the singer, but not, it feels, the singer we hear in the other songs on the album. It's as if the regular singer has gone a step further than acknowledging a fellow lost-but-finding-itself soul and is stepping aside to allow one of his fellows to speak for himself. The hobo is something of a self-made loser, but his opening self-representation lends his fate a universal resonance:

*I am a lonesome hobo*
    *without family or friends*
*Where another man's life might begin*
    *that's exactly where mine ends*

This is to suggest that our kinship with each other is not something we can lose but something we may never find in the first place. Turning on his brother–the crime that precipitated his "fatal doom"–is less a violation of an established spiritual order than an affirmation of an all-too-human natural order the spiritual order, if and when established, will override.

Thus, in the final verse, when the hobo bequeaths his hard-earned wisdom to whoever will listen, he's trying to establish a kinship his words tell us he has despaired of finding. The substance of his bequest is worth pondering:

*Stay free from petty jealousies,*
*live by no man's code,*
*And hold your judgment for yourself*
*lest you wind up on this road.*

"Hold your judgment for yourself" is expected, given what has preceded it. "Stay free from petty jealousies" may seem oddly random, except that "petty jealousies" is likely the crime for which this once enviably wealthy man "carried [his brother] to blame."* To offer it as part of his warning, without recrimination, is thus itself an act of generosity. But what do we make of "live by no man's code." Does he mean no other man's code–no code, that is, but your own? I don't think so–not after having consulted John Wesley Harding on the matter. Does he mean no human code–no code, that is, but a divine revelation? Yeah, maybe–"Love your neighbor as yourself" certainly comes to mind here. But that does not seem to be his main point. After all, the metrical and

* Reading W. T. Lhamon's *Raising Cain* as I was preparing this book for publication, I discover that Dylan's hobo is a descendant of the blackface Cain: "There is in Cain, then, the primary doubleness that his infamous act meant to annihilate. In slaying Abel, Cain struck a reflex blow against preferential differentiation. . . . Cain did not resolve the issues. Rather, he became their sign. He wanders forever betokening doubleness: the cursed man who is protected; the brother-killer who evokes brotherhood; a once-rooted man of agriculture now hoboing through cities; a divided self whose experience broadens the need for fraternal love" (*Raising Cain*, p. 125).

musical stress here is on "code," not on "man." Codes, human or divine, are the things we often invoke to assure ourselves that everything is in order.

Well, kind ladies and kind gentlemen, everything is not in order! Never has been, never will be. That's why humankindness is always so beleaguered a spiritual treasure. Everyone is always in a panic to find someone to blame so it can all be set right, once and for all, just like it used to be, back in that time no one can quite remember. If you don't believe me, just ask the drifter.

"Dear Landlord" and "I Pity the Poor Immigrant" comprise another pair of companion songs. Indeed, the figures of the landlord and the immigrant are deeply related to a pair we have already met, Judas Priest and Frankie Lee. Dylan's landlord is both any landlord, literal or figurative, and *the* Landlord, the Devil to whom our souls are so far merely in hock. Dylan's immigrant, likewise, is both any number of self-alienated folks and the anti-community of resident aliens–"isolatoes," Melville called us–we humans often seem hell-bent on establishing on earth.

These two songs are also the first on the album in which the singer seems to be fully in possession of his voice, to speak both for himself and as himself. Indeed, "Dear Landlord" is all about voice: the singer's voice here is one that St. Augustine would recognize as that of a "gifted King." The lyric conveys a sense of summoning a tremendous courage of address, of superbly steeled nerve and a formidable presence of mind in the face of an adversary who would deny him that very freedom of voice with which he sings:

*Dear landlord,*
*Please don't put a price on my soul.*
*My burden is heavy,*
*My dreams are beyond control.*
*When that steamboat whistle blows,*
*I'm gonna give you all I got to give,*
*And I do hope you receive it well,*
*Dependin' on the way you feel that you live.*

A large part of the effect is carried in the way, in each verse, the lines grow progressively longer, culminating in the first two verses in a final line that stretches the capacity of a single breath to its limit. (It's this metrical stretching, I suspect, that led Dylan to turn "Dear Landlord" into a piano song.) But as the lines grow in length, they also grow in what we might call their forensic finickiness, so that they convey the singer's insistence upon saying the full measure of what he has to say. For that reason, in the last line of the opening verse, quoted above, the interpolated "you feel" delivers a kind of knock-out punch–even before we begin to ponder what it adds to the singer's meaning.

The final line of the concluding verse does a strikingly abrupt about-face, returning for finale to the comparatively laconic common meter of the other songs in this ten-song suite:

*And if you don't underestimate me*
*I won't underestimate you.*

Many listeners apparently hear in this a compassionate gesture of fellowship, an offer of mutual respect anchored in some democracy of the spirit. I certainly wouldn't rule this out, and many lines in the song do suggest that the singer is keeping at least one eye on actual landlords, so that the song often seems to be an effort to democratize an essentially feudal social relationship. But my own sense is that the singer also has one eye–and his good eye at that–on a greater adversary. To my ears, the singer here is merely giving the devil his due–even as, somewhat devilishly himself, he knows the devil won't be happy to concede "what was meant to be" and allow the singer the freedom of his own gifts.

The voice of compassion does, on the other hand, lie at the core of "I Pity the Poor Immigrant." Its drama lies in the search for this voice, a drama that strikes me, somewhat paradoxically, as both unconscious and as a bit mechanical. And this is not a pleasing paradox: this song has never completely won me over. The singer's imaginative relationship to the immigrant shifts, in each successive verse, from a disdainful distancing to an uncomfortable empathy to a genuine compassion that reaches its fruition in the wonderfully distilled final line: "I pity the poor immigrant when his gladness comes to pass." As Christopher Ricks has pointed out, "comes to pass" here is a brilliant pun, blending the phrase's biblical sense (happens) with its apparent meaning in literal English (ceases to be).* The result is to telescope the coming and going of the immigrant's "gladness" in a single perception that accents its vanity, so that his ill-founded happiness does not merely "shatter like the glass" but constitutes its own shattering.

There is something truly piercing about that final image, but for some reason I can't put my finger on, the song as a whole does not seem to keep up with it. The singer never seems–even perhaps in this wonderful final line–to purge himself fully of his self-regard. The immigrant clearly starts out as a self-projection of some sort, a figure for or reminder of what the singer has been, or might become, or even is, but he never fully emerges as someone in his own right, a character who casts his own shadow. And this failure seems to block the song's deepest aspirations for itself.

Perhaps the singer holds back from a fully persuasive realization of his compassion because he is not prepared to assume the mantle of prophecy with which such a voice would burden him. Of course, in saying this, I am referring not to Dylan's fictitious singer but to Dylan himself. Remember the "wicked messenger," who could express his prophetic voice only in a note–that is, in writing. Remember that Dylan wrote these songs before he found the music–which includes the voice–for them. Remember, too, how in talking about this album, Dylan emphasized "dealing with fear" as a central theme, and how in making the record his only concern was to "get the words right."** Remember, too, that Dylan made this record–a self-conscious and conscientious return to the role of public poet, singer, and musician–after having spent the better part of a year making some of the best music of his life in private cahoots with his friends.

How does all this add up? Well, here's my story: *John Wesley*

* "Clichés That Come to Pass," in *All Across the Telegraph*, pp. 27-28.

** Cott, "Bob Dylan: The *Rolling Stone* Interview Part II," p. 60.

*Harding* is an album about itself, about the struggle of a reluctant prophet to return to his audience and tell them that he's still with them in spirit, that he loves them, that he's sorry if he has failed them in any way, and that he certainly feels their pain, but they're gonna have to get by on their own for the time being because he just isn't up to it anymore, not now anyway.

Dylan's singer does confront and perhaps master his fears, but in the end he declines to reclaim his prophetic voice. The songs on *John Wesley Harding* conspire to suggest that he does this largely out of some deep mistrust of himself, but the placement of "The Wicked Messenger" at the end of the 10-song suite I have been examining strongly implicates a crisis of faith in his audience. The singer has managed, over the course of this suite, to recover his moral bearings, his sturdiness as a self-reliant simple, separate person. But that is as much, it seems, as he can manage, or even imagine for himself. Returning himself to the world as a "moderate man," the singer abdicates *his* deepest identity, opting instead to take his own prophetic advice and go *his* way accordingly to make and raise a family with the one he loves.

## IV

*Nashville Skyline* and *New Morning* both have reputations–inexplicably to me–as celebrations of domestic bliss, but for my money, Dylan has only written two songs that fully warrant that description and persuasively realize its promise. Those are the two songs that close this album; two songs that are, in their own way, as surprising a departure from the songs that precede them on the album as the album itself is from Dylan's previous work. For one thing, they possess a musical fluency and grace–not only as songs but as poems too–that turns their words into a procession of sparkles the music releases.

And in a brand-new development for Dylan, those words are truly simple. The plainness of the diction in the preceding songs was simply a matter of the way they eschewed the figurative. Despite its plainness in this sense, however, it maintained a lively specificity and singularity ("foolish move," "gifted kings and queens," "soulful bounding leap," "multiplied the smallest matter") that we normally associate not just with poetic language but even good journalism. Now suddenly, we begin to hear what sounds an awful lot like cliché: "my true love," "bundle of joy," a mockingbird that "sail[s] away," and a moon that shines "like a spoon." Moreover, this simplicity of diction is accompanied by a simplicity of tone, an ordinariness of voice, that, in the context of Dylan's career up to this point, is simply astonishing. The singer in these songs may, as he appears to, believe that his life and being are in the hands of some transcendent power, but there is nothing transcendent about him. Nothing at all. Our boy has finally, for better or worse, climbed down from that high horse.

"Down Along the Cove" and "I'll Be Your Baby Tonight" are wonderful songs–wonderful minor songs, certainly, although it feels merely churlish to bring that up. "Down Along the Cove" is especially easy to underestimate, a mechanically programmed love song (I love my baby, my baby loves me, we love each other) that does not feel the least bit mechanical. Indeed, it feels like a miracle:

*Down along the cove,*
*I spied my true love comin' my way.*
*Down along the cove,*
*I spied my true love comin' my way.*
*I say, "Lord, have mercy, mama,*
*It sure is good to see you*
*comin' today."*

Its affect seems to derive largely from the fact that it is cast, poetically and musically, as a blues, which lends to the vision of "my true love comin' my way" a darkish cast, as if his delight in her were almost too much to confront or bear. Thus "Lord have mercy, mama" is no cliché; he means it. And the kick the apparently bland final line delivers lies in the way it releases that tension or anxiety by finding words to bear and confront his delight. Indeed, the meter–which sorts "comin' today" as a sort of metrical bow that ties up the verse–conspires to throw up, for the finale, a freshened image of that delight that moderates the sense of emotional safety. A moderate man indeed!

The second verse seems merely to repeat this process, substituting "bundle of joy" for "my true love comin' my way," until we get to a punch line that reverses the perspective:

*She said, "Lord, have mercy, honey,*
*I'm so glad*
*you're my boy!"*

Suddenly, we realize that to be the "bundle of joy" someone is planning to unpack might be every bit as intimidating (and, of course, dangerous) a blessing as it would be to possess that "bundle of joy" for yourself.

In the final verse, it is their walking together "hand in hand" that creates the tension, a tension that is released, with a delightful imaginative leap, by dissipating the electricity of their togetherness into the larger world that watches and understands them. "Down along the Cove," we only now recognize, is a wedding song, an exchange of "I do's" followed by a presentation of the couple to the community that both sustains and is itself enriched by their marriage. Wow! And all without lifting a Dylanesque finger. Double wow!

"I'll Be Your Baby Tonight" is a wedding night song. If ever there was a lyric that speaks for itself, this is it. The song is a limpid invitation to the singer's beloved (and, in the third verse especially, to himself) to let the self go into the other's company ("close your eyes," as often in Dylan, carries the sense also of "close your I's"). The near redundancy of the first two verses–and the way the singer worries the word "worry" by placing his caesura in the middle of it–underscores the pleasure (and perhaps the residual difficulty as well) of the experience of letting go. The triumphant concluding pun on "bottle" (bottle of whiskey, bottle of milk, or even the bottle that you are to me) is so transparent as hardly to function as a pun at all. The singer is having his impossible way, a man at last and a child again. The song is dream made real, or made to seem so anyway. And not any dream, but the dream of dreams that Dylan's singers have been pursuing since the first one hit the highway, a long time coming and a long time gone.

But what are we to make of the bridge and its extravagant banalities:

*Well that mockingbird's gonna*
*sail away*
*We're gonna*
*forget it*
*That big fat moon is gonna*
*shine like a spoon*
*We're gonna let it*
*you won't regret it*

This is banal, even though it's not entirely clear what it means, a neat trick in itself. The mockingbird's departure and the moon's fat shining both seem to be bad things, aspects of reality that need to be tolerated or ignored. Perhaps they are images of the outside world's–or more narrowly, nature's–abandonment of and intrusion upon human purposes. Together then, their going and coming could be said to represent the excesses or perhaps simply vicissitudes of the way the world in which we live impinges upon our lives. The lovers are not going to worry about this, we are to surmise, because they are complete in being alone together.

So far, so good. But having the mockingbird "sail away" and the moon shine "like a spoon" also reduces them to cartoons, non-birds and non-moons, mere words, so that the words fail to realize within themselves the realities they invoke. Apparently–and this seems to me the deeper point of this bridge–we aren't going to let that bother us anymore either. Poetry, art, human ambition and struggle are all being chucked out the window as well, it seems. The infantilization of the singer and his lover seems to be quite thorough. But since we recognize it here as what Hart Crane termed an "improved infancy," we are likely to be persuaded, as the singer clearly aims us to be, that it's a superb bargain. It's an even better bargain, of course, in the context in which we ordinarily hear this song, which is that of a happy couple–half of which is not necessarily a poet–bedding down for the night. In this context, the mockingbird and moon come across as stylized interior decor, like mobiles hanging above an infant's crib, emblematic, in their very stylization, of the couple's freedom now to ignore them. In interpreting the song as I do here, in the context not only of this album, haunted as it is by the question of the poet-prophet's vocation, but also of Dylan's poetic career generally, I am undoubtedly exaggerating its fearsome underside.

I would also suggest that we could have seen this coming. The whole aim of Dylan's art, I would argue, has been to attain the blessed state this song invokes. The best gloss on all this is "Eternal Circle," a superb 1963 song that remained officially unreleased until it was included in the 1991 *Bootleg Series*. It is Dylan's most straightforward song about the motives of song, and it identifies that motive as the conjuring of its own muse–what Wallace Stevens calls a poem's "interior paramour"–as a palpable visitation. It's a lovely song, at once Blakean in the fine particularity of its visionary reach and Keastian in the bright boyishness of its hushed melancholy. Its moral is that this unnameable "she" emerges in the graspable form of a "girl" only in the moment she is gone, which is the very moment he finishes his song.

One imagistic detail connects the two songs. The singer in "Eternal Circle" first notices the girl as she emerges "from the shadows" into the "light" that "my silver strings spun," and he realizes her phantom nature only when, his song finally done, he discovers that "her shadow was missin'." In "I'll Be Your Baby Tonight," when the singer urges his love to "shut the shade," we are permitted to hear a banishment of the shadows–the limitings–of their bodies, but not of their bodies themselves. He is, after all, having his cake and eating it, too. "I'll Be Your Baby Tonight" can be heard as a song addressed to its most intimate audience–the Muse Dylan finds listening to him in "Eternal Circle"–but it is primarily addressed, in a way no other Dylan song really is, to a listener who longer needs–for her sake or for his–to listen to it at all.

"I'll Be Your Baby Tonight" is thus a valedictory of sorts. *John Wesley Harding's* first ten songs prepare the way for the final two by finding an honorable way to announce a farewell to prophecy. "Down Along the Cove" and "I'll Be Your Baby Tonight" might be said to constitute the briefest of Dylan's artistic phases. They are butterflies that flutter by and are gone, leaving behind only the fullness of silence.

# 10

## *Nashville Skyline*

### Country Cooking

*Nashville Skyline* is a strange record. Perhaps the strangest thing about it is that so immaculately conventional a record could seem strange at all. But then, it is a country record, and country music, for all its reputation for tacky banality, can be a very strange thing indeed.

It has always struck me that what distinguishes country music from the blues is that while the blues singer is committed to thwarting and overturning his fate, the country singer is either simply resigned to his, or, more interestingly, determined to persuade himself that he chose it. While the blues can seem meaner than the meanest truth, country music can be sweeter than the sweetest lie. That's clearly an oversimplification–country music, especially, is too mongrel a phenomenon to submit to any generalization–but that does describe the kind of country music–a kind of genteel honky-tonk–that I hear on this record.

*Nashville Skyline* was recorded during a period in Dylan's life when, as perceived then and now, he was a disgustingly happy family man. It may seem odd to suggest that such a fortune is a fate to which anyone might have to resign himself. But for the poet in him, it must have felt that way. I don't believe that poetry arises only from unhappiness, but I do believe that the sort of poetry Dylan writes–a spiritual quest for a freshness of imagination–does require something unattained for which to quest. As you may recall, *John Wesley Harding* concludes with a celebration of marriage that is also a muted farewell to poetry. There is nothing left to quest for.

Or so it seemed. What happens if you find yourself as happy as you may have imagined in your marriage and–inexplicably–burdened with an itch to resume the quest, as if something remained obscurely unattained? What happens, if you are a quester named Bob Dylan, is *Nashville Skyline*, is a brand of country music that intrigues precisely because it is generally impossible, in listening to it, to know whether Dylan's singer is trying to persuade us (and himself) that he has chosen his fate or that he hasn't. He appears to be lying both ways at once.

Before beginning a discussion of specific songs, let me acknowledge a crucial fact. The poetry of *Nashville Skyline* is for the most part rather threadbare. Dylan is certainly attentive to what his singer is saying, but most of the time and in most ways he is not paying all that much attention to the language in which he is saying it. The language is not careless or inept, but neither is much of it inspired or inspiring. My test of this is pragmatic: memorizing the lyrics is mostly a wearisome chore and not–as I find with the best of Dylan's songs–a largely effortless by-product of assimilating the spirit and feeling of a song and making it my own. It would be tedious to do anything but simply ignore the subpar poetry of these songs, and I intend to focus instead primarily on those places where their poetry does grab your attention.

So where was I? Oh yes, lying both ways. It's easiest to see this in the two songs that revisit the poet-killing scene of "I'll Be Your Baby Tonight." These two songs approach that scene from opposite directions: "To Be Alone with You" approaches it from behind, as memory, while "Tonight I'll Be Staying Here with You" approaches it from the front, as desire. Moreover, unlike "I'll Be Your Baby Tonight"–indeed, unlike almost every Dylan song that addresses "you" directly–the listening by the "you" addressed in these songs does not shape their lyrics in any way, so that each song comes across not as one end of a conversation but as a soliloquy pointedly holding conversation at arm's length.

The best things about "To Be Alone with You" are its title, a marvelously evocative vernacular paradox, and the lyric's tone, which refuses to choose between a delight in being "alone with you" and a delight in the *idea* of being "alone with you." And although casual listeners, if they notice it at all, might see this as a happy having-your-cake-and-eating-it-too, the singer knows better:

*They say that nighttime is the right time*
*To be with the one you love*
*Too many thoughts get in the way in the day*
*But you're always what I'm thinkin' of*

This is the bridge, a frequent site of more than usual poetic intensity on this album. What gets a listener's attention here is the last line, and especially its initial "but." The "too many thoughts" that plague his workaday life apart from her turn out, upon reflection, to be various thoughts of her. Indeed, this very song is surprisingly revealed, at the beginning of the final verse ("I wish the night were here") to be one of those thoughts, a product of the "working day" for which she–and not merely the idea of her–will be the "sweet reward." By the conclusion of the song we realize that this wife is really (or also) a muse, at once the inspiration for and the end of the singer's imaginative work.

To be sure, "to be alone with you" is not the final end, since this muse is also the wife he goes home to every night and says goodbye to every morning, when he returns to his work. (I'll call her his wife, because that's what she seems to be, but she is never explicitly identified in any of these songs and should not be reductively equated with the songwriter's actual wife.) But since his work is that of wooing her, it's hard to imagine this happy alternation of working day and rewarding night going on for very long without the work of the day losing its sap and turning into a kind of make-work. This darker view of the matter seems to be the explicit subject of the very silly song "Peggy Day," where the singer admits that he wants to spend the night with Peggy

Day and the day with Peggy Night. "Peggy Day" I take to be his name for the girl he cultivates in his imagination during his working day, and "Peggy Night" the girl he has at night. It's notable that Peggy Night disappears from the song after the verse that introduces her; it seems that if forced to choose, the singer would prefer the girl in his imagination to the real girl whose presence renders his working mind superfluous, even to himself.

In "To Be Alone with You" this view of things emerges more subtly, and much more ambiguously, in the sly grammatical indeterminacy of the song's closing couplet: it's unclear whether he will "thank the Lord" for his "sweet reward" or for granting him, against growing odds, yet another productive "working day." In fact, if I had put money on it, I'd go with the latter: after all, his work, not the Lord's intervention, has earned his "sweet reward."

"Tonight I'll Be Staying Here with You" is a considerably more substantial song, the result, no doubt, of a fictive premise that forces into the open the psychic division within the singer. This premise is no longer the accommodating natural cycle of night and day but the hard choice between the open road and domesticity. It's a choice the singer has made before the song begins, so that the full sense of the title is "Tonight (at last and forever after) I'll Be Staying Here with You." The "ticket," "suitcase," and "troubles" he tosses out into the street in the opening verse are emblems of an old life he readily, willingly abandons in return for what he no longer has to tell us is his "sweet reward."

The second verse introduces a troubling note: "I should have left this town this morning," apparently intended to mean "ordinarily I would have left this town this morning," carries more than a whiff of residual reluctance, and there is a suggestion too that his will has been overpowered ("more than I could do") rather than persuaded. This darker side remains an undertone, however, until we come to the bridge:

*Is it really any wonder*
*The love that a stranger might receive.*
*You cast your spell and I went under,*
*I find it so difficult to leave.*

The crucial line here is the first, which, I suggest, we would expect to be something along the lines of "It is really quite a wonder." By framing it as a question, he raises the possibility that there is no "wonder"–in any sense of the word–to this love he is about to accept. But if there is no "wonder" to it–if it's just another predictable chapter from the old story of the mating game–then is it a very good bargain? If there is no "wonder" to it, does the singer, who is the wondering kind, perhaps really remain the "stranger" to her he was when they first met? Yet by framing it as a question, he leaves both possibilities open, so that the final line of the bridge is able to have it both ways: you can hear it as a despairing cry for help and as an ironic cry for help from a man savoring the exquisite pleasures of surrender.

In any case, in the final verse, the images of the old life he is about to abandon–the "whistle blowin'," the "stationmaster," and the "poor boy on the street" to whom the he bequeathes his old "seat"–possess by this point in the song a more than merely nostalgic claim on his soul. But he willingly turns down that claim, choosing instead to "be staying here with you." The repetition, for conclusion, of the first verse reaffirms the freedom of this choice, now made in full knowledge of all that he has *not* freely chosen. But it does leave unresolved that troubling question: "Is it really any wonder?" The song merely tosses that question–along with the rest of his troubles–out the door. What both we and the singer still don't know is whether his troubles were an affliction from which she has rescued him or a vital core of his being from which his acceptance of her has severed him.

I want to look closely at one more song–"I Threw It All Away"–but first let me clear the deck. The lyric of "Tell Me That It Isn't True," its seductive soulfulness of the music (and Dylan's recorded vocal) notwithstanding, doesn't do anything at all for me. Here the singer sounds not so much divided against himself as merely hypocritical: it's all crocodile tears. The hypocrisy is transparent, and thus harmless. The song simply wallows in the tenderness of the singer's vulnerabilities, and yes, it's all very pleasant.

Although it's always been one of Dylan's most popular love songs, "Lay Lady Lay" just rings false:

*Whatever colors you have*
*in your mind*
*I'll show them to you*
*and you'll see them shine*

Wonderful lines, a superb definition of the powers of romantic poetry, and a delightful visionary summary of what a woman might hope to receive from her husband. But there's something fishy here: the lady's reluctance to yield feels like a red herring. What we hear most vividly, I think, is the singer's anxiety that marriage to this woman might *not* afford sufficient scope for the exercise of his powers to make things "shine." "Why wait any longer for the world to begin"–the question is addressed to her, but it sounds like it is addressed by the singer to himself. The answer seems to be that he is deeply worried–as he should be!–that either of them "can have your cake and eat it too." "Lady Lady Lay" comes into its own only in the outrageously raunchy 1976 Rolling Thunder Revue rewrite (available on the live album *Hard Rain*) in which it is addressed to a woman the singer probably has never seen before and never intends to see again.

"Country Pie" is a song for which, I must confess, I have always felt an absurdly strong affection. It is little more than a silly trifle–it pains me to say that–but, for one thing, this is precisely how a married romantic poet might talk to his wife, whether he's complimenting her during the day for her country cooking or at night for her "country cooking." That is, his gratitude for these domestic pleasures is just slightly–or maybe not so slightly–too intense for the occasion. His intensity finds its fullest outlet by resorting to one of Dylan's oldest and favorite tropes–negation (and the negation of a negation to boot). The result is what is easily the most potent single line in the whole album: "I won't throw it up in anybody's face." Imagine your husband saying that to you from across the picnic blanket! Such is the startling foreplay of the poet.

The lyric of "Country Pie" sounds like it a cleaned-up version of something that may have strayed here from the Basement Tapes sessions, and it's worth noting that one could assemble from those sessions a good start toward an album's worth of similarly spirited songs that would not suggest, as *Nashville Skyline* does, that domesticity might be incompatible with the poetic spirit. I'm thinking of "You Ain't Going Nowhere," "Apple Suckling Tree," "Odds and Ends," "Don't Ya Tell Henry," and even, from one of the funkier corners of domestic life, "Please Mrs. Henry." All of these songs have their dark side, but then what doesn't? What's curious, though, is how "Country Pie" found its way into the world of *Nashville Skyline*, and once it did, why it doesn't have any companions in spirit on the album. I have no answers to these questions.

"One More Night" and "I Threw It All Away" are the only two of the eight new songs on *Nashville Skyline* that are about the problems not of gaining but of losing love, a theme they share with "Girl of the North Country," the *Freewheelin'* song that makes a return appearance to open the album in Dylan's raggedly charming duet with Johnny Cash. What also links these three songs–and separates them from the all the others on the album except "Peggy Day"–is that they are all man-to-man songs, songs with which we imagine the singer regaling either himself or a close male friend. And, interestingly, Dylan sounds much freer here than in most of the album's man-woman songs. His singing is more open and looser, with none of the hints of anxiety and buried tensions we find elsewhere, and the writing has more snap and verve and rhythmic fluidity:

*One more night*
*the stars are in sight*
*But tonight I'm as*
*lonesome as can be*
*Oh the moon is shinin' bright*
*lighting everything in sight*
*But tonight no light will*
*shine on me*

Not that all this makes "One More Night" an especially memorable song. It's actually an interesting lyric, if you're willing to study it, but the conventional counters Dylan employs here–the night and the sky, the moon and the light, etc.–don't stand up and cast shadows the way similarly conventional tropes do in, say, "Tonight I'll Be Staying Here with You" or even "Country Pie."

"I Threw It All Away" is another matter, clearly the best song on the album. Unlike in "One More Night," we are completely convinced that the singer regrets the loss of his beloved–the exquisitely sensuous melancholy of the first two lines takes care of that–but we also notice–or maybe we don't, but we should–that the singer has not the slightest inclination to repent whatever exigency impelled him to "treat her like a fool." (Perhaps that's because, as seems likely, he knows he can only fully appreciate the "mountains" and "rivers" after he's lost them.) Instead, in the final verse, and in a most surprising move, he passes the burden of his experience onto his listener. But he does that only after, in the bridge, he has distilled his experience into this resonant yet limpid pearl of wisdom:

*Love is all there is*
*it makes the world go round*
*Love and only love*
*it can't be denied*
*No matter what you*
*think about it*
*You just won't be able to*
*do without it*
*Take a tip from*
*one who's tried*

There is nothing in the least saccharine about this, especially in its context, where "go round" refers not only to the impulse that attracted him to the girl he has now lost but also to whatever made him throw her love away. (The image of love making things "go round" also covers the final verse, in which the singer, on his way out, passes the baton over to his anonymous listener, on his way in.) Love sucks you into its orbit and then hurls you back out; love spins you around. This notion recalls that most provocative couplet from "One More Night," a couplet that also served at that song's bridge:

*I was so mistaken when I*
*thought that she'd be true*
*I had no idea what a*
*woman in love would do!*

"Love," it appears, made her cast his love aside, even as in "I Threw It All Away," "Love" seems to have made him throw hers away.

"I Threw It All Away" is in some ways the simple unfolding of the hidden logic of its title, so that, by the end of the song, what we first heard perhaps as "I *Threw* It All *Away*" we now hear as "I Threw *It All* Away." The words "it" and "all" are the stitching that hold the song together, and Love itself is the "it all," impersonal and universal, the fate in which we inscribe our lives, a fate that keeps us coming and going. This Love is not romantic, let alone Christian love, but Lucretian, primordial and paradoxical. It is not merely attraction but attraction-repulsion. There are no contradictions in love, no negations ("it can't be denied"), or as Dylan so gnomically glossed it 30-odd years later on the *Love and Theft* song "Sugar Baby," "Love is pleasing, love is teasing, love's not an evil thing."

For once on *Nashville Skyline*, then, the singer unequivocally embraces his fate. But we do not feel that, in what I have characterized as the country manner, he has persuaded himself that he has chosen it. The split between what we "do" and what we "think" is central to the song. The lyric exposes Love as something we would never, given a choice, freely choose; it is an offense to thought. The song itself, however, is a thought, a fully realized expression of the singer's power of free thought, which remains unhampered by the spell of any fate, including those, like Love, the singer himself cannot escape.

Perhaps that is just a fancy way of saying that despite its somber coloring, "I Threw It All Away" is not in the end a sad song. It is exhilarated and exhilarating. In country music–at least country music of the conventional sort that this album generally emulates–knowledge is treasured as a mode of psychic mastery. In "I Threw It All Away," a song in which Dylan's Hermetic genius raises its unruly head for the first time since *Blonde on Blonde*, knowledge figures as spiritual freedom.

# Bibliography

## The Songs

The most complete official collection of the lyrics to Bob Dylan's songs is at the web site bobdylan.com. The principal print sources are *Lyrics, 1962-1985* (Alfred A. Knopf, 1985) and numerous songbooks, which include those published for each official album release and various collections. In whatever format, the published lyrics often differ–sometimes trivially, sometimes significantly–from either the original recordings or subsequent performances. There is no standard or variorum edition of Dylan's songs, and since it probably doesn't make sense to attempt a definitive edition as long as Dylan is roaming the stages of the world tinkering with his texts, I'm in no hurry to see one.

Below is a list (with official release date) of the albums that include songs that are the subject of this study. All of Dylan's albums are still available on Columbia Records.

*Bob Dylan* (March 19, 1962).

*Freewheelin'* (May 27, 1963).

*The Times They Are A-Changin'* (February 10, 1964).

*Another Side of Bob Dylan* (May 1, 1964).

*Bringing It All Back Home* (March 22, 1965).

*Highway 61 Revisited* (August 30, 1965).

*Blonde on Blonde* (May 16, 1966).

*Bob Dylan's Greatest Hits* (March 27, 1967).

*John Wesley Harding* (December 27, 1967).

*Nashville Skyline* (April 9, 1969).

*Bob Dylan's Greatest Hits, Volume 2* (November 17, 1971).

*Hard Rain* (September 1, 1976)

*Biograph* (November 7, 1985).

*The Bootleg Series, Vol. I-III* (March 26, 1991)

*The Bootleg Series*, *Vol. IV: Live 1966* (October 13, 1998).

## Secondary Sources

Note: Some of the material included here can be found only in back issues of hard-to-find (*On the Tracks*, *Series of Dreams*, and *The Bridge*) and defunct (*The Telegraph*) fanzines or in out-of-print books. Much of this elusive material–and lots more–can be purchased from the collector's catalog of the mail-order service Rolling Tomes (P. O. Box 1943, Grand Junction, CO 81502), which also publishes *On the Tracks* and *Series of Dreams*.

Interviews, press conferences, news profiles, and essays included in books listed here are not listed separately unless they have been cited in my text.

————. "Bob Dylan '65: Meeting the Press," Ben Fong-Torres, ed., transcribed in *Rolling Stone Rock 'n' Roll Reader* (New York: Bantam, 1974), 214-230.

Bauldie, John, ed. *Wanted Man: In Search of Bob Dylan* (New York: Citadel Underground, 1990).

———. "Stranded." *The Telegraph* 15, 31-38.

———. "Visions 2." *The Telegraph* 9, 49-54.

———. *The Ghost of Electricity: Bob Dylan's 1966 World Tour* (Romford, England: privately published, 1988).

Benson, Carl, ed. *The Bob Dylan Companion: Four Decades of Commentary.* (New York: Schirmer Books, 1998).

Bowden, Betsy. *Performed Literature: Words and Music by Bob Dylan* (Bloomington: Indiana University Press, 1982).

Bronstein, Martin. Interview. CBC Radio, late Feb., 1966. Transcribed in Bauldie, *The Ghost of Electricity,* 20-23.

Cable, Paul. *Bob Dylan: His Unreleased Recordings* (London: Scorpion/Dark Star, 1978).

Cartwright, Bert. "Talkin' Devil with Bob Dylan." *The Telegraph* 49, 76-99.

———. *The Bible in the Lyrics of Bob Dylan* (Bury, England: Wanted Man, 1985).

Cohen, Scott. "Don't Ask Me Nothin' About Nothin' I Might Just Tell You the Truth: Bob Dylan Revisited." *Spin* (Dec. 1985), 37-40, 80, 81.

Cott, Jonathan. "Bob Dylan: The Rolling Stone Interview Part II." *Rolling Stone* (Nov. 16, 1978), 57-62.

———. "Standing Naked: The Rolling Stone Interview." *Rolling Stone* (Jan. 26, 1978), 38-44

Day, Aidan. *Bob Dylan: Escaping on the Run* (Bury, England: Wanted Man, 1984).

———. *Jokenman: Reading the Lyrics of Bob Dylan* (Oxford, England: Blackwell, 1988).

de Somogyi, Nick. *Jokermen & Thieves: Bob Dylan and the Ballad Tradition* (Bury, England: Wanted Man, 1986).

Dunnett, Hugh [pseudonym]. "Weary Hugh Tonight." *The Telegraph* 23, 92-97.

Fiedler, Leslie. "Walt Whitman: Portrait of the Artist as a Middle-Aged Hero." in *No! in Thunder* (Boston: Beacon Press, 1960), 61-77.

Flanagan, Bill. "Bob Dylan." *Written in My Soul: Rock's Great Songwriters Talk about Creating Their Music* (Chicago: Contemporary Books, 1986), 87-112..

Gray, Michael, and John Bauldie, eds. *All Across the Telegraph: A Bob Dylan Handbook* (London: Sidgwick & Jackson, 1987).

Gray, Michael. *Song and Dance Man III: The Art of Bob Dylan* (London & New York: Cassell, 2000).

Gunderson, Edna. "Dylan's Melodies Always Are A-Changin'." *USA Today* (July 16, 2001), section C, p. 1.

Hajdu, David. *Positively Fourth Street: The Life and Times of Joan Baez, Bob Dylan, Mimi Baez Farina, and Richard Farina* (New York: North Point Press, 2001).

Harvey, Todd. *The Formative Dylan: Transmission and Stylistic Influences, 1961-1963* (Lanham, MD & London: The Scarecrow Press, 2001).

Hentoff, Nat. "The Playboy Interview: Bob Dylan." *Playboy* (March, 1966), 41-44, 138-142. Reprinted in McGregor, *A Retrospective,* 124-145.

Herdman, John. *Voice without Restraint: Bob Dylan's Lyrics and Their Background* (New York: Delilah, 1982).

Heylin, Clinton. "'Freeze Out,' 'Visions of Johanna,' and the Nightingale's Code." *The Telegraph* 16, 80-81.

———. *Bob Dylan: Behind the Shades Revisited* (New York: William Morrow, 2001).

———. *Bob Dylan: The Recording Sessions 1960-1994* (New York: St. Martin's Press, 1995).

Hilburn, Robert. "I Learned That Jesus Is Real and I Wanted That." *Los Angeles Times* (Nov. 23, 1980). Reprinted in Benson, *The Bob Dylan Companion*, 161-167.

Kermode, Frank, & Stephen Spender. "Bob Dylan: The Light at the End of the Funnel." *Esquire* (May 1972), 110, 118, 188. Reprinted in Thomson and Gutman,*The Dylan Companion,* 155-162

Kleinman, Bernard. "Dylan on Dylan." Westwood One radio broadcast, Nov. 17, 1984. An excerpt is reprinted in Benson, *The Bob Dylan Companion*, 30-40.

Krogsgaard, Michael. "Bob Dylan: The Recording Sessions (Parts 1-6)," *The Telegraph* 52, 68-131; *The Telegraph* 53, 54-119; *The Telegraph* 55, 111-143; *The Telegraph* 56, 150-175; *The Bridge* 1, 31-60; *The Bridge* 2, 68-90.

Krogsgaard, Michael. *Positively Bob Dylan: A Thirty-Year Discography, Concert, and Recording Session Guide, 1960-1991* (Ann Arbor: Popular Culture Ink, 1991).

Landau, Jon. "Bob Dylan: John Wesley Harding." *It's Too Late to Stop Now: A Rock 'n' Roll Journal* (San Francisco: Straight Arrow, 1972), 43-64. Reprinted in McGregor, *A Retrospective*, 248-263.

Lhamon, W. T. Jr. "Dylan's Living Lore." *The Telegraph* 37, 102-131.

———. *Raising Cain: Blackface Performance from Jim Crow to Hip Hop* (Cambridge: Harvard University Press, 1998).

Lindley, John. "Reels of Rhyme." *The Telegraph* 36, 86-102.

Loder, Kurt. "Bob Dylan: The Rolling Stone Interview." *Rolling Stone* (June 21, 1984), 14-18, 23, 24, 78

Marcus, Greil. "Bob Dylan After the 1994 Congressional Elections." *Double Trouble: Bill Clinton and Elvis Presley in a Land of No Alternatives* (New York: Picador USA, 2000), 104-107.

———. *Invisible Republic: Bob Dylan's Basement Tapes* (New York: Henry Holt and Company, 1997).

———. *Mystery Train: Images of America in Rock 'n' Roll Music* (New York: E. P. Dutton, revised edition, 1982).

McClure, Michael. "The Poet's Poet." *Rolling Stone* (Mar. 14, 1974), 33-34.

McGregor, Craig, ed. *Bob Dylan: A Retrospective*. (New York: Morrow Paperback, 1972).

Pichaske, David. "Bob Dylan and the American Dream." *The Telegraph* 26, 36-102.

———. "Bob Dylan and the Search for the Past." *The Telegraph* 14, 14-20.

Rees, Garth. "Thinking about Bob Dylan: Disguise." *The Telegraph* 56, 98-114.

Ricks, Christopher. "Cliches That Come to Pass." *The Telegraph* 15, 14-25. Reprinted in Gray and Bauldie, *All Across the Telegraph: A Bob Dylan Handbook*, 22-29. Revised and expanded into two chapters of *The Force of Poetry* (Oxford, England: Oxford University Press, 1984), "Cliches," 356-368, and "American English and the Inherently Transitory," 417-441. The Dylan-related excerpts are reprinted in Thomson and Gutman, *The Dylan Companion,* 163-172.

——— "The Lonesome Death of Hattie Carroll." *The Telegraph* 42, 77-82.

Rosenbaum, Ron. "The Playboy Interview." *Playboy* (Mar. 1978), 61-62, 64, 69-74, 78-82, 86-90.

Saal, Hubert. "Dylan Is Back." *Newsweek* (Feb. 26, 1968). Reprinted in McGregor, *A Retrospective*, 243-247, and (with additional material from Saal's report of the same interview in the Apr. 28, 1986 Chicago Tribune) in *The Telegraph* 56, 43-49.

Saluszinsky, Imre. "Bob Dylan and the Professors." *The Telegraph* 45, 39-46.

Saluszinsky, Imre. "Chimes of Freedom Flashing." *The Telegraph* 45, 48-57, and *The Telegraph* 49, 23-37.

Scaduto, Anthony. *Bob Dylan* (New York: Signet, 1973).

Scobie, Stephen. "No Prophet's Son." *The Bridge* 2, 7-20.

———. *Alias Bob Dylan (*Red Deer, Alberta: Red Deer College Press, 1991).

———. *Visions of Johanna* (privately published, no date).

Selerie, Gavin. "Tricks and Training: Some Dylan Sources and Analogues." *The Telegraph* 50, 155-179.

Shelton, Robert. "The 1966 Airplane Interview." *The Bridge* 6, 6-39; 7, 6-30, & 9, 6-20.

———. *No Direction Home: The Life and Music of Bob Dylan* (New York: Beech Tree Books/William Morrow, 1986).

Sounes, Howard. *Down the Highway: The Life of Bob Dylan* (New York: Grove Press, 2001).

Spitz, Bob. *Dylan: A Biography* (New York: McGraw-Hill, 1989).

Steen, Margaret. "Not You, Bob Dylan.!" *Toronto Star Weekly* (Jan. 29, 1966). Reprinted in Bauldie, *The Ghost of Electricity*, 10-12.

Sumner, Carolyn. "The Ballad of Dylan and Bob." *Southwest Review* (Winter, 1981). Reprinted in *The Telegraph* 14, 38-52.

Thomson, Elizabeth M, and David Gutman, eds. *The Dylan Companion: A Collection of Essential Writings about Bob Dylan* (New York: Delta, 1990).

Thomson, Elizabeth M, ed. *Conclusions on the Wall: New Essays on Bob Dylan* (Prestwish, England: Thin Man, 1980).

Trager, Oliver, and David C. Barrett. "Black Cross: Lord Buckley, Joseph S. Newman, and the Bob Dylan Connection." *On the Tracks* 15, 18-24.

Ventura, Michael. "Music to Know America By." *Austin Chronicle* (Vol. 16, issue 14), 86 & 87.

Williams, David R. "Dylan and Dickinson." *On the Tracks* 13, 24-26.

Williams, Paul. *Bob Dylan: Watching the River Flow: Observations on His Art-in-Progress, 1966-1995* (London: Omnibus Press, 1996).

———. *Performing Artist: The Middle Years, 1974-1986* (Lancaster, PA: Underwood-Miller, 1992).

———. *Performing Artist: The Music of Bob Dylan, Vol. 1, 1960-1973* (Lancaster, PA: Underwood-Miller, 1990).

Wissolik, Richard and Scott McGrath, eds. *Bob Dylan's Words: A Critical Dictionary and Commentary* (Greensburg, PA: Eadmer Press, 1994).

Zollo, Paul. "Bob Dylan: The SongTalk Interview." *SongTalk* (Winter 1991), 35-39.

# Index

# COPYRIGHT ACKNOWLEDGEMENTS